EARLY EXPERIENCES AND
THE PROCESSES
OF SOCIALIZATION

SOCIAL PSYCHOLOGY

A series of monographs, treatises, and texts

EDITORS

LEON FESTINGER AND STANLEY SCHACHTER

Jack W. Brehm, A Theory of Psychological Reactance. 1966

Ralph L. Rosnow and Edward J. Robinson (Eds.), Experiments in Persuasion. 1967

Jonathan L. Freedman and Anthony N. Doob,
Deviancy: The Psychology of Being Different. 1968

Paul G. Swingle (Ed.), Experiments in Social Psychology. 1968, 1969

E. Earl Baughman and W. Grant Dahlstrom, Negro and White Children:
A Psychological Study in the Rural South. 1968

Anthony G. Greenwald, Timothy C. Brock, and Thomas M. Ostrom (Eds.),
Psychological Foundations of Attitudes. 1968

Robert Rosenthal and Ralph Rosnow (Eds.), Artifact in Behavioral Research. 1969

R. A. Hoppe, E. C. Simmel, and G. A. Milton (Eds.), Early Experiences
and the Processes of Socialization. 1970

Richard Christie and Florence Geis, Studies in Machiavellianism. 1970

Paul G. Swingle (Ed.), The Structure of Conflict. 1970

Alvin Zander, Motives and Goals in Groups. 1971

Stanley Schachter, Emotion, Obesity, and Crime. 1971

Charles A. Kiesler, The Psychology of Commitment:
Experiments Linking Behavior to Belief. 1971

Jacobo A. Varela, Psychological Solutions to Social Problems:
An Introduction to Social Technology. 1971

David C. Glass and Jerome E. Singer, Urban Stress:
Experiments on Noise and Social Stressors. 1972

In Preparation

Ivan D. Steiner, Group Processes and Productivity

Shelley Duval and Robert A. Wicklund, A Theory of Objective Self Awareness

EARLY EXPERIENCES AND
THE PROCESSES
OF SOCIALIZATION

edited by

RONALD A. HOPPE
University of Victoria
Victoria, British Columbia

G. ALEXANDER MILTON
University of Victoria *et al*
Victoria, British Columbia

EDWARD C. SIMMEL
Miami University
Oxford, Ohio

1970   ACADEMIC PRESS   New York and London

ACADEMIC PRESS, INC.
111 Fifth Avenue, New York, New York 10003

United Kingdom Edition published by
ACADEMIC PRESS, INC. (LONDON) LTD.
Berkeley Square House, London W1X 6BA

LIBRARY OF CONGRESS CATALOG CARD NUMBER: 74-97486

Second Printing, 1972

PRINTED IN THE UNITED STATES OF AMERICA

LIST OF CONTRIBUTORS

Numbers in parentheses indicate the pages on which the authors' contributions begin.

SIDNEY W. BIJOU, *Child Behavior Laboratory, University of Illinois, Urbana, Illinois* (43)

BRIAN COATES, *Department of Psychology, University of North Carolina, Chapel Hill, North Carolina* (109)

CATHERINE FELKNOR, *University of Colorado, Boulder, Colorado* (167)

LUCY RAU FERGUSON, *Psychological Clinic, Michigan State University, East Lansing, Michigan* (59)

JOHN L. FULLER, *The Jackson Laboratory, Bar Harbor, Maine* (7)

SAM GLUCKSBERG, *Princeton University, Princeton, New Jersey* (149)

WILLARD W. HARTUP, *Institute of Child Development, University of Minnesota, Minneapolis, Minnesota* (109)

O. J. HARVEY, *University of Colorado, Boulder, Colorado* (167)

ECKHARD H. HESS, *Department of Psychology, University of Chicago, Chicago, Illinois* (19)

RONALD A. HOPPE, *University of Victoria, Victoria, British Columbia* (207)

ROBERT M. KRAUSS, *Department of Psychology, Livingston College, Rutgers University, New Brunswick, New Jersey* (149)

G. ALEXANDER MILTON, *Department of Psychology, University of Victoria, Victoria, British Columbia* (39, 145)

ROSS D. PARKE, *University of Wisconsin, Madison, Wisconsin* (81)

EDWARD C. SIMMEL, *Miami University, Oxford, Ohio* (3)

PREFACE

The outcome of the 1968 Miami University Symposium on Social Behavior is presented in this volume. Socialization—the process by which individuals become members of groups—has been a broad topic for an assortment of theories, researches, and recommended practices. Viewing the assortment suggests that there are interrelationships and possibilities for integration among the approaches to the study of socialization. The present volume presents some of these approaches in order to promote integration and synthesis, as well as to illustrate the diverse richness which is currently present in the studies of the topic. Each chapter is not a verbatim transcription of the contributor's presentation at the time of the symposium, but rather is a revision by the author who attempted to take into account comments made during the formal and informal discussions at the time of the symposium. In addition, the editors have attempted some integation.

In order to make the present undertaking feasible, not all approaches to the study of socialization could be represented. However, from the assortment of research strategies, several representatives have been drawn who exemplify the current concerns of social and natural scientists. Also, recommendations for child-rearing practices have not been considered, although the intrepid reader may be able to induce a few.

The present work is based on the second Miami University Symposium on Social Behavior and is not unrelated to the first symposium which explored the relationships between social facilitation and imitative behavior (Simmel, Hoppe and Milton: *Social Facilitation and Imitative Learning*). In the previous work, social facilitation was considered from the standpoint of the influence of the simple presence of another individual of a species on a member of that species. In one sense, this is basic to socialization because it is obvious that almost all of socialization occurs in the presence of another.

Another connection this volume has with the earlier one is the topic of imitation. It has long been clear to students of socialization that imitative behavior is an important aspect of the developmental process. In fact, for some, the concept of imitation serves as a model to use for understanding all the essentials of socialization. The relationship of imitation to socialization is expounded in a chapter to follow.

In the first symposium, animal and human studies were compared and contrasted, increasing the overall understanding of both social facilitation and imitation. The socialization of both animals and human beings is explored in the present work in hopes that similar benefits will result.

In the quest of integration within the study of socialization, contrasting methodologies are presented as well as broad and small theoretical constructs. Further, recent data collected by the contributors and others are presented. From the exposition of this variety and the exploration of similarities and differences, we hope to achieve some synthesis.

We wish to thank the National Science Foundation for making the symposium possible with grant GS2233.

The efforts of a large number of people, in addition to the contributors to the symposium, produced the present book. The diligent work of the following graduate students was very much appreciated: Elaine Baker, Mike Colligan, Marty Hahn, Connie Harris, David Lauffenburger, Stan Lewin, Doug Lewis, Doug Lindquist, Maurice Moore, Millard Reschke, Dick Reynolds, Steve Schmidt, Gary Schneider, and Steve Walters. James H. Davis is to be thanked for his capable performance as a chairman during the symposium. For excellent clerical work and typing under stress, Mrs. Marcie O'Hara and Elaine Grushas are to be commended.

January 1970   R. A. Hoppe
                                                             G. A. Milton
                                                             E. C. Simmel

CONTENTS

PART II

CURRENT EXPLANATORY CONCEPTS USED
TO UNDERSTAND SOCIALIZATION

PART III

ADULT CHARACTERISTICS AND
CHILDHOOD SOCIALIZATION

EARLY EXPERIENCES AND THE PROCESSES OF SOCIALIZATION

PART I

BIOLOGICAL ASPECTS OF SOCIALIZATION AND IMPLICATIONS OF ANIMAL STUDIES

The Biology of Socialization

*Edward C. Simmel**

The proverb says it well: "To arrive at simplicity, one must first recognize complexity." Before we may attain a more elegant, more comprehensive understanding of mice or men, we must first recognize, and then struggle through, the myriad variables present at a number of different levels. Until quite recently, with a few prominent exceptions, the potential contributions of biologically-oriented explanations to social development, as to social behavior in general, were either ignored or referred to in such grossly over-simplified terms as to be of little value.

First of all, what is meant by the term "biological" in the present context? Not, to be sure, physiological reductionism, or simplistic explanations of complex processes directly from Mendellian genetics, or mere extrapolation to higher organisms of findings from those more easily studied. Instead, an emerging subdiscipline, which might be termed *social*

* Miami University.

3

psychobiology, is concerned with those aspects of social behavior more or less directly related to "evolutionary significance" (i.e., the adaptiveness of organisms, both individual and species). Looked at another way, it is concerned with biological "determinants" of social behavior, whether these be genetic, species-characteristic, or physiological. While more specific examples are abundant in the first two chapters of this book, a brief look at representative areas may illustrate the relevance of the biological approach to the study of socialization.

BEHAVIOR GENETICS

There can be little question that every form of behavior has a genetic basis. Crudely speaking, the determination of just how, and how much, is the task of the behavior geneticist. Obviously, it is genes that are inherited, not behavior; and the search for genotypes and how behavior is affected by them is a complex but fruitful process. Less fruitful are the evasive truisms which even today are sometimes passed off as explanation, such as "heredity interacts with the environment . . ." Organisms from two different populations may respond to a given situation in exactly the same way, and yet the major proportion of the variance may be genetic in one case, and experiential in the other. The determination of which behaviors and traits of known genetic determinants are influenced by which types of environmental conditions, and at what stages of development, are of inestimable import for an understanding of socialization processes. An interesting and illuminating example of this may be found in Fuller's paper (Chapter 1).

SPECIES-CHARACTERISTIC BEHAVIOR

Species-characteristic behavior has been found especially interesting by many studying socialization in that it is concerned at a most basic level with just what *is* a Pekin duck, or a Peromyscus, or a man? This phenomenon is sometimes referred to as "species-specific" behavior, and it probably is more specific and is certainly more easily studied in lower than in higher species, but the potential of the findings and the research strategies for explanations of socialization cannot be ignored. This point will be better appreciated after reading Hess' paper (Chapter 2).

COMPARATIVE STUDIES

Comparative studies, using a variety of species, contribute to basic knowledge of the evolution of all forms of behavior. A point often missed by laymen is that one does not generalize in any simple fashion from lower to higher levels of organisms, but rather that a thorough understanding of the similarities and differences, especially the latter, among many species is needed to place in context and understand the behavior of any species, including man. Indeed, it has been the comparative psychologist (most notably the late T. C. Schnierla) who has warned against the misleading analogy and the overly generalized extrapolation from simpler to more complex organism: The error of *zoomorphism* is seemingly becoming more prevalent than anthromorphism in this day of *The Naked Ape* and *The Territorial Imperative*. An appreciation of differences between species of any sort of behavior cannot help but contribute to an understanding of the evolutionary significance of many sorts of behavior.

As interest in the biological aspects of socialization has increased, and the realization of its importance has grown, a natural but most fortunate consequence has been the acceleration of interdisciplinary research and communication (the symposium from which this volume is derived being but one example of the latter). Ethologists, behavior geneticists, and comparative psychologists have found that they have something to say to developmental and social psychologists, and many of the latter want to listen, and vice versa. Both cause and outcome of such interdisciplinary activity has been the rise in the level of sophistication in the use of biologically derived concepts and explanations, as the simplistic cliché falls into disfavor and disuse.

1

GENETIC INFLUENCES
ON SOCIALIZATION

*John L. Fuller**

One can look at human societies and argue convincingly that the patterns of social behavior are similar in all. Each group provides for the propagation and care of children, and a modicum of community cooperation in economic production and territorial defense. The ways these can be accomplished are limited. Within any one society, however, individuals differ in the roles they play, and heredity is a potential contributor to such variation. In part, social roles are determined by age and sex. The influence of these factors is considered by Ferguson in her discussion of the concept of dependency in Chapter 4 in this volume. Sex may be considered a type of genetic influence, but the question of the relative importance of biological and cultural influences in the assumption of masculine or feminine social roles will not be specifically examined in this paper. Instead variables unrelated to age and sex, with emphasis on the interaction of genetic factors and mode of rearing, will receive major attention.

EXPERIMENTS WITH PUPPIES

The first part of the paper presents an account of a series of experiments with dogs performed over a decade, largely in collaboration with Dr. Lincoln D. Clark of the College of Medicine, University of Utah. The primary interests in this series of experiments were: (a) the effects of experiential deprivation upon later behavior, and (b) discovery of means by which the deleterious effects might be counteracted. In addition a genetic variable was introduced by comparing two breeds of dogs, wire-

* The Jackson Laboratory, Bar Harbor, Maine.

7

haired terriers and beagles, that were subjected to similar degrees of deprivation. This phase of the study led to a reconsideration of the logic of the heredity-environment problem.

This reconsideration made apparent the semantic pitfalls involved in distinguishing between "innate" and "learned" behavior. The interpretation of the origin of maladaptive behavior in animals reared under social restriction was also changed. These points will be discussed later.

In all studies (Fuller, 1963, 1967; Fuller and Clark, 1966a) a similar basic isolation procedure was used. Puppies were removed from their mother at three weeks of age, the earliest at which they can survive independently without special handling. They were placed in chambers about 60 by 75 cm interior dimensions, designed so that feeding, watering, and removal of wastes was accomplished without physical or visual contact with a human being. The chambers were furnished with a one-way observation window and were constantly lighted. Ventilation was furnished by a blower which provided some masking of external sounds. Upon this monotonous background a number of procedures were superimposed—introduction of objects, rearing in pairs, removal for special handling and observation at specified ages. The method has been called "scheduling of experience" (Fuller and Waller, 1962).

The principal means of evaluating differences between subjects has been the arena test, during which the subject's responses to a human handler, to toys, and to another puppy are recorded for 7.5 minutes. The arena was 3.5 meters square and was surrounded by an opaque barrier 1 meter high. The floor area was divided into nine equal squares by painted stripes.

In the majority of experiments, behavior in the arena was recorded in a "code for observational description" (COFOD) (Fuller and Clark, 1966b). Observers write out at regular intervals, generally 6 seconds, a five-letter word which provides a "snapshot" of the subject at that instant of time.

Letter one of each COFOD word denotes the stimulus toward which the subject is responding; letter two describes the nature of the response. Location in the testing area is indicated by letter three, and type and level of activity by letter four. Letter five denotes any one of various indicators of emotional arousal. For example, HMAJT describes a dog "manipulating" (M = pawing or mouthing) the handler (H). The dog is in the arena (A), jumping (J) up and down, and wagging its tail (T).

A useful feature of COFOD is a numerical transformation for letters two and four. Response intensities are graded from orientation through approach, investigation, contact, and manipulation. Adding the numerical values of these letters for each test provides a response index (RI) which is a measure of the average intensity of responses directed toward identifiable stimuli. Response indices can also be calculated for individual stimuli. Similarly, numerical equivalents of letter four increase with an increase in level of activity, from lying down through sitting, standing, walking, running, and jumping. The sum of these numerical equivalents yields an activity index (AI). Practiced observers obtain interjudge rank order correlation coefficients of about .90 on ratings of RI and AI. Observing is easier and agreement is better when subjects make relatively stereotyped responses, but satisfactory records can be obtained from all subjects.

General Effects of Experiential Deprivation

The major emphasis of the following discussion is upon the differences between beagles and wirehaired terriers—the two breeds employed in our research—in response to experiential deprivation. Before taking up the matter of interaction between genotype and treatment, the general effects of the isolation procedure upon dogs will be summarized, and a description of some of the differences in the behavior of beagles and terriers when reared under more standard conditions in the laboratory will be given.

Dogs isolated from three to fifteen weeks of age make fewer and less intense contacts with other dogs, persons, or toys than do pet-reared animals. Mobility is sometimes decreased, sometimes increased. It will be seen that the genotype affects the direction of the change. Isolates remain in a small transport cage after it is opened to the arena for long periods of time; pet-reared animals emerge from the transport cage almost immediately after it is opened.

Bizarre posture and episodes of approach-avoidance conflict are common among the isolates. Often the manifestations during the fourth through fifteenth week of isolation are observed for many weeks following termination of confinement. However, the symptoms of the postisolation syndrome do moderate as animals are given regular handling and experience in the arena. Individual differences in persistence of deviant behavior are great. Relatively brief breaks in isolation counteract the effects of experiential deprivation to a high degree. Animals given 15 minutes handling per week in two equal periods are more like pet-reared than isolated animals.

On the basis of observations on the changes of the postisolation behavior in successive arena tests, and the ameliorating effect of treating isolates with a tranquillizer at emergence, Fuller and Clark (1966a) and Fuller (1967) concluded that the syndrome was best described as a response to stress-emergence. More emphasis is placed on the strangeness of the arena for the experientially deprived dog than on possible failure of normal perceptual development because of the low level of stimulation during isolation. Further evidence (Fuller, 1966) for this view is provided by an experiment in which experiential isolation was found to be compatible with effective performance on a reversal learning task. The majority of isolates, in fact, performed as well as pet-reared controls. To be sure, a few isolates performed poorly and depressed the group average. Experiential deprivation undoubtedly contributes to depressed learning ability, but it is not sufficient in itself to produce significant impairment.

Beagles and Terriers

An extensive body of data on the behavior of beagles and terriers reared in litters in large open pens was obtained by Scott and Fuller (1965). Both breeds performed similarly on discrimination tests; on an emotional reactivity test, beagles were more vocal than terriers; terriers had higher muscle tension and showed more panting than beagles. A major difference in social behavior is the stronger dominance hierarchy set up in terrier litters in contrast to the beagle litters. Terrier litters often were subdivided in order to avoid serious injury to the lower ranking members; this was never necessary in beagle litters. Despite their appearance of greater muscle tension, terriers were more readily trained to inhibit jumping down from a platform in an "obedience test" than were beagles.

What happens to these breed differences when puppies are reared in isolation for twelve weeks? Three aspects of this question will be discussed: (a) the dose-effect relationship, that is, the effect of differing amounts of socialization on the postisolation behavior of beagles and terriers, (b) the quality and persistence of the postisolation syndrome in beagles and terriers, and (c) the modification of dominance-submission relationships within the two breeds as a result of isolation.

In the dose-effect experiment (Fuller, 1963) the amount of arena experience was varied by interposing different numbers of arena tests in otherwise continuous isolation. Beagles and terriers were isolated at three weeks of age, and there were four treatment groups of each breed receiving respectively 4, 2, 1 or 0 breaks (10-minutes of arena experience) per week. At fifteen weeks of age, all groups were removed from isolation. Figures 1 and 2 are a summary of observations made on the fourth week after isolation was terminated following a series of 12 arena tests. Thus the differences between treatment groups represent relatively persistent effects of isolation. It should be noted here that in their general behavior and their performance on the arena tests, the four break-per-week groups were really not different from pet-reared animals. The differences between the beagles and terriers are shown on the same figures. On three of the seven scores which have been selected as illustrative of the data as a whole, there are strong breed differences (Fig. 1). These are: strong handler contacts (pawing, mouthing), contacts with the towel when another dog is present (a measure of dominance), and locomotion as measured by the number of squares entered. All of these scores were also significantly affected by varying the number of isolation-breaks. Figure 2 presents the four measures which did not show a breed difference, and these were, in general, less affected by changes in the amount of experience.

The lesson to be learned is that behaviors cannot be divided into two exclusive classes, one genetically programmed and insensitive to en-

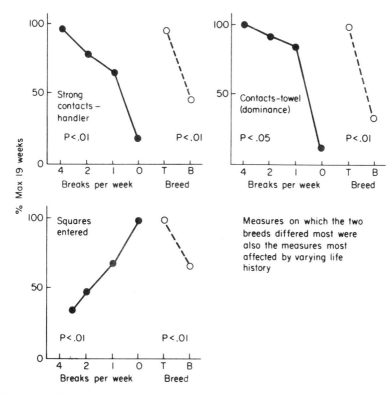

Figure 1. Observations in which 19-week-old isolated terriers and beagles differed four weeks after isolation was terminated. The scores have been adjusted so that the experimental group which gave the highest score was given 100 and the others are shown in comparison to it.

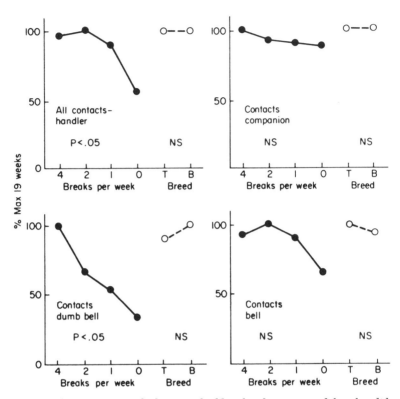

Figure 2. Observations in which 10-week-old isolated terriers and beagles did not significantly differ four weeks after isolation was terminated. The scores have been adjusted so that the experimental group which gave the highest score was given 100 and the others are shown in comparison to it.

vironmental manipulation, the other experientially programmed and insensitive to changes in the genotype. Actually, it seems that those behavioral characteristics which are most affected by genotypic differences are the very ones which are most easily shifted by differences in the amount of experience, and those characteristics which are unrelated to genotypic differences are less sensitive to changes in experience. It is suggested here that there is synergism rather than antagonism between genetic and environmental effects upon behavior.

A second example (Fuller and Clark, 1968) of breed differences concerns the changes in behavior of beagles and terriers during a five-week period following emergence from twelve weeks of complete isolation. A comparison group of pet-reared littermates was also observed on a similar schedule. Pet-reared dogs were maintained in isolation cages as were isolates, but twice a day when the attendant serviced the cages, they were removed and allowed to run freely about the laboratory. Thus they were handled frequently and habituated to open space and to contact with companions. Their behavior, in the opinion of experienced observers, was indistinguishable from the behavior of puppies reared as pets in a home or small kennel.

The effect of isolation upon the two breeds can be demonstrated in terms of the activity indices (AIs) and response indices (RIs) as described earlier.

Figure 3 shows the average activity indices for the four groups during the series of 20 tests. Terriers were consistently more active than beagles. From the third week of testing, terriers reared in isolation were more active ($p < .05$) than those reared as pets. Throughout the tests, beagles reared in isolation were less active than those reared as pets. Thus it appears that isolation magnifies the breed differences in activity seen in dogs reared in standard fashion. The descriptive terms at the right in Fig. 3 provide a guide to the actual observations, but it must be noted that a mean value of 2.0 does not indicate continuous walking but indicates a mix of standing, walking, jumping, and so on, in varied proportions.

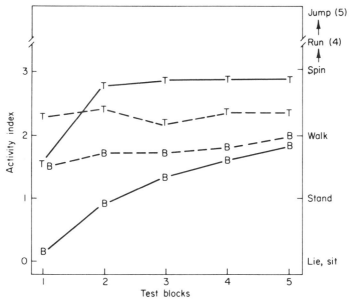

Figure 3.   Mean activity indices of isolated and pet-reared beagles (B) and terriers (T). The solid lines refer to dogs reared in isolation and the broken lines refer to those reared as pets. (Reprinted from *Science,* December 29, 1967, **158**, No. 3809, pp. 1645–1652. Copyright 1967 by the American Association for the Advancement of Science.)

Similarly, we may compare the response indices for the four groups (Fig. 4). Here the curves for terriers and beagles reared as pets do not differ. But, after isolation, terriers consistently responded more intensely than beagles to the arena stimuli, and, from the second week of testing, their responses were indistinguishable from those of pet-reared litter mates. The beagles raised in isolation had not come close to responding as freely as their pet-reared litter mates by the end of the experiment. By this measure, too, isolation enhanced the difference between the two breeds.

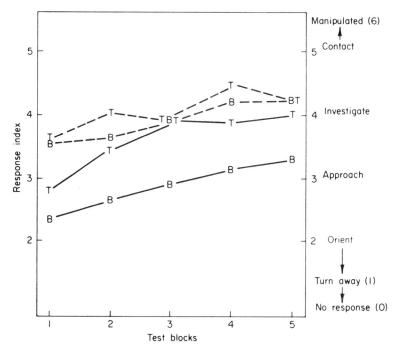

Figure 4. Mean indices of response intensity of isolated and pet-reared beagles and terriers. The solid lines refer to dogs reared in isolation and the broken lines refer to those reared as pets. (Reprinted from *Science,* December 29, 1967, **158**, No. 3809, pp. 1645–1652. Copyright 1967 by the American Association for the Advancement of Science.)

It is apparent, therefore, that genotype is one determinant of the direction, duration, and intensity of the isolation effect. If living in a more open environment, typified by the arena, is taken as a desideratum, beagles would appear to be more vulnerable than terriers to the disruptive effects of isolation.

The response index includes many social components. Among these the towel possession score has especial interest as a measure of dominance. The procedure is very simple. A hand towel is thrown into the arena between two puppies. Every six seconds, for one minute, each animal is recorded as not responding, orienting, contacting or chewing the towel. Ordinarily, one member of the pair is clearly in control of the object at a given moment; occasionally, both are recorded as sharing possession. The difference between the possession scores of the pair members was used as an index of the degree of dominance difference between them. In this study covering four tests, the potential range of dominance difference was 0 to 40.

Figure 5 shows the results of pairings between two isolates and between an isolate and a pet-reared puppy. The experimental unit here is a pair of animals and we are looking for possible genetic effects upon social interactions between animals of the same breed. Pawlowski and Scott (1956) demonstrated clearly with pet-reared dogs that dominance in terrier litters was stronger than in beagles. When both members of a pair are isolates, the same relationship is found. The mean difference between paired terriers is twice that between paired beagles. However,

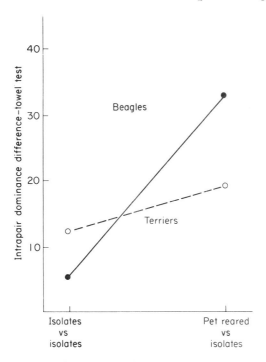

Figure 5. Mean intrapair dominance difference scores for isolated and pet-reared beagles and terriers.

when isolate-pet-reared pairs are considered, the beagles showed significantly greater differences in dominance. In every case the pet-reared member was the dominant animal.

Thus when pairs are composed of animals with similar life histories, be it pet-rearing or isolate-rearing, terriers show stronger dominance differentiation. When pairs are made up of pet-reared and isolate-reared animals, beagles show stronger intrapair differentiation. The result is clearly a function of more severe and lasting depression of dominance producing behavior in beagles.

HEREDITY-ENVIRONMENT: DICHOTOMY OR SYNERGISM

It is not difficult to find abundant material from animal experiments which demonstrates that variation in social behavior is in part genetic. Fruitflies, mice, rats, and dogs show heritable variation in mating speed and selectivity; the mammals, at least, show variation in fighting, dominance, caretaking, and other aspects of social behavior (Fuller and Thompson, 1960; Hirsch, 1967; Parsons, 1967). Few studies have dealt with the dynamics of the development of social behavior. Much more is needed to supplement the start that has been made in studying the heredity-environment synergism. The possible strategies for such research programs are as follows.

Genetic differences can be considered as treatments whose influence upon some behavior of interest is evaluated by standard experimental procedures. As treatment, genes have special attributes, but so do techniques of stimulus deprivation, surgical alteration, and drug administration. Although these points are of great importance in designing behavior-genetics experiments they will not be dwelled upon here. Instead an emphasis will be placed on the nature of the conclusions which can logically be drawn when two strains differ in behavior even though treated alike. We can properly say that the genetic difference is a cause of the observed variation in behavior, but we cannot call the behavior pattern as a whole *innate*. It seems essential that the same care in terminology be taken in studies of early experience. The demonstration that changes in aggression of mice are related to mode of rearing does not prove that aggressive motor patterns can be learned by any organism. There is no way of excluding the genotypic substrate as a necessary condition for the behavior.

Both genes and variations in early experience have the difficulty of being historical rather than proximate causes of behavior. Theoretically a perfected science of psychology could predict the response to any stimulus by considering only the immediate state of the stimulated organism. The life history of the organism would be irrelevant to such a prediction; so also would be the DNA of the cell nuclei. It seems impossible that such a psychology will ever develop, but nevertheless the concept has value in calling attention to the limitations of historical explanations.

From this point of view both Ashley Montagu's (1968) statement that "aggression is a learned way of responding to certain conditions" and Konrad Lorenz's (1966) concept of an instinctive need to express aggressions seem equally in error. The predictability of aggression, given certain conditions, carries the implicit assumption of a genetically determined substrate which is ready to be programmed for fighting. Without such an assumption there is no reason to expect consistency of response, no way to insure that structuring experience in a particular way will have predictable effects upon enhancing or reducing aggression.

Paradoxically, the ardent environmentalist (and there are still a few) needs rigorous biological uniformity to make his theories work. Quite properly he dissents from applying the term "innate" to behavioral phenotypes, but he fails to recognize that his assumption of uniformity in the truly innate characteristics of an organism—its array of genes—is in conflict with facts. A species is not a collection of uniform genotypes, but a group of individuals sharing enough genes in common to enable reproduction. Always under natural conditions there is significant genetic variation within the species.

Such experimental evidence as we have supports the view that the same nurturing procedures yield different results with different genotypes. To achieve satisfactory socialization for a given individual requires attention to the biological substrate as well as to the desired objectives. In a species as genetically heterogeneous as man, no one can tell whether a newborn baby is a "beagle" or a "terrier." Yet the effects of understimulation might be very different in the two cases. Perhaps a continuous monitoring of the child's development can provide adequate care.

This view is in sharp contrast to some educators who feel that children should be considered as innately (their word, not mine) equal. Though the motivation of such advocates is praiseworthy, the logical conclusion of their assumption is that no right of a child is violated by training him for any socially useful vocation his tutors desire, since all of his special interests and aptitudes are acquired. The conflict in viewpoint is not merely academic; it involves the structuring of child care and education of young children in a fundamental way. It is time we rid ourselves forever of the heredity-environment dichotomy and begin to study gene-experience synergisms.

REFERENCES

Fuller, J. L. (1961, 1963). Effects of experiential deprivation upon behavior in animals. *Proc. 3rd Cong. Psychiat., Montreal*, **3**, 223–227.

Fuller, J. L. (1966). Transitory effects of experiential deprivation upon reversal learning in dogs. *Psychonomic Sci.*, **4**, 273–274.

Fuller, J. L. (1967). Experiential deprivation and later behavior. *Science*, **158**, 1648–1652, December 29.

Fuller, J. L., and Clark, L. D. (1966a). Genetic and treatment factors modifying the postisolation syndrome in dogs. *J. Comp. Physiol. Psychol.*, **61**, 251–257.

Fuller, J. L., and Clark, L. D. (1966b). Effects of rearing with specific stimuli upon postisolation behavior in dogs. *J. Comp. Physiol. Psychol.*, **61**, 258–263.

Fuller, J. L., and Clark, L. D. (1968). Genotype and behavioral vulnerability to isolation in dogs. *J. Comp. Physiol. Psychol.*, **66**, 151–156.

Fuller, J. L., and Thompson, W. R. (1960). *Behavior genetics*. Wiley, New York.

Fuller, J. L., and Waller, M. B. (1962). Is early experience different? In E. L. Bliss (Ed.), *Roots of experience*. Hoeber, New York.

Hirsch, J. (Ed.) (1967). *Behavior-genetic analysis*. McGraw-Hill, New York.

Lorenz, K. (1966). *On aggression*. Bantam, New York.

Montagu, A. (1968). Review of D. Morris, *The naked ape*. In *Psychology Today*, **1**, 11–15.

Parsons, P. A. (1967). *The genetic analysis of behavior*. Methuen, London.

Pawlowski, A. A., and Scott, J. P. (1956). Hereditary differences in the development of dominance in litters of puppies. *J. Comp. Physiol. Psychol.*, **49**, 353–358.

Scott, J. P., and Fuller, J. L. (1965). *Genetics and the social behavior of the dog*. Univ. of Chicago Press, Chicago, Illinois.

2

THE ETHOLOGICAL APPROACH
TO SOCIALIZATION*

Eckhard H. Hess†

Two things are of paramount importance to ethologists in studying any behavior: the *context* in which it occurs and its *adaptive value.* Social behavior and socialization processes are not exempt from these considerations.

Social behavior is of sufficient value for the survival of the species that, while there may or may not be learned features, there are always innate, built-in ones. There is social behavior in every species even if just for brief or indirect contact for reproductive purposes during the breeding season. In such cases the complete dependence upon innate built-in mechanisms for the behavior to occur is especially clear, as the animals in such cases have had no opportunity to learn. In one case there may be a concerted release of sperm by males that will fertilize eggs, earlier or simultaneously, deposited in the vicinity by females.

Another example is that of the male mantis who stalks the female in a very specific manner and then jumps on her back in such a way that each one of the four walking feet lands upon one of the four slots situated upon her back (Lorenz, 1958). These slots are equipped with sense organs which will cause her to become temporarily motionless when they are stimulated by the male's feet. If the male makes any mistake in performing "this elaborate chain of behavior patterns," according to Lorenz, the female will eat the male. Such a male would therefore have no second chance to correct any errors or to leave any progeny.

* The research reported in this paper was supported by Grant 776 of the United States Public Health Service, National Institutes of Mental Health and by the Wallace C. and Clara A. Abbott Memorial Fund, The University of Chicago.

† The University of Chicago.

GENETIC BASES OF LEARNING

In social species where there is appreciable parent-young contact (un-like butterflies, earthworms, or turtles), we do find that learning plays a definite role in social behavior. This learning, especially at young ages, is what is commonly meant by _socialization_. Ethologists, particularly Konrad Lorenz (1961, 1965), have recently adopted the view that during the process of phylogeny a species not only acquires adaptive innate behaviors but also acquires the _ability_ to learn certain adaptive behaviors during ontogeny. That is, the species becomes, during evolution, so constituted that the individual members can learn specific kinds of things. And, of course, it must be of greater adaptive value to the species in such cases if learning of some sort is the mechanism by which an individual animal comes to respond in particular situations, than if the individual members are innately constituted to give a specific response to such a situation. And, of course, as has been mentioned, there are cases where an innate response has a greater adaptive value in a particular situation than a learned response would have. All behaviors, whatever their process of origin, either have or have had adaptive value serving toward the survival of the species or the individual, just as all morphological features have or have had adaptive value, whether obvious or not.

Social imprinting as it occurs in certain avian species, notably chicks and ducks, is a socialization process that is an extremely clear form of a kind of learning whose occurrence is _genetically programmed_. It is true, of course, in all cases of socialization, that the learning in question must occur if the particular species is to survive, in terms of the ability of the offspring to reach sexual maturity and reproduce. In this light it is not very surprising that there are innate features that serve to guarantee that the socialization will take place. With social imprinting, however, the urgency for the learning to take place _quickly_ arises because of the fact that the young chicks or ducks are not motorically helpless but can very soon move about. They, however, need to be attached to a parent object so as to have protection from the elements and from predators. Hence, if they do not have the drive to be with a parent object and learn the qualities of that parent object during the first day of life, their chances of survival are very slim unless they are kept in artificial brooders.

IMPRINTING AND LEARNING

My 15 years of research on imprinting in chicks and ducks has shown that during the first 16 hours of life the drive of these animals to learn the parent object is so strong that its processes are contrary to the usual ones found in other cases of learning. There are six fundamental ways in which we have found the processes of social imprinting in chicks and ducks to be different from the laws of association learning that have been deduced by experimenters working in the areas of discrimination or rote learning processes.

CRITICAL PERIOD

The first is the fact that imprinting occurs most efficiently during a specific sensitive period which lasts only during the first day of life in chicks and ducks. Because of the brevity of this sensitive period, it is called a "critical period." There is, in fact, a period of greatest sensitivity to the effects of an imprinting experience during the period of 13 to 16 hours after hatching in these animals, and we have used the term "critical period peak" to describe this maximal effectiveness (see Figs. 1 and 2). While there have been many indications of optimal and sensitive learning periods in the life of organisms, these have in general been rather extensive periods of time, frequently amounting more or less to the proposition that young animals (but usually not including neonates) often can learn more quickly and permanently than can those that are much older. In other words, for many well-known association learning situations, the age of the animals in terms of hours, days, or even weeks is normally not a crucial factor in determining whether the animal learns at all. With imprinting in chicks and ducks, however, it is clear that after the first day of life has passed it is relatively very difficult to produce an attachment for the parent surrogate on the part of the young. This is because in natural conditions the chick or duck species have no need of an ability to learn rapidly the characteristics of the parental object, during the second day of life or afterwards, for the simple reason that those that have not learned this before then are dead.

The concept of sensitive periods in the development of behavior is one that ethology has brought forcefully to the attention of psychologists in this country, although it may also be said that Sigmund Freud's notions regarding stages in the psychosexual development of the child are certainly highly related. They prepared us toward the understanding of the sensitive period notion as applied to behavior and not just to the morphological development of the embryo. Certainly also, John Bowlby's (1951) studies on the effects of age of institutionalization of orphaned children upon their social behavior development reflected a serious examination of the possibilities of sensitive periods in the socialization of human beings.

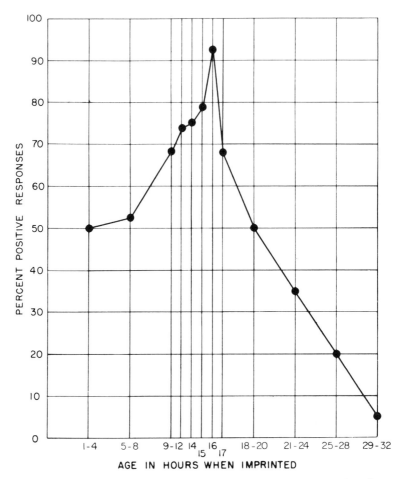

Figure 1. The critical period peak for imprinting in mallards expressed as the mean
percentage of positive responses scored in the imprinting strength test,
conducted at a later hour, by ducklings that were subjected to the imprinting experience at various ages in hours after hatching. (From Hess,
1957.)

Returning to the subject of social imprinting proper, we can find that
the relationship between the environment of the chick or duck and the
ability to imprint gives us a clue as to why some species show less imprinting ability than do others. For example, as we have shown (Hess,
1959), Leghorn chicks are poor imprinters while Vantress broiler chicks
are very good imprinters. Leghorns are a breed which has been selected
on the basis of the lack of brooding of eggs since hens that do not brood
eggs will lay more of them, thus making greater profits for the poultry-

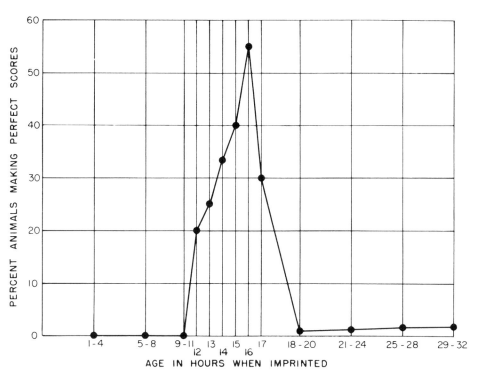

Figure 2. The critical period peak for imprinting in mallards expressed in another way: in terms of the percentage of animals in each imprinting age group that made a perfect response score of 100% in the later test for imprinting strength. (From Hess, 1957.)

man. This breed remains in existence only through the artificial incubation and brooding of fertile eggs and hatched young. Vantress broilers, on the other hand, have been bred for meat qualities. Since Leghorn hens are so unmaternal, it is not at all surprising that their artificially incubated offspring should be quite unfilial. The natural brooding behavior of Vantress broilers has not been altered by selection on the part of animal breeders, and the chicks of this breed are also possessed with a marked filial drive. Once again it becomes obvious that the ability to be socialized to the species and to the parent is genetically determined.

It can be pointed out in passing that neither chicken breed is artificially fed (since they must, on their own, recognize and ingest food objects) and both show the food imprinting phenomenon which takes place optimally at the age of 3 days (Hess, 1962, 1964). This is yet another indication of the importance of a behavior's survival value in its perpetuation.

PRIMACY VS. RECENCY

A second fundamental difference between imprinting and most association learning processes is that, while in discrimination and rote learning experiments, that which has been most recently performed has the most potent influence in determining what the animal does subsequently; in social imprinting it is the first-learned object that is learned the most completely. In other words, it is the primacy of experience, rather than its recency, that promotes the likelihood of its having been learned. We have taken ducks at the peak of the sensitive period, 13 to 16 hours old, and successively exposed them to two different-looking models (Hess, 1959). Half of the animals saw one object first and the other half saw the other object first. The majority of the subjects showed imprinting toward the first-seen object, not to the most recently seen one, when tested 24 hours later.

Ducklings and chicks were exposed at an early age to their siblings with no parental object present and then later an attempt was made to imprint them to a parental object (Polt and Hess, 1964, 1966). The attempt failed even when the exposure took place during the critical period peak itself because the exposure to their agemates had caused them to be already imprinted by the time they first met a parental object; that is, the ability to learn new input had been shut off by the exposure to agemates. This primacy effect is, again, a mechanism having a high survival value in the case of imprinting, because in natural conditions the first active social object is highly likely to be the parent (with the siblings present, of course), and the sooner the imprinting to this parent is completed the less likely it is that imprinting will occur toward any other objects, for if the latter were the case the young would end up being away from its parent and not showing avoidance behavior in response to potential predators. Our research (Hess and Hess, 1969) has shown that the simultaneous exposure to the parent and to siblings in natural conditions does not hinder imprinting to the parent. Perhaps one reason for this is the fact that the parent would be the dominant social object in the environment at the time of the earliest exposure to siblings and parent.

LAW OF EFFORT

The third fundamental difference is described by our *Law of Effort*. In most association learning problems, such as memorizing a list of

words, running a maze, or discriminating between two differently colored boxes for food reward, it has been found that when learning trials
are spaced adequately, the learning is more efficient than when many
learning trials are massed close together. It has been suggested that this
may have some relationship with the formation of discrete memory traces
relevant to the task in question. However, with imprinting, spacing of
practice trials does not improve the efficiency of the learning. Extreme
spacing of trials, of course, would be expected to be affected by sensitive
period factors as well. However, in comparing the effects of a short
interval between two 6-minute imprinting trials with those of a continuous 12-minute imprinting trial during the critical period, there is no
difference in the strength of imprinting displayed on a later test, as
shown by Fischer (1966).

Our investigations have shown, furthermore, that it is not the amount
of time that a duckling or chick spends with the parental object that
determines how strongly it is imprinted to that object; rather it is how
much effort it has expended to be with the mother object or to follow it
(Hess, 1957, 1959). If a duckling followed the decoy for 50 feet, it made
no difference at all whether it was given 10, 20, or 30 minutes in which
to do this much following (see Fig. 3). There appears, furthermore, to be

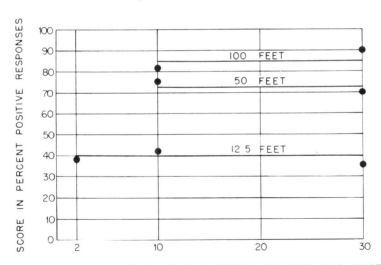

Figure 3.   The law of effort: the mean percentage of positive responses scored in
the imprinting strength test, conducted at a later hour, by ducklings that
were permitted to follow the model for different distances during a 10-
minute imprinting session occurring at the age of 12 to 17 hours. (From
Hess, 1957.)

a logarithmic relationship between amount of following and strength of imprinting, so that marked differences in imprinting strength are observable between animals that have followed 50 feet and those that have followed for lesser distances, whereas there is not much difference in imprinting strength in animals that have followed 50 feet and those that have followed for 100 feet (see Fig. 4). The relationship between effort and imprinting strength can be described as follows: $I_s = \log E$, that is, imprinting strength is a logarithmic function of the amount of effort expended.

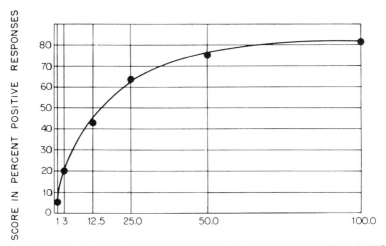

DISTANCE IN FEET FOLLOWED DURING 10 MINUTE IMPRINTING PERIOD

Figure 4. The law of effort: the mean percentage of positive responses scored in the imprinting strength test, conducted at a later hour, by ducklings that were permitted to follow the model for different amounts of time when the distance of following was held constant during an imprinting session. (From Hess, 1957.)

While my Law of Effort has been one of the most debated topics in imprinting literature, there has been, in my opinion, no experimental evidence that disproves it, and our own subsequent research and that of other laboratories have confirmed it in various ways. It is, of course, possible to reinterpret the Law of Effort by pointing out that it may actually be directed *visual* experience which determines imprinting strength and not just motor effort, as Bateson (1966) has suggested. Even so, the relationship between amount of directed following and strength of imprinting still stands.

EFFECTS OF PUNISHMENT

Fourthly, we have made a finding bearing on Ross Parke's (1970) discussion of punishment in socialization. This is the astonishing fact that aversive stimulation from the parental object positively enhances imprinting toward that object! We first noticed this whenever we accidentally stepped on the toes of a duckling we were trying to imprint on ourselves. Though our stepping on their toes surely was painful to them, this experience never caused the ducklings to become afraid of us or to run away from us as would be expected on the basis of the many aversive escape/avoidance learning experiments that have been conducted and that show that an animal will tend to avoid an object or an action which is associated with, or results in, aversive stimulation. Instead, they stayed even closer to us, a fact which made it even more difficult for us to be careful not to step on them.

Later we carried out a formal experiment (Kovach and Hess, 1963) with Vantress broiler chicks in which the chicks were electrically shocked while following a decoy around a runway. When the chicks were at the critical age peak, the shocks actually *increased* the amount of following they did, as long as the shocks were not so strong and so frequent that the subjects became somewhat incapacitated. After the critical period peak, however, the shocks served to *depress* the amount of following engaged in by experimentally naive subjects. This would seem to indicate that, after the peak of the critical period, regular association learning processes begin to take over and the imprinting processes decline after having reached their maximum intensity at 13 to 16 hours of age. This age, it may be pointed out, is one at which most chicks and ducklings have acquired optimal locomotion powers, and therefore it becomes imperative that the parent object be learned. Furthermore, this fits in well with the notion that imprinting involves a supra-individual learning of the species, and the association learning which succeeds imprinting enables the young to know the characteristics of its own individual parent in distinction from other members of the same sex and species as the parent.

Of course, it should be pointed out that traditional learning theory notions regarding the effects of aversive stimulation upon behavior have not satisfactorily explained learning in many other situations. For example, a parent may smack his child for some misbehavior. Since the parent is the agent of the punishment, learning theory would lead us to expect that the child would thereafter avoid the parent. But this is not the case; what he usually does is to avoid performing the misdemeanor which caused the parent to chastise his child. We all know children do not run away from their parents when they are spanked, and yet there are not really too many of us who have reflected on the incongruity of this fact with traditional association learning laws.

Not only that, but there are some people that actually seek aversive stimulation, and this pathological situation is called masochism in the clinical literature. Menaker (1956), for example, has discussed the child that is ruled harshly by an unloving and domineering parent and yet such a child can show an extremely strong and idealized devotion toward the parent. This intensified filial behavior toward the punitive parent appears very similar to the intensified following behavior seen in shocked chicks or ducklings whose toes have inadvertently been stepped on. Actually, however, the strengthening of filial drive and behavior by means of aversive stimulation has a very real and strong adaptive advantage for the survival of the species under natural conditions. This is because if hatchlings should be attacked by predators or encounter some other dangerous situation, it would be disastrous to the young to desert the parent at this time: survival is far more likely through maintenance of attachment to the parent.

DRUG EFFECTS

The fifth difference between imprinting processes and other association learning processes is the effect of meprobamate or carisoprodol upon the retention of learning when the experience takes place under the influence of that drug. Discrimination learning experiments were performed in which chicks learned which of two differently colored food boxes they could see at two ends of a Y-maze contained feed, and the results showed that neither the rate of learning nor the degree or retention was affected by whether the chicks had learned the problem under the influence of meprobamate or of carisoprodol (Hess, Polt, and Goodwin, 1959). But if 13 to 16 hour-old experientially and experimentally naive chicks were exposed to the imprinting object while they were under the influence of either drug, they acted as if they never before had been exposed to the imprinting object when they were tested the next day. In contrast, if imprinting had taken place normally, the influence of meprobamate or carisoprodol during testing did not affect the filial bond they had formed toward the imprinting object. Carisoprodol and meprobamate have also been found to prevent the acquisition of food imprinting in chicks in the sensitive period phase for food imprinting (Hess, 1962, 1964). Hence it appears that the biological basis of the learning process in imprinting is extremely sensitive to certain pharmacological disturbances that do not at all influence learning processes of other kinds.

PRIMARY REINFORCEMENT

The sixth, and final, difference found in comparing imprinting with other forms of association learning is that, in the case of imprinting, the object to be learned is precisely the agent that provides the rewarding properties of the entire situation; that is, the learning is of the *primary* object since the imprinting stimulus both releases *and* rewards the filial behavior. Paradoxically, then, the imprinting object not only has to be learned but acts as an unconditional stimulus! What really happens in imprinting, in contrast to other association learning situations, is that initially there is a rather large number of characteristics which will elicit filial behavior in a young chick or duck, but only the ones that were experienced while the individual is in a sensitive phase will retain this property and the others will lose it. If no imprinting experience has occurred, on the other hand, then the animal will not respond with filial behavior toward any characteristics since no reinforcement has been associated with any of them. Other association learning situations, on the contrary, cause the animal to make certain responses to objects or to sensory characteristics that have not before elicited such responses. In such cases the presence of an unconditional reward agent must be associated with such objects or sensory characteristics, so that the learning is of a *secondary* object.

This sixth difference provides a crucial clue as to why imprinting processes—of either social or food objects—should have some properties which are the converse of those possessed by other association learning situations. We are now in a position to make the prediction that whenever an object to be learned innately releases *and* reinforces unconditionally a particular response, that is, the object is *both* a CS and UCS, then the laws of the learning that take place with respect to this object will be different from the laws of other association learning. In addition, it will be the strongest possible learning, especially in terms of relatively permanent retention and difficulty of being entirely erased. The genetic program of the species, in other words, is responsible for this difference since the animal is so constituted as to *respond innately* to certain kinds of objects during a specific age period, to *be reinforced* for responding and to *learn* the specific object experienced as a permanent elicitor of the behavior.

GENETIC PROGRAMMING OF IMPRINTING

It is not true that any object can serve as a parental object or as a food object. While there have been recurrent observations in the literature that different social objects are not equal in their potentiality for eliciting filial behavior, a recent study (Hess and Hess, 1969) demonstrated that social imprinting is indeed a genetically programmed learning process. Small groups of naive hatchling ducklings were imprinted to either an inanimate duck decoy or to a human being. The half-hour exposure to the social object was repeated ten times over a period of three weeks. After this had been done, the ducks were tested individually for a choice between the decoy and the human being, simultaneously present. The interesting thing about the results was that while every single duckling chose to go to the object to which it had been imprinted, the majority of those that had been imprinted to the decoy dashed to it immediately, while those imprinted to the human being took one or two minutes to make their choice. It is clear that even though the duck decoy is inanimate, cannot move its body parts, and provides no consistent feedback or coaxing to the young ducklings, they imprint more strongly to it. Since its visual characteristics more closely approximate those of the natural parent than the human being does, it therefore follows that ducklings possess an innate, phylogenetically acquired knowledge of what the parent looks like. To rephrase an earlier statement, not all objects are equal to the young duckling in search of a parent.

Since food imprinting exists in a phylogenetically old species, the turtle (Burghardt and Hess, 1965), it may be that the imprinting process, aside from social or food situations, is an ancient form of learning which can be applied in the service of learning things which are highly related to the survival of the species, but which must be learned quickly during a rather limited period of time.

GENETIC BASES OF PARENTAL BEHAVIOR

The importance of the socialization process for the survival of the species in which socialization occurs can also be seen in the fact that it is not a unilateral process depending solely on what the young experiences and does. In species in which prolonged parent-young contact occurs, the parent that cares for the young must adequately perform parental behavior in order for the offspring to be reared properly.

Parental behavior itself possesses innate features in the same way as filial behavior. Lorenz (1943) has pointed out that the qualities of "babyishness" in the young serve as ubiquitous releasers of parental behavior in the animal kingdom wherever there is rearing of the offspring by adults. Figure 5 illustrates these qualities of the facial features of young in comparison with adults of the same species. It is these distinguishing qualities that constitute "babyishness."

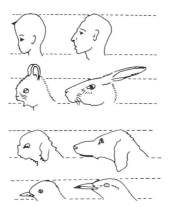

Figure 5.   Young and adult heads of four different species, showing the nature of visual stimuli from the young that serve to elicit parental caretaking reactions. (From Lorenz, 1943.)

These features of "babyishness," as described by Lorenz, include a large bulbous forehead, eyes down farther on the face in keeping with the enlarged forehead, a receding chin, large eyes.

As is readily seen, such "babyish" features also apply with ease to the human species. These are the qualities that have been emphasized by Walt Disney to construct his appealing cartoon creations. Manufacturers of dolls and toys also use them profitably. We all can observe the tremendous visual appeal of baby animals to most people, especially women. Apparently, then, this releaser also operates among humans and had great survival value for the human species when there were no cultural pressures for parents to bring up their children. There is no question that most people will bring up their children, customs or no customs. There are abnormal people who lack these innate responses to their children and, from my impressions of the occasional articles I have run across in psychiatric literature, it seems clear enough that not even social sanctions are able to make them be successful parents. Such a mother may, for example, respond to a pediatrician's tactful suggestion that a baby "needs more company" by propping it up in a stroller so that it can see the passers-by from a window, thus obeying the suggestion to the letter and not to the spirit.

Since normal and healthy babies of a species are morphologically constituted as to elicit optimal parental responses from their caretakers this, then, is another phylogenetically derived insurance that the socialization process will take place, since the parent must be there with the baby if the baby is to become socialized. And, of course, normal and healthy adults of the species are behaviorally so constructed as to respond innately to features of babyishness.

It can be seen, then, that in the ethological viewpoint it is not by chance that the socialization process occurs. This learning occurs because of the concerted effects of several different phylogenetically, and therefore genetically, based processes going on simultaneously to ensure the survival of the species through the rearing and socialization of offspring. The morphological and behavioral development of an individual is programmed to follow certain broad paths, with individual variations in genetic bases and experiences serving to adaptive advantage in the survival of the species. Neither the morphology nor the behavior of the individual can be entirely free of structural direction from the genetic constituents either inherited from the ancestors or derived from chance mutation. Otherwise survival would not be possible. Swallowing and breathing are two examples of such indispensable behavior.

In sum, then, socialization is seen by ethologists as one aspect of a total system. The origins of social behavior are several: the young and parent have innate responses to certain stimuli, and both are more likely to learn certain kinds of things than others. In fact, it may be said, adopting fully Lorenz's (1965) notions regarding the phylogenetic and ontogenetic bases of behavior, that socialization occurs at *both* the *phylogenetic* and *ontogenetic levels*. The phylogenetic level exists throughout the animal kingdom and the role of the ontogenetic level varies for different species.

ETHOLOGICAL ANALYSIS OF SMILING BEHAVIOR

As an example, let us take the smiling response of babies, a behavior which has been rightly held important in the relationship between mother and child. Smiling behavior is indulged in by babies of every single culture known (Darwin, 1872) and is present before birth since it has been observed in premature babies (Wolff, 1963). Visual stimulation is not the sole factor bringing about smiling, since it occurs in blind babies (Eibl-Eibesfeldt, 1967). From the ethological point of view, smiling is an innate fixed action pattern that has high survival value for young babies since their smiling behavior promotes the parental-filial bond. The studies of Spitz and Wolf (1946) and Kaila (1932) have shown that smiling behavior in normal babies is initially elicited by very simple schematic stimuli and progressively requires more specific and detailed stimulation to be set off. Ambrose (1961, 1963) has suggested that smiling behavior has the same kind of function in the socialization of the child as following behavior has in the socialization of the chick or duckling. The similarity, of course, would have to be strictly analogous and not at all homologous, since there is no evidence of a progression of forms of the behavior from following to smiling in related species between birds and humans, as there is in the case of the wing and the arm.

Smiling behavior, though a fixed action pattern, shows vicissitudes with respect to the object to which it is directed, thus showing very clearly the influence of learning on the *elicitation* of smiling, but not as much on the actual *form* of the smiling pattern. The same is true with many other fixed action patterns. The smiling behavior readily serves as a means of indexing the infant's social development and responsiveness toward its environment. As the child becomes more and more attached to one or two specific parents, there emerges an increasingly sharper distinction between the familiar parent and others less often encountered. In many cases the child will show marked fear behavior toward any stranger, whereas previously every person was smiled to broadly. Thus, we may say, an innate behavior serves to indicate the course of a specific learning process while it is taking place. The changes in smiling behavior, it may be pointed out, are similar to the fact that in social imprinting the chick or duckling is at first potentially responsive to a great many stimuli, and afterwards only to its parents.

AGGRESSION

Because of the current widespread interest in these violent times on aggression and its origin, a few comments on the ethological position regarding aggression are in order since it is in social contexts that agression occurs. The ethological position, as stated most clearly by Lorenz (1963, 1966), has been misunderstood even by highly intelligent people. Most commonly these people believe that the ethological findings on and notions of aggression lead to a pessimistic attitude that nothing can be done about the undesirable destruction occurring around us.

This most definitely is not Lorenz's (1966) opinion: "With humanity in its present cultural and technological situation, we have good reason to consider intraspecific aggression the greatest of all dangers. We shall not improve our chances of counteracting it if we accept it as something metaphysical and inevitable but, on the other hand, we shall perhaps succeed in finding remedies if we investigate. Whenever man has achieved the power of voluntarily guiding a natural phenomenon in a certain direction he has owed it to his understanding of the chains of causes which formed it" [pp. 29–30]. Lorenz (1966) also has said, "I believe in the power of human reason as I believe in the power of natural selection, I believe that reason can and will exert a selection pressure in the right direction" [p. 299].

Through the observation of many species of animals, ethologists have come to the conclusion that aggression, broadly considered, is primarily an innately based behavior, and not one that is due to "bad environment" (*destructiveness* is due to bad environment). In fact, the ethologists have found that in most respects aggression is a behavior that has high positive value for the survival of the species under natural conditions. In the case of predators, aggression serves as a means of obtaining food, certainly not of causing destruction or of expressing fear or anger. It is not to the predator's advantage to exterminate all members of the prey species because then it would no longer have any food resources. In the case of prey animals, aggression serves as a means of defense and also, therefore, of maintaining the proper predator-prey balance. Hence the survival value of aggressive behavior is obvious in the case of predators and of prey.

However, the survival value of aggression directed toward members of the same species is rather less obvious. Lorenz (1966) and other ethologists have pointed out the importance of optimal spacing of the members of a given species over the available habitat so that the maximal number may be supported properly. Thus territorialism, as manifested by aggression, serves the positive means of maintaining species survival in that the maximum number of the species in question may be provided for by the environmental resources. Lorenz and many other ethologists have noted that intraspecific aggression in lower animals under natural conditions does not lead to the killing or even any serious injury of fellow members. Usually, aggression consists of symbolic threat actions or highly ritualized fighting.

Another positive advantage of aggression is seen in the defense of the family. In the animal kingdom, if only one sex cares for the brood, it is that sex which is aggressive toward other members of the species. In nomadic ungulate species there are rival fights between males for the female. The rival fight in these species not only results in the strongest male becoming the father of the offspring, but also in the strongest male becoming the defender of the family. Thus the rival fight has evolved stronger males in the species.

Social ranking hierarchies among animal societies are based on who may show aggression toward whom. The social structure of the particular group thus has some individuals serving as "leaders" or "authorities" that make decisions on behalf of the entire group.

The positive value of aggressive behavior does not, Lorenz (1966) emphasized, "negate the fact that under unnatural conditions, for example, confinement, unforeseen by the 'constructors' of evolution, aggressive behaviors may have a destructive effect" [p. 47]. The potential destructiveness of aggression is a feature which is true of other innately based behaviors.

Aggression, like any other innately based behavior, is so rooted biologically that it can be expressed spontaneously and not just in reaction to external conditions. The problems in eliminating destructiveness cannot be solved by concentrating solely on the elimination of aggression. Rather it lies in the understanding of aggression as one component of a complex system of interacting drives, of identifying the pathological conditions which cause aggression to have destructive rather than constructive consequences, and of finding adequate means for channeling aggression into constructive lines. To accomplish this, the needs of the organism in terms of environment and experience must be recognized and properly provided for, so that there is a smooth functioning of the various behaviors in the entire complex.

Lorenz (1966) has emphasized the importance of recognizing the interaction of drives in behavior. It would not be possible to predict the consequences of attempting to make any one of them disappear entirely. Aggression exists in many of our daily acts, and serves as an initiator in getting us to tackle our tasks, in promoting our self-esteem, ambition, creative activity, and so on. Lorenz has asserted that even the ties of personal friendship and marital bonds appear to depend upon the existence of aggression for their origin, although they can, as in the case of Greylag geese, become autonomous of aggression—a fact which he considers hope-inspiring in our search for ways to deal with aggression constructively and for the benefit of mankind.

REFERENCES

Ambrose, J. A. (1961). The development of the smiling response in early infancy. In B. M. Foss (Ed.), *Determinants of infant behaviour*. First Tavistock Seminar on Mother-Infant Interaction, London, 1959. Wiley, New York.

Ambrose, J. A. (1963). The concept of a critical period for the development of social responsiveness in early human infancy. In B. M. Foss (Ed.), *Determinants of infant behaviour II*. Second Tavistock Seminar on Mother-Infant Interaction, London, 1961. Wiley, New York.

Bateson, P. P. G. (1966). The characteristics and context of imprinting. *Biol. Rev.*, 41, 177–220.

Bowlby, J. A. (1951). *Maternal care and mental health.* World Health Organization, Geneva.

Burghardt, G. M., and Hess, E. H. (1966). Food imprinting in the snapping turtle, *Chelydra* serpentina. *Science*, 151, 108–109.

Darwin, C. (1872). *The expression of the emotions in man and animals.* Murray, London.

Eibl-Eibesfeldt, I. (1967). Neue Wege der Humanethologie. *Homo*, 18, 13–23.

Fischer, G. (1966). Distribution of practice effects on imprinting. *Psychonom. Sci.*, 5, 197–198.

Hess, E. H. (1957). Effects of meprobamate on imprinting in waterfowl. *Ann. N.Y. Acad. Sci.*, 67, 724–732.

Hess, E. H. (1959). Imprinting. *Science*, 130, 133–141.

Hess, E. H. (1962). Ethology. In R. Brown, E. Galanter, E. H. Hess, and G. Mandler. *New directions in psychology.* Holt, New York.

Hess, E. H. (1964). Imprinting in birds. *Science*, 146, 1129–1139.

Hess, E. H., and Hess, D. B. (1969). Innate factors in imprinting. *Psychonom. Sci.*, 14, 129–30.

Hess, E. H., Polt, J. M., and Goodwin, E. (1959). Effects of carisoprodol on early experience and learning. In J. G. Miller (Ed.), *The pharmacology and clinical usefulness of carisoprodol.* Wayne State Univ. Press, Detroit, Michigan.

Kaila, E. (1932). Die Reaktionen des Säuglings auf das menschliche Gesicht. *Ann. Univ. fenn. Aboensin.* Series B., 17, 1–114.

Kovach, J. K., and Hess, E. H. (1963). Imprinting: effects of painful stimulation upon the following response. *J. Comp. Physiol. Psychol.*, 56, 461–464.

Lorenz, K. Z. (1943). Die angeborenen Formen möglicher Erfahrung. *Zeitschrift für Tierpsychologie*, 5, 235–409.

Lorenz, K. Z. (1958). The deprivation experiment: its limitations and its value as a means to separate learned and unlearned elements of behavior. Paper presented at the Downing Hospital, Illinois.

Lorenz, K. Z. (1961). Phylogenetsche Anpassung und adaptive Modifikation des Verhaltens. *Zeitschrift für Tierpsychologie,* 18, 139–187.

Lorenz, K. Z. (1963). *Das Sogenannte Böse.* Zur Naturgeschichte der Aggression. Borotha-Schoeler Verlag, Vienna.

Lorenz, K. Z. (1965). *Evolution and modification of behavior.* Univ. Chicago Press, Chicago, Illinois.

Lorenz, K. Z. (1966). *On aggression.* Harcourt, Brace, New York.

Menaker, E. (1956). A note on some biologic parallels between certain innate animal behavior and moral masochism. *Psychoanalyt. Rev.*, 43, 31–41.

Polt, J. M., and Hess, E. H. (1964). Following and imprinting: effects of light and social experience. *Science*, 143, 1190–1192.

Polt, J. M., and Hess, E. H. (1966). Effects of social experience on the following response in chicks. *J. Comp. Physiol. Psychol.*, 61, 268–270.

Parke, R. D. (1970). The role of punishment in the socialization process. Chapter 5 this volume.

Spitz, R. A., and Wolf, K. M. (1946). The smiling response: a contribution to the ontogenesis of social relations. *Genet. Psychol. Monographs*, 34, 57–125.

Wolf, P. H. (1963). Observations on the early development of smiling. In B. M. Foss, (Ed.), *Determinants of infant behaviour* II. Second Tavistock Seminar on Mother-Infant Interaction, London, 1961. Wiley, New York.

PART II

CURRENT EXPLANATORY CONCEPTS USED TO UNDERSTAND SOCIALIZATION

Current Concepts of Socialization

*G. Alexander Milton**

Manifestly it might appear that the four chapters in Part II deal with four different sets of explanatory concepts regarding the socialization processes. A thoughtful reading of these chapters, however, gives quite the opposite impression. Progress is being made in eliminating alternative explanations and a gradual consensus is emerging. For example, we find expressed doubt as to the explanatory power of the primary biological drive reduction hypothesis of socialization, and a zeroing in on the importance of imitation. These authors represent their positions clearly and ably. No preceding summary statement seems required, but at least two points appear which may profitably be noted.

The first point involves the possible significance of a process which might be termed *alter-imitation*. Ferguson notes the existence of *reciprocal matching responses*, e.g., a kind of mutual imitation process where

* University of Victoria.

the parent and child are imitating each other. She goes on to suggest the possibility, and provide anecdotal support for the idea, that a parent's imitation of a child is pleasurable for the child. Hartup and Coates elaborate upon this point in hypothesizing that initial instances of imitation are deliberate matching of the child's behavior by the parent, i.e., the parent imitating the child. Combining these two observations with Bijou's insistence that imitation is a class of discriminative operants, we are left with the intriguing possibility that the *imitation by the parent of the child's behavior* may not only reinforce the child's specific behavior but may also set up an operant reinforcement cycle which ultimately *reinforces the act of imitation* on the part of the child as well. This certainly warrants careful developmental study.

A second point which may need emphasis has to do with the relation between the preceeding section and this one. None of the contributors to Part II would really fit Fuller's earlier classification of the "ardent environmentalist," in that they all grant the contribution of genetic factors to the social development or organisms. Even Bijou explicitly names genetic variables as being among the important conditions contributing to the development of a child's unique personality. Furthermore, Ferguson emphasizes the extremely interesting finding that mother-infant relationships among monkeys show sex differences similar to those which are attributed to social-cultural factors when observed in humans, which more probably would be regarded as a characteristic of the species in subhuman interaction.

These authors, however, have elected to study, through their various strategies, the contribution of environmental factors to the process of socialization, and have in effect adopted the dichotomous view of the heredity-environment controversy and ignored the effective possibility of "gene-experience synergisms." It may well be that many of the discrepancies and inadequacies noted by the authors of this section will be resolved with attention to the synergistic relationships. Even more important, perhaps, this attention may help account for large "error" variances found within methods of socialization. If Fuller is right, differences among the responses of individuals to a given parental practice may be due not to random error, nor to individual difference variation, but to genetic differences not clearly visible in the phenotypes of the individual. The exploration of this possibility makes for an interesting research ideal which is difficult to actualize because we cannot identify the "beagles" and the "terriers" among our human infant subjects. It may be that crude progress in this direction is being made by the studies of sex differences in reaction to socialization conditions ably summarized by Ferguson, and by Hartup and Coates. It may be that gene-experience synergisms underlie the interactions between cognitive structure and effectiveness of punishment found by Parke or even the cognitive systems noted by Harvey in the next section.

In any event, despite the progress toward convergent solutions among the explorers of the social environment represented by the papers in the current section, Fuller's challenge awaits them and may provide impetus for further progress in the development of current concepts for explaining socialization, by offering a place to look for the lost variance in our studies of the social environment.

3

REINFORCEMENT HISTORY
AND SOCIALIZATION*

Sidney W. Bijou†

The unique personality of each child evolves, to a considerable extent, from his own special reinforcement history. That is to say, the specific interrelationships which constitute the child's reinforcement history modify him in such ways that in the future, under specific circumstances, he will behave in ways characteristic of him. This formulation seems straightforward, yet it is easily misunderstood. It may be taken to mean that one's reinforcement history, *as such,* is the cause of his personality development. For example, it is meaningless to say, "Johnny is a hostile and aggressive boy because of the way he has been reinforced in the past." The phrase, ". . . because of the way he has been reinforced in the past," merely asserts that psychological events have historical antecedents. It does not indicate the specific interrelationships that have generated a hostile and aggressive boy. Furthermore, "hostile and aggressive" are not descriptions of Johnny's actual behavior; they are personality traits.

To say that the child's personality stems to a considerable extent from his reinforcement history is a recognition that other conditions also play a part in this development. Among these conditions are: (*a*) other segments of the child's history, (*b*) genetic variables, and (*c*) conditions, especially motivational, in the current living situation. A complete analysis of personality development includes all of these conditions together with the processes which account for changes.

Before discussing the consequences of a child's reinforcement history

* The formulation presented in this paper grew out of research supported by the Division of Research, Bureau of the Handicapped, U.S. Office of Education, OEG–0–9–2322030–0762(032).

† University of Illinois.

as a part of the socialization process, we shall expand on the meaning of these two terms. Reinforcement history refers both to the sequences of stimulus pairings in respondent (classical) conditioning and the contingencies of reinforcement in operant conditioning. The actual ingredients of a history of respondent conditioning are: a description of the stimuli and responses involved, their temporal relationships, the schedule of stimulus pairings, and the setting factors, especially satiation and deprivation when conditioning involves primary appetitive stimuli (e.g., food). The constituents of an operant conditioning history are: a description of the antecedent stimuli, the form of the response, a description of the reinforcers, the criterion for a reinforcement contact (whether it is the character of the antecedent stimulus, the form of the response, or both), and the schedule of reinforcement contingencies. All these factors are taken into account because laboratory research has shown that sequences of operant reinforcement establish the discriminative and reinforcing stimuli and the form of the response, and maintain them in strength through schedules of reinforcement.

In our analysis of reinforcement history, we separate respondent and operant interactions, but it should be understood that they are always interrelated and particularly so in the events of everyday living. For example, when the operant behavior of bringing food to the mouth is strengthened by the food actually in the mouth, the food is also functioning as an unconditioned stimulus eliciting the salivary response. Neutral stimuli paired with the food become conditioned stimuli for that response.

We turn now to the concept of socialization which, as Clausen (1968) points out, has many meanings. "Current usage in the literature varies; most often socialization designates a general area of interest, not a sharply definable process. Sharper delimitation is possible when one speaks of a subarea such as political socialization or socialization to a particular group or role relationship, but even here clear delineation of boundaries is difficult. Often other words or phrases which refer to important aspects or segments of socialization will do as well as 'socialization' to designate a focus of interest—child rearing, social orientation of the child, education, enculturation, role learning, occupational preparation, preparation for marriage and parenthood, adaptation or adjustment to changing individual powers or changing social demands, changing reference groups or reference sets. As a subfield of behavioral science inquiry, socialization comprises all of these. It encompasses the learning of motives and feelings as well as skills and cognitive sets. The concept of socialization embraces equally the efforts of society's formally designated socialization agents (parents, teachers, elders, preachers) to transmit and secure adherence to existing norms, and the mutual efforts of participants in all sorts of relationships (peer group, courtship, marriage, work group) to establish stable expectations" [pp. 5–6].

Here, we shall use the term socialization to mean the study of those conditions and principles involved in the development of social behavior. By social behavior we mean "the behavior of two or more people with respect to one another or in concert with respect to a common environment" (Skinner, 1953, p. 297); by conditions we mean the social, physical, and organismic (physiological) events which are effective for an individual. Social events are conditions involving people, either directly (talking to a child) or in their roles as mediators of nonsocial stimuli (bringing a toy to a child). The principles pertaining to the development of social behavior are the same as those in the development of nonsocial behavior. To say that the principles of development for social and nonsocial behavior are the same is not to imply that social behavior has all of the same characteristics as nonsocial behavior. Two differences may be mentioned: first, social behavior tends to range over a greater variety of stimuli, mainly because of the way verbal behavior can mediate among diversified classes of stimuli. Second, social behavior tends to be more flexible than nonsocial behavior. Social responses are more sensitive to subtle changes in stimuli because many of the contingencies supporting social behavior are on schedules *tied to the way* the individual responds. This is rarely the case in relationships with physical and organismic contingencies. For example, a certain type of social behavior may be supported by an increasing or decreasing ratio schedule of reinforcement, depending on the speed of response. In teaching a child the names of animals from pictures, the teacher may be observed to be reinforcing by saying "that's right" with low frequencies when the child's responses are prompt, and with high frequencies when they are delayed.

The relationships included in one's reinforcement history encompass a broad area, too broad to consider as a single unit of analysis. It is therefore necessary to break it down into components. We shall discuss various aspects of reinforcement history as they pertain to the development of (*a*) stimuli and response "meanings" (functional properties), (*b*) cultural forms of behavior (differentiations), and (*c*) cultural patterns of behavior and personality traits (chained sequences).

REINFORCEMENT HISTORY AND STIMULUS-RESPONSE "MEANINGS"

Reinforcement history gives "meanings" to stimuli and responses. In technical terms, a sequence of reinforcement contacts establishes and maintains the *functional properties* of stimuli and responses. The concept of stimulus and response functions is an important one for psychology because it offers a solution to the problem of how to relate the consequences of one's history to his interactions in the present. Before discussing further the concept of stimulus and response functions, let us present some background on the problem of relating past and present events.

In recent years, systematists have recognized (*a*) that practically all of the subject matter of psychology is historical; hence the history of previous interactions must be taken into account in any adequate analysis of behavior; (*b*) that past interactions influence present interactions only insofar as they modify the individual, the environment, or both; and (*c*) that past interactions have influence only at the time of current interactions. However, a troublesome question has persisted. How can one adhere to these three assumptions and remain within the framework of the natural sciences?

Hull (1943) offered one solution. He suggested that psychologists use the hypothetico-deductive method to construct a general theory which would account for past events in hypothetical variables and relationships which bridge the gap between stimulus input to a subject and his response output. He believed that these hypothetical variables and relationships would eventually be shown to coordinate with biological variables and processes, and that ultimately psychological phenomena would be accounted for in the terms of neuroanatomy and neurophysiology. As recent history has shown, Hull's system did not fare well. The reasons are various; probably the most critical was his attempt to construct a general theory by the hypothetico-deductive method which required uniformities in the basic data not yet achieved.

Lewin (1935) proffered another solution, one that is representative of the phenomenological and cognitive approaches. He suggested that we account for the influences of history by an analysis of the individual's "psychological world", i.e., by determining what the current situation means to him. According to Lewin's theory, evaluation of an individual's psychological world means interpreting information from retrospective accounts, tests, interviews, and personal accounts of how the subject feels about the current situation. It also means synthesizing the findings and correlating them with what the subject does in the situation. Since, in this approach, one set of responses is correlated with another set of responses, only *group* (actuarial) predictions are possible. Functional analyses between stimulus and response events are precluded, and so are the possibilities for advancements in the prediction and control of *individual* behavior.

We now turn to the solution suggested by Kantor (1924) and Skinner

(1938) in terms of stimulus and response function and we start with the concept of stimuli. Stimuli have been defined in so many ways (Gibson, 1950) that some psychologists are wont to say that psychology as a science is still so primitive that we do not know as yet what stimuli really are. To a large extent, confusion in defining the term stems from the dualistic philosophical concept of man: man is assumed to be a creature who has a mind which is in communication with the subjective world and a body in communication with the objective ("real") world. One way to eliminate this definitional difficulty is to replace the dualistic concept with a monistic or unitary concept of man: man is a unified biological system interacting with stimuli which have both physical *and* functional properties. If there is a duality, it is not in the psychological nature of man but in the fact that stimuli may possess both physical and functional dimensions at one and the same time.

The physical properties of stimuli are expressed in the usual space and time units employed in the measurement of physical objects. The functional properties of stimuli are described in terms of their effects on the behavior of an individual under specific conditions. For example, one might ask: does the stimulus set an occasion for the person to perform a specific class of operant behavior (e.g., opening a door or answering a question)? If so, what is its strength? Does the same stimulus elicit respondent behavior? If so, what is its strength? It follows that a class of stimuli, identified by its physical characteristics, may have (*a*) the same functional properties for different individuals, (*b*) different functional properties for different individuals, and (*c*) few or many different functional properties for an individual, depending on his history with that class of stimuli.

This leads us to the concept of response function. A response, in psychology, is a discernable movement of a total-functioning organism. In some studies, the movement itself is the response (frequency of head-banging behavior); in others, the results from a sequence of movements are the response (uttering a sentence); and in still others, the effect on the environment is the response (frequency of turning a dial). In each case, a response, like a stimulus, may be measured in terms of its physical and functional dimensions. With regard to the latter, turning the head to the side might have the function of avoiding a flying object; saying the Spanish word for newspaper to a boy in Madrid, the function of producing a newspaper; and jumping out of a window, the function of escaping from smoke and fire. As is apparent from these examples, a response function is the *reciprocal* of a stimulus function. Some response functions have names such as avoiding, attending, and escaping; others have not as yet been designated.

The Development of Social Stimulus and Response Functions

The experimental studies by Lipsitt and Kaye (1964) on classical conditioning, and Kron (1966), Siqueland (1968), and Siqueland and Lipsitt (1966) on operant conditioning strongly indicate that both respondent and operant processes are operative during the neonatal period. On the basis of their data, we may conclude that the development of stimulus and response functions, social and otherwise, probably start soon after birth.

In all probability, social stimuli with eliciting, discriminative, and reinforcing functions are initially established in relation to the mother or caretaker since she is involved in all, or almost all, of the positive and negative reinforcing contingencies inherent in child-rearing practices. In the act of mediating nonsocial reinforcers and administering reinforcing and eliciting stimuli, her appearance and behavior assume specific and generalized conditioned reinforcing properties. Examples of the latter include proximity of the mother to the infant, paying attention to the baby, being affectionate with the baby, and so on.

Social stimuli take on additional functions when the baby develops first-level motor (Bijou and Baer, 1965) and verbal skills (Rheingold *et al.*, 1959) since they enable him to interact, more and more, with other members of the family, relatives, and friends. The baby's relationships with these individuals do not start *de nouveau*. They have stimulus and response functions generalized from the baby's history with the mother. On the basis of the specific interactions with others, some of these generalized functions undergo modification, and new ones are established.

During the preschool years—the basic stage of development (Bijou and Baer, 1961)—the rate of acquiring new stimulus and response functions increases rapidly. At the same time some of the previously acquired functional properties are maintained while others are modified or extinguished. This acceleration in development is probably linked with the relative decrease in rate of biological growth, the increase in efficiency of biological functioning, and the increase in opportunities for exploration provided by enhanced skills in locomotion, talking, and manual dexterity (Bijou and Baer, 1965). For example, within the class of discriminative stimulus functions, a chair may provide an occasion for the baby to pull himself to an erect position; later, it may provide him with an opportunity to sit prior to eating at a table; still later, it may provide him with an object for climbing, standing, and reaching for a box of raisins on a high shelf. And still later, the chair may be a convenient object upon which to sit after strenuous activity.

Along with his increased mobility and ability to manipulate the environment, the child comes in contact with new physical objects and social events, some with reinforcing, and some with aversive consequences. Hence, many discriminative operants with aversive contingencies are established, perhaps for the first time, during this period. Digging in the dirt in one situation (sandbox) may be reinforced; digging in the dirt in another situation (flowerbox) may be punished.

With the development of verbal behavior comes training in complying with verbal instructions and this training has a direct bearing on the rapid extensions of stimulus and response functions. For example, a mother may give a glass of water to her child and tell him to drink it, and he is expected to do just that. Or she may hand him a glass of water after he brushes his teeth and tell him to rinse his mouth, and he is expected to swish the water around in his mouth and spit it out. The glass of water has two functional properties for this child and he is required to respond to it differentially, depending on the verbal instructions.

Furthermore, mothers in the middle and upper socioeconomic classes have a strong inclination to teach their youngsters all sorts of abstract concepts through informal, and often subtle, discrimination training. Through this process, an aspect of an object or an event in the social, physical, and biological worlds acquires functional properties. The reinforcement contingencies arranged by mothers are usually social, in the form of "that's right," "yes, that's a dog," "no, that is a cow," and so on.

Training during the preschool years has at least two prominent features. First, the frequent use of imitation *to prime* operant behaviors coupled with high rates of social reinforcement to strengthen them. Imitation (a class of discriminative operants which have a topographical similarity between the discriminative stimulus and the operant) is effective in priming new behavior insofar as a child has an imitative repertoire. It is likely that a child begins to develop an imitative repertoire very soon after he can discriminate social (especially verbal) stimuli. (See Chapter 6 in this volume for a comprehensive analysis of the role of imitation in childhood socialization.) Second, the reinforcing function of social stimuli, in the form of parental behavior, is probably more powerful during this stage of development than at any other time in the life of the child. This has been documented by studies in the home and in the nursery school which have shown that the social behavior of preschoolers changes rapidly when the mother (Hawkins *et al.*, 1964) or nursery school teacher (Harris *et al.*, 1964) stops reinforcing undesirable behavior and starts reinforcing desirable behavior.

During later childhood and adolescence—the societal stage—the development of stimulus and response functions focuses on social relationships, with a heavy emphasis on speech and language. Some of the stimulus and response functions related to adults are modified and new ones develop on the basis of contingencies largely under the control of peers. Since the behaviors which are reinforced and punished in an adult-dominated group may be reversed in a peer-dominated group, stimuli and responses may acquire conflicting functions.

REINFORCEMENT HISTORY AND CULTURAL FORMS OF SHAPED BEHAVIOR

The reinforcement history of the child is critical to the formation of many of the manners, customs, and skills cherished by a culture. Since these forms of behavior are shaped on the basis of consequences occurring in family living, they are not only characteristic of the culture, but they are also typical of the geographical and sociological subdivisions of a society. The establishment, modification, and maintenance of the prescribed ways of behaving rest upon two processes: (a) differential reinforcement contingent upon the form of a response, and (b) schedules of reinforcement (planned or situationally derived) establishing stimulus-response chains. Although both processes are involved in the development of cultural forms of behavior, we shall, for purposes of this analysis, discuss them separately. Shaping of cultural forms of behavior will be considered here; establishing stimulus-response chains will be covered in the next section on reinforcement history, cultural patterns, and personality traits.

The shaping of cultural behavior refers to the procedure of delivering reinforcers contingent upon the topography of a response class rather than upon an occasion, as in discrimination training (Skinner, 1953). The history can be such that reinforcement is contingent on an identifiable class of responses within the repertory of the child. A history of this sort produces a learned act. Or the history can be such that reinforcement is contingent upon responses which are successively closer to some desired form of behavior. A history of this type results in a skill. In the simple and highly controlled conditions of laboratory research, an act or a skill is established in short order and can be maintained indefinitely. In the complex and changing relationships of a natural setting, they develop at a slower rate; they may stabilize at a low level of development, and they may deteriorate. Some forms of behavior arise through physical and organismic contingencies, as in picking up a small object and bringing it to the mouth. Some evolve mostly through social contingencies. The arrangements of social reinforcements may be informal, such as those in which the mother or teacher gives social contingencies while she is engaged in something else. Or they may be formal (often called an instructional program) in that someone provides contingencies for proper responses according to some plan. Needless to say, both informal and formal types of training may be ineffective because of other exigencies and because of limited knowledge about shaping principles.

The Development of Cultural Forms of Shaped Behavior

Like stimulus and response functions, the shaping of operant behavior begins within the first month after birth. For example, the turning of an infant's head and eyes toward a source of sound, orienting toward his mother's steps, will probably be reinforced, while orienting in the opposite direction will probably not be. The relationship between the topography of a response and differential reinforcement is more clearly apparent after the infant develops stronger bones and muscles, and improved sensory-motor coordination.

During the first year and a half of life, simple motor skills are developed rapidly and the child grows more adept at managing the parts of his body, moving about, manipulating objects, and imitating vocal stimuli. Reinforcers may be physical (inherent in the properties of the stimuli manipulated), social (the behavior of parents—what they do and say and how they do and say it), organismic (sensory stimulation from the behavior), or some combination of the three. The rapidity of shaping usually observed during this period is attributed to the fact that most of the contingencies are physical and organismic in origin; hence they tend to occur immediately and consistently after each response. A more detailed analysis of the development of the initial body skills is given by Bijou and Baer (1965).

Speech, like gross motor skills, is also shaped during the first 18 months, on the basis of differential reinforcement. However, the course of speech development is not parallel to the course of motor development because of the differences in circumstances. One difference is in the composition of the two classes of responses. Most forms of verbal behavior are made up of the products of movements rather than the movements themselves. As a result contingencies for certain parts of speech are more likely to be delayed. A second difference is in the degree of obscurity of some of the response components. Many of the components of verbal behavior are not easily observable and, consequently, imitative procedures, which ordinarily play a major role in the shaping of motor responses, are less effective for bringing the *detailed* aspects of verbal behavior under reinforcement control. A third difference is in the number of dimensions in each response class. Speech seems to have many more dimensions. When a segment of verbal behavior is differentially reinforced, strength is added to the form of the verbal unit (from syllable to sentence), to its particular enunication, timbre, tempo, and auditory quality.

During the preschool years, training in higher-order motor and verbal skills takes place, not only in the child's home, but also in the homes of relatives and friends, and often times in the nursery school. The behaviors shaped center around the culturally proper ways of eating, speaking, toileting, dressing, etc. In most families, opportunities are provided for the further development of locomotor skills such as tricycling, skating, and climbing, and manual skills such as drawing, cutting, and block building.

During childhood and adolescence extended forms of behaving are established by contingencies controlled by peers. Some of the behaviors developed by those contingencies may be aversive to the adult group; hence, conflicts may arise—the extent and severity depending on the history of the individual and his current situations. Other behaviors strengthened by peers take the form of high-level social and athletic skills, highly prized during these periods. Acquisition and maintenance of such skills often become central to the person's "personality structure."

REINFORCEMENT HISTORY, CULTURAL PATTERNS, AND PERSONALITY TRAITS

Many cultural patterns of behavior and personality traits are established, modified, and maintained by that part of the reinforcement history which pertains to schedules-of-reinforcement contacts. In daily living, reinforcement contingencies occur in intricate, concurrent schedules involving time and responses. The composition of these schedules varies from situation to situation (e.g., those in effect at the dinner table in contrast to those in effect on the playground) and changes within situations as the individual grows biologically and develops socially. (Among other things, the intervals between reinforcers usually increase.) Since the schedules in an individual's history are unique to him, the cultural behaviors generated are also unique to him, although they vary around a "cultural norm."

Some of the behavior patterns that evolve from schedules of reinforcement may rightly be called personality traits. Traditionally, an analysis of personality traits is based on a clinical evaluation or on the results from personality tests. In a typical clinical evaluation, inferences about traits are drawn from psychiatric examinations, psychological tests, social and medical histories, and the like; and a theory of personality, such as psychoanalysis, is used to integrate these traits into a personality structure. In the traditional analysis of traits by means of tests, responses to the test items are intercorrelated, and the clusters of responses that result are given names such as extroversion, anxiety, dominance, and so on. Test-derived traits are generally attributed to hereditary factors, hypothetical mental variables and relationships, and the consequences of history, especially those parts which describe the resolutions of critical conflicts. Although the analyses of traits by clinical and test procedures have been serviceable for diagnostic classification and for job placements, they do not tell us anything about the specific conditions that produce stable forms of individual social behavior. A functional analysis is required for that purpose.

Schedules of reinforcement and their characteristic patterns of behavior have been studied extensively in the experimental laboratory (e.g., Catania, 1966; Ferster and Skinner, 1957; Kelleher, 1966; and Morse, 1966), and Ferster and Skinner (1957) have named and classified the schedules that they have explored. In these studies, the subjects have for the most part been pigeons and rats. However, studies with adult subjects (Weiner, in press), and with normal and retarded children (Long, 1963; Long et al., 1958; and Orlando and Bijou, 1960) have produced results consistent with those obtained with infrahuman subjects.

Because the laboratory is a situation in which relatively simple, single, and concurrent schedules of reinforcement can be studied under highly controlled conditions, it has been possible to show clear-cut relationships between schedules of reinforcement and patterns of behavior. The simple covariations demonstrated in the laboratory would not be expected to be found in the natural ecology because of the complexities in relationships existing there. However, the concepts and principles derived from the laboratory research would certainly be expected to apply.

It is not enough to expect experimental laboratory findings on schedules of reinforcement to pertain in natural settings. Research must be carried on in the natural ecology to demonstrate that the principles do in fact apply. Looking at the whole developmental cycle, one might suggest, for example, that a study be devoted to the relationships among the dominant concurrent schedules in one or two of the major living situations and the child's rate of verbal and motor development. We are assuming that complex concurrent schedules generate behaviors that may be ordered on a scale of flexibility-rigidity. Behavior described as flexible would be expected to facilitate learning, while behavior described as extremely rigid would be expected to hamper it. A second area of research on general development is an analysis of the relationships between concurrent schedules in a given situation and length of sustained sequences of behavior. Indices of development are based not only on the number of stimulus and response functions in the child's repertory and the topographies of his behaviors in social situations (e.g., see the items on the Vineland Social Maturity Scale), but also on his ability to maintain long sequences of behavior, such as working steadily at a task, preparing for an activity, etc.

The Development of Cultural Patterns and Personality Traits

The consequences of concurrent schedules of reinforcement should be apparent in the behavior of the infant within several weeks after birth. This is a reasonable expectation considering (a) that schedules of reinforcement include continuous reinforcement (reinforcement occurring after each response), extinction, and intermittent reinforcement made up of an almost infinite combination of intervals and numbers of responses (Ferster and Skinner, 1957); and (b) that the reinforcement schedules are usually established within weeks after birth in feeding, cleansing, bathing, and preparing the baby for sleep.

The relationship between the schedules-of-reinforcement child-rearing practices and the cultural behavior and personality traits developed from them has been emphasized in the psychoanalytic literature, in cross-cultural studies, and in infant-care research. However, investigations to date have produced little data that permit definite conclusions. The difficulty of obtaining adequate data has been attributed to the complexity of the situations which involve the interaction of schedule effects with (a) the primary and social reinforcers in the schedules, (b) other schedules of reinforcement in effect at the same time, and (c) other stimuli and setting factors. Inadequate research methodology has also been a factor (Caldwell, 1964).

Schedules of reinforcement emanate not only from child-rearing practices but also from the physical, organismic, and social circumstances of development. For example, the location of an infant's crib may establish a characteristic schedule. If, in a small home, the crib is in the kitchen where the mother is working, social reinforcement from the mother will after a time, probably be on a small variable interval or ratio schedule. If, on the other hand, the crib is in a distant bedroom down the hall or on the second floor, it is quite likely that the baby's responses will be reinforced on a large variable interval or ratio schedule. The responses required for social reinforcement under each set of circumstances would establish a characteristic form and chain of responding. How well and how long the pattern would persist would depend on the concurrent schedules in that situation and the schedules in effect under future similar conditions. Changes in the organismic status of the baby also alter the character of the schedules of reinforcement. For example, being more biologically mature and having adequate locomotor equipment and skill to rove about the house independently, the baby comes in contact with many objects and physical situations that produce physical consequences on a continuous schedule, some positively reinforcing, some aversive. The consequent behavior patterns would be long or short chains of exploratory behaviors depending on the other schedules in effect, the availability of things to explore, and their responsiveness to manipulation (Rovee and Rovee, in press). Finally, changes in the social situation providing opportunities to interact with people other than the mother generate new schedules not only because of the differences in the histories (personalities) of the other people, but also because the settings would probably be quite different. For instance, a babysitter is expected to devote all of her attention to the needs of the baby. If she does, the infant has an almost continuous schedule of social reinforcement. The influence of this constant attention on the formation of a pattern of social behavior depends upon many factors, particularly on how often and for how long the babysitter is with the baby, on how much she herself is reinforced by the baby's behavior, and on the effectiveness of her reinforcers for the baby.

A similar analysis can be made for reinforcement schedules in the home during the basic stage of development but it would take into account the increase in complex relationships existing at that time. In addition, the child's participation in informal playgroups in the neighborhood and possibly in the nursery school provides occasions for new and different schedules of social reinforcement. For example, the reinforcement schedules controlled by the nursery school teacher are sure to differ from those controlled by the mother by virtue of the fact that the teacher is required to distribute her attention among all the children and in ways consistent with her school program. The child now also responds to the schedules of social reinforcement arranged by his one or two close friends and by other groups of children in the school as well as those by the teacher. Obviously, then, the youngster's behavior patterns evolve from concurrent schedules under the control of each and all of them. Gavalas and Briggs (1966) and Speer *et al.* (in press) have studied, in a nursery school setting, some relationships between concurrent schedules of reinforcements and patterns of behavior (labeled dependence and competence) in four-year-old children. (See Chapter 4 in this volume for a discussion of the behaviors associated with dependency.)

During the societal stage of development, social reinforcement contingencies in peer groups become powerful. As peer groups become more autonomous and more specialized (social, athletic, academic, etc.), each tends to generate characteristic reinforcement schedules, some with aversive consequences. Patterns of behavior strengthened in one situation may be aversive to the members of another peer group or to an adult-dominated group.

It is also during the societal stage that reinforcement schedules establish interactional chains which involve more than one response system of the *same* individual. These revolve around conflict situations, i.e., situations in which the immediate consequence of a response is positively reinforcing while the remote consequence is aversive, or vice versa. Under conflicting conditions, chains may be formed in which one class of a person's responses changes the circumstances so that another class of his responses is activated. Stated in another way, the individual engages in a series of reactions in which one class of his responses manipulates stimuli to affect the strength of another class of responses. Controlling one's temper in an athletic contest is an example.

SUMMARY

Basic to this presentation is the thesis that the child becomes a unique personality largely because of his reinforcement history. A child's reinforcement history consists of the sequences in interactions that strengthen and weaken both operant and respondent behaviors through reinforcement contacts. Three consequences of reinforcement history are stressed: (a) the development of "meanings" or stimulus and response functions, (b) the shaping of cultural forms of behavior, and (c) the formation of cultural patterns and personality traits (interactional chains). For the most part, stimulus and response functions evolve from reinforcements contingent on occasions (discriminative stimuli); shaping of cultural forms of behavior emerge from reinforcements contingent on topographies of responses; and cultural patterns and personality traits result from reinforcement schedules.

This conception of reinforcement history is applied to the socialization of the child through an analysis of the conditions that prevail at three stages of development—universal, basic, and societal. Greater emphasis is given to the interactions during the early periods. The concepts and principles of an empirical behavioral analysis (Bijou and Baer, 1961 and 1965) are employed throughout.

REFERENCES

Bijou, S. W. and Baer, D. M. (1961). *Child development: A systematic and empirical theory.* Vol. 1. Appleton, New York.

Bijou, S. W. and Baer, D. M. (1965). *Child development: Universal state of infancy.* Vol. 2. Appleton, New York.

Caldwell, B. M. (1964). The effects of infant care. In M. L. Hoffman and Lois W. Hoffman (Eds.), *Review of child development research.* Russell Sage Foundation, New York.

Catania, A. C. (1966). Concurrent operants. In W. K. Honig (Ed.), *Operant behavior: Areas of research and application.* Appleton, New York.

Clausen, J. A. (Ed.) (1968). *Socialization and society.* Little, Brown, Boston.

Ferster, C. B. and Skinner, B. F. (1957). *Schedules of reinforcement.* Appleton, New York.

Gavalas, R. J. and Briggs, P. F. (1966). Concurrent schedules of reinforcement: A new concept of dependency. *Merrill Palmer Q.,* **12,** 97–121.

Gibson, J. J. (1950). *The perception of the visual world.* Houghton, Boston.

Harris, J. R., Wolf, M. M. and Baer, D. M. (1964). Effects of adult social reinforcement on child behavior. *Young Children,* **20,** 8–17.

Hawkins, R. P., Peterson, R. F., Schweid, E. and Bijou, S. W. (1966). Behavior therapy in the home: Amelioration of problem parent-child relations with parent in a therapeutic role. *J. Exp. Child Psychol.,* **4,** 99–107.

Hull, C. L. (1943). *Principles of behavior: An introduction to behavior theory.* Appleton, New York.

Kantor, J. R. (1924). *Principles of psychology.* Vol. 1. Principia Press, Bloomington, Indiana.

Kelleher, R. T. (1966). Chaining and conditioned reinforcement. In W. K. Honig (Ed.), *Operant behavior: Areas of research and application.* Appleton, New York.

Kron, R. E. (1966). Instrumental conditioning of nutritive sucking behavior in the newborn. *Recent Advances in Biol. Psychiat.,* **9,** 295–300.

Lewin, K. (1935). *A dynamic theory of personality.* McGraw-Hill, New York.

Lipsitt, L. P. and Kaye, H. (1964). Conditioned sucking in the human newborn. *Psychonom. Sci.,* **1,** 29–30.

Long, E. R. (1963). Chained and tandem scheduling with children. *J. Exp. Analaysis of Behavior,* **6,** 459–472.

Long, E. R., Hammack, J. T., May, F. and Campbell, B. J. (1958). Intermittent reinforcement of operant behavior in children. *J. Exp. Analysis of Behavior,* **1,** 315–339.

Morse, W. H. (1966). Intermittent reinforcement. In W. K. Honig (Ed.), *Operant behavior: Areas of research and application.* Appleton, New York.

Orlando, R. and Bijou, S. W. (1960). Single and multiple schedules of reinforcement in developmentally retarded children, *J. Exp. Analysis of Behavior,* **4,** 339–384.

Rheingold, H. L., Gewirtz, J. L. and Ross, H. W. (1959). Social conditioning of vocalizations in the infant. *J. Comp. Physiol. Psychol.,* **52,** 68–73.

Rovee, C. K. and Rovee, D. T. (in press). Conjugate reinforcement of infant exploratory behavior. *J. Exp. Child Psychol.*

Siqueland, E. R. (1968). Reinforcement patterns and extinction in human newborns. *J. Exp. Child Psychol.,* **6,** 431–442.

Siqueland, E. R. and Lipsitt, L. P. (1966). Conditioned head-turning in human new-borns. *J. Exp. Child Psychol.*, 3, 356–376.

Skinner, B. F. (1938). *The behavior of organisms.* Appleton, New York.

Skinner, B. F. (1953). *Science and human behavior.* Macmillan, New York.

Speer, D. C., Briggs, B. F. and Gavalas, R. J. (in press). Concurrent schedules of social reinforcement and dependency behavior among four-year-old children. *J. Exp. Child Psychol.*

Weiner, H. (in press). An analysis of inter-subject variability under fixed-interval schedules with humans. *J. Exp. Analysis of Behavior.*

4

DEPENDENCY MOTIVATION
IN SOCIALIZATION

*Lucy Rau Ferguson**

The process of socialization may be broadly conceived as one in which parents, schools and other agents and institutions of society exert influence on the developing social behavior of children. The prolonged physical dependence of the young of the human species makes it possible for child-care agents to control many very basic sanctions and incentives. It has been rather generally accepted, however, that the emotional dependency which the child develops on parents and other significant persons is an even more important source of influence. The fact that children, and adults for that matter, value the presence, attention, and approval of significant others, and fear their loss, has been considered a most powerful motive for conformity to the expectations of these others, for imitation and identification, for the acquisition of values, for the internalization of behavioral controls, for academic achievement, and for many other aspects of socialization. This general process of social influence can be studied from two different perspectives, one of which has been adopted in studies of dependency and the other characterizing the many recent experimental studies of social reinforcement. One can ask the question: "What are the effects of manipulating such social reinforcers as attention, approval or the mere presence of an adult, and what are some of the determinants of these effects?" Or one may ask: "What current or antecedent conditions are associated with the tendency to seek attention, company, approval or help, and what other behaviors can we predict from such a tendency?" Each of these research problems is, in a sense, the reciprocal of the other. The research strategies and some of the assumptions are different, but in each case we are looking at the same set of social interactions.

* Michigan State University.

59

The use of the concept of "dependency" does imply that we are dealing with a more or less enduring set of response dispositions, which may vary from one individual to another and may be evoked to varying degrees by different situations or environmental events. In other words, the term "dependency" usually refers not only to specific responses but to a general trait. In addition, it has also been defined as an inferred motive or drive, assumed to underlie the overt manifestations of dependency. These usages of the term "dependency" as they apply to an account of the socialization process will be critically examined in the following pages.

Objections to the definition of "dependency" as a motive have reflected in part the general theoretical position that motivational constructs are unparsimonious and unnecessary in functional accounts of behavior and behavior development. More specifically, they have also taken issue with the traditional account, put forth by Sears *et al.* (1957 and 1965) and others, of dependency as a derived or secondary drive, based on the association of the caretaker with the satisfaction of more "basic" or primary biological drives. Without becoming embroiled in the more general question of the usefulness of the drive concept, which seems beyond the scope of this paper, some aspects of the second issue will be briefly reviewed. The social learning theorists explained the development of the "derived" drive or motive of dependency on the basis of the association between the mother's presence and the reinforcement provided by the reduction of such "primary" biological drives as hunger, thirst, cold, pain and discomfort, etc. It seems fairly clear that the psychoanalytic theory of the "oral" period influenced these theorists to focus especially on the feeding situation as crucial in the mother-infant interaction. The psychoanalytic notion of sucking as intrinsically gratifying and providing instinctual pleasure was modified to allow for an increase of drive strength through practice and through the association of sucking with the reduction of hunger and thirst. There is indeed some evidence (e.g., from Davis *et al.*, 1948; Sears and Wise, 1950; Sears *et al.*, 1957) that the "oral" drive is in part a learned or secondary drive, which increases in strength with greater amounts of reinforced practice, and that amount of sucking experience is related to such measures of drive strength as upset over weaning. There have also been some studies relating early oral experiences to later oral behavior and symptoms, and even a few (e.g., Goldman-Eisler, 1953) purporting to demonstrate a relationship between early oral experience and "oral" character traits in adults (optimism vs. pessimism). However, the bulk of the evidence from studies relating infant care practices to measures of social behavior even in preschool children (Sears *et al.*, 1957, 1965; Caldwell, 1964) fails to demonstrate any stable or significant relationship between experience in the feeding situation and dependency in young children. These studies are beset by a number of methodological problems, but it seems that the main difficulty is that the preoccupation with orality inherited from psychoanalytic theory led to a focusing on the wrong aspects of mother-infant interaction.

The recent experimental work on the determinants of social responsiveness and factors which shape particular social responses such as smiling and vocalization, as well as the more naturalistic studies of the development of attachment, seem to be converging in a way which will be much more productive of meaningful relations between infantile experience and the development of dependent behavior. Certainly the evidence from these studies suggests that the infant's response to social objects does not depend on their association with the reduction of "primary" biological drives, such as hunger or thirst, although the function of contact with the mother in reducing generalized distress may be important (cf. Bronson, 1968). Rather, such stimuli as the smiling human face or a familiar voice are in themselves the most effective elicitors and reinforcers of the infant's smiles and vocalizations. Further, the strength and specificity of attachment seems to be much more a function of the amount of contact and responsive attention which has characterized the mother-infant relation than of the mother's purely instrumental functions. Before examining some of the implications of the work on attachment and social responsiveness for later dependent behavior, however, a closer look at the behaviors to which the term "dependency" refers is in order.

A brief survey of a number of recent studies of social development reveals that the following behaviors have been classified under the general rubric of dependency: seeking attention (including both positive and negative forms of attention-seeking behaviors), seeking recognition or approval, seeking comfort and reassurance, seeking physical proximity to another person, seeking or maintaining physical contact (touch and holding, clinging), seeking help, protest at separation or separation anxiety, anxiety over loss of nurturance, passive reaction to frustration. A number of authors have followed Heathers' (1955) distinction between "emotional" and "instrumental" dependency, and the latter has often been contrasted with independence or self-sufficiency. Other researches, which seem to involve observation of behaviors identical with or very similar to some listed above, have been carried out under the conceptual labels of "attachment" or "affiliation." Some of Schacter's (1959) work on affiliation, for instance, measured the subjects' preferences for the company of others as opposed to remaining alone in an anxiety-provoking situation. In one of the best known naturalistic studies of the development of attachment, Schaffer and Emerson (1964) used the infant's protest at separation as their primary index of specific attachment.

Faced with this rather diverse set of behaviors (and a more thorough search of the literature might well have revealed more), the question arises whether a single behavior system or at least an empirically and theoretically coherent set of response dispositions is involved. A rational analysis of these behavioral labels, coupled with a consideration of the intercorrelations among the observational categories used in a number of the studies of dependency in the literature, leads to the conclusion that at least three major sets of response dispositions are involved, namely (a) the *activity-passivity* dimension, (b) *instrumental dependency*, or help-seeking as opposed to self-sufficiency, and (c) a variety of behaviors designed to *elicit or maintain contact with and positive response from others*. The intercorrelations between these behavioral dimensions are not necessarily positive in all subject populations, and there is evidence that they reflect the operation of different sets of antecedents.

ACTIVITY-PASSIVITY

The only major study of social development to include passivity with other measures of dependency is the Kagan and Moss (1962) analysis of the Fels longitudinal data, and they do not make clear how passivity intercorrelates with the other dependency variables in childhood, although it does seem to show some predictive relationships, e.g., to dependency on love objects in adult women. These authors conclude that while passivity shows considerable stability, especially in women, from infancy into adult life, it is probably a trait primarily determined by constitutional factors rather than by social experience. Direct observations of individual differences in response patterns among infants (e.g., the work of Thomas *et al.*, 1963) tend to confirm the view that some such general dimension of responsivity as activity vs. passivity appears as a relatively stable trait shortly after birth, and shows some association with sex, males being more active. Bell (1968) suggests that such individual differences in activity level or "assertiveness" may well exert an important influence on the mother-infant interaction and the infant's resulting social experience, rather than being a product of social experience, as has often been assumed. Some recently published observations by Mitchell (1968) of mother-infant interaction in the rhesus monkey would tend to support this view. He found significant differences between the sexes in amount and kind of maternal contact. Mothers of female infants engage in more nonpunitive physical contact with them and protect them more, while mothers of male infants are more likely to withdraw from them and also more likely to engage in aggressive play with them. Similar observations on human mother-infant interaction might plausibly be explained on the basis of the mother's culturally determined attitudes towards the sex of her child. For instance, in a study of identification in five-year-olds (Sears *et al.*, 1965), it was found that the mother's acceptance of sexuality was more highly positively correlated with permissiveness for aggression in boys and permissiveness for dependency in girls. However, if Mitchell's observations prove generalizable to human as well as other primate species, they suggest that the congenitally less active female infant is more likely to receive reinforcement for contact and comfort-seeking, a factor which may well be important in determining the typical sex differences in the development of attachment which will soon be discussed.

Thus, while passivity may prove to be positively correlated with emotional dependency, these variables may reflect quite different determinants.

INSTRUMENTAL DEPENDENCY

Beller (1959) reports a measure of instrumental dependency, seeking help, to be consistently and quite highly positively correlated with measures of his subjects' tendencies to seek attention, contact and recognition. The help-seeking variable also shows substantial negative correlations with measures of autonomous achievement-striving, although his other dependency measures do not. Beller is the only major investigator in this area to report such a substantial relationship between instrumental and emotional dependency, and his measures have frequently been criticized as being based on global ratings by nursery school teachers, and thus subject to halo effects, or contamination by the raters' preconceptions of how these behaviors ought to be related. Another problem in Beller's data, which may be even more relevant to his findings, concerns his subject population. His studies were carried out on a sample of moderately disturbed children attending the therapeutic nursery of the Child Development Center in New York. As compared to well-adjusted preschoolers, these children were presumably characterized by relatively high levels of anxiety. Highly anxious children are likely both to be lower in self-sufficiency and autonomous coping ability and also to seek contact and reassurance from adults to a relatively greater extent than other children. Walters and Parke (1965) have suggested that the increases in affiliative behavior in social isolation experiments may well be a function of the anxiety aroused by these experimental procedures, and one may argue that the "emotionally disturbed" child carries around a relatively chronic vulnerability to stress. Beller's own data clearly indicate that his high-dependency children both increase in attention and contact-seeking and decrease in self-sufficiency under conditions of even mild frustration. It is also possible, of course, that requests for help from an adult are indeed instrumental, not so much in the completion of the task or the attainment of some nonpersonal goal, but rather in securing the attention or proximity of the adult. One can observe the reinforcement of this connection between emotional and instrumental dependency in any first grade classroom. The child who hangs around the teacher's desk just to be near her will usually be sent promptly to his seat, but if he can produce a question about his schoolwork or some other problem with which he needs help, he is much more likely to be allowed to stay. As many a teacher has regretfully discovered, however, the result of such reinforcement is usually that the child seems to need more, rather than less, help in completing his work.

What is being stated here is that instrumental dependency or low self-sufficiency is not *necessarily* closely related to other aspects of dependency, and should probably not be considered part of the same behavior system. Help-seeking, attention-seeking and contact-seeking may come to covary closely in certain subpopulations of children, either because high levels of anxiety both interfere with the development of autonomous coping skills and reflect disturbances in the normal development of attachment, or because helplessness has become instrumental in securing attention and contact, just as some children seem to develop patterns of accident-proneness or frequent minor illness for the same reason. Again, it seems to me that the assumption that instrumental and emotional dependency must necessarily be closely related derives mainly from the secondary drive notion of dependency, that emotional attachment develops because the caretaker satisfies the biological needs of the helpless infant. Studies of institutionalized babies who have experienced insufficient or inconsistent interpersonal contact (see Yarrow, 1964), Harlow's (1961) work with monkeys, and the experimental studies of social reinforcement (e.g., Rheingold et al., 1959) all combine to suggest strongly that the affectional response system develops somewhat independently of the satisfaction of survival needs.

The relationship between instrumental and emotional dependency becomes considerably more complicated if one considers not just the data from cross-sectional studies of nursery school children, but the continuities and changes over successive developmental periods. Kagan and Moss (1962) report that, while in women passivity and a close emotional relationship to one's family in childhood tend to be maintained through adolescence and into adulthood, the opposite is true for men, and there is even a negative correlation between instrumental dependency in early childhood and in adolescence. Also, males are more likely to show shifts in the objects of emotional dependency from family to friends, and these shifts seem to be correlated with the development of self-reliance. On the other hand, self-reliance and autonomous coping ability in middle childhood and later developmental stages may be facilitated by a close attachment in infancy and early childhood. In a study of achievement behavior in second-graders, Rau *et al.* (1964) found that boys who were more self-sufficient, and showed generally better interpersonal and academic coping skills, had mothers who had been more accepting in their attitudes towards them when they were in kindergarten as well as more supportive of their independence strivings. It is not known, of course, that maternal warmth, as measured by parental attitude scales administered during the child's preschool or early school years, is necessarily postdictive of a positive mother-infant relationship, although the Bayley and Schaefer (1964) data would suggest some such developmental continuities, especially for boys.

In a set of studies recently completed in the Psychological Clinic at Michigan State University, Rowland (1968) selected contrasting groups of boys judged by their teachers as either high or low in self-sufficiency as compared to their classmates. The boys were then observed with their mothers in an interaction situation structured so as to present them with a frustrating problem-solving task, and the mothers were administered a set of parent-attitude questionnaires developed by Winder and Rau (1962). The boys judged more self-reliant by their teachers did indeed show more constructive reactions to frustration in the experimental situation. The mothers of the more self-reliant boys not only expressed more positive attitudes towards them (i.e., received lower Rejection scores on the questionnaire), but also interacted with them in more positive and supportive ways in the frustration situation, encouraging their independent attempts at problem solving and engaging in much less interference and criticism than the mothers of the less self-reliant boys. An incidental observation of the experimenter is one of the most interesting aspects of the study. The high self-reliance group were much more likely than the other group, whose attempts to cope with frustration were less constructive and more likely to be aggressive or regressive, to engage in self-instruction and self-reinforcement in the course of working on the problem. Thus the self-reliant eight- or nine-year old, while struggling with a difficult problem in the presence of an attentive and supportive but non-interfering mother, engages in behavior towards himself which may well be imitative of her behavior towards him at earlier developmental

periods. This observation, in conjunction with studies of exploratory behavior in infants, suggests that the development of self-reliance is facilitated by the establishment of a secure attachment at earlier stages.

A study carried out some years ago by Celia Stendler (1954), although
based on a very small sample, illustrates the rather distinct antecedents
of instrumental and emotional dependency, at least in extreme cases. She
selected a group of 20 first graders who were judged according to a
number of criteria to be "overdependent." They received extreme scores
on a number of teacher ratings of both help-seeking and contact-seeking
behaviors, especially reluctance to be separated from the mother. The
mothers of 6 out of the 20 cases met the criteria for maternal over-protec-
tion, as described by Levy (1943); they encouraged the child's dependence on them and thwarted any attempts at self-sufficiency. These
children tended to be "physically dependent," i.e., low in self-reliance.
The other 14 children presented a rather different pattern of high *emotional* dependency. To a much greater extent than either the physically
dependent children or the control group, they had experienced serious
discontinuities in care in the period between six months and three years
which Bowlby (1951) considered critical for the development of attachment. Their mothers also tended to be inconsistent in their current handling of the child's dependency, thus presumably increasing anxiety and
the tendency to seek reassurance through further dependent solicitations.
The implication is that inconsistent nurturance, whether brought about
through separations or through erratic maternal behavior, may lead to
extreme emotional dependency.

EMOTIONAL DEPENDENCY

In studying the socialization process, not only are the extremes of
dependent behavior of interest, but also the conditions which lead to a
degree of emotional dependency sufficient to account for the child's
susceptibility to the influence of socializing agents. As was indicated
earlier, once there is focus on those behaviors which are generally taken
to be indices of *emotional* dependency—such as seeking physical proximity, attention or approval—rather than on such behaviors as instrumental
dependency or passivity, the most fruitful line of evidence would seem
to come from the studies of Schaffer and Emerson (1964), Ainsworth
et al. (1967) and others (e.g., Cox and Campbell, 1968) on the development of *attachment* in infants and young children. Indeed, if we allow
for the differences in response repertoires attributable to the different age
levels of the subject populations used, then the terms "attachment" and

"emotional dependency" seem to refer to essentially the same cluster of interpersonal behaviors.

If it is assumed that the clues to the development of emotional dependency and affiliation in later childhood and the adult years lie in the establishment of attachment and its vicissitudes in infancy and early childhood, then a number of the inconsistencies and discontinuities in dependent behavior which have seemed puzzling to previous investigators may become explicable. If dependency is thought of as a system of behaviors or as a trait, the implication is that there should be consistency in the overall level of dependent behavior which an individual shows as compared to other individuals. The data of most studies, however, do not fit this assumption. A given child's status on a given measure of dependency will depend both on the particular response being measured and on the interpersonal situation in which he is being observed. Sears *et al.* (1965) report the intercorrelations among a number of measures of dependency in a sample of 40 five-year-olds based on extensive time-sample observation through eight weeks of nursery school and on two periods of mother-child interaction. For girls, there is some tendency for such aspects of dependent behavior in the nursery school as attention-seeking, seeking physical closeness, and seeking comfort and reassurance, to be positively interrelated and to predict demands for attention from the mother, but there is no such consistency for boys. Forms of dependency which involved seeking physical contact or proximity seemed more closely related to each other than to attention-seeking, and the authors suggest that the latter may be a more mature form of dependent behavior for five-year-olds. Attention-seeking was also found to predict the child's tendency to engage in behavior which was imitative of typical adult actions (adult-role behavior). This was true for both boys and girls when the measures of adult-role behavior involved engaging in adult work; for boys alone, however, behavior which seemed imitative of adult nurturance was correlated with the more immature forms of dependency (physical contact-seeking). The data also indicated that when dependent behavior was directed towards peers, the object tended to be a child of the same sex. This differentiation is found even more strongly among somewhat older children.

A more recent study by Radke-Yarrow *et al.* (1968) also examines the generality of dependent behavior in nursery school children (sample of 43 four-year-olds of each sex) by comparing intercorrelations of sets of items from different sources. Mother-interview items measuring attention and closeness wanted and separation reactions intercorrelated well, but questionnaire items did not. (It may be that interview items are more susceptible to halo effects.) Teachers' ratings of the degree to which the child sought closeness and attention from them intercorrelated well, but correlated essentially zero with the child's reaction to separation from the mother. The only item which yielded clear correspondence across different sources of information was the one on the child's reaction to separation from the mother. These data would seem pretty clearly to reflect not a generalized trait of dependent behavior but a specific attachment to one person in the child's life, the mother, which does not necessarily generalize to other adults such as nursery school teachers.

In view of such findings, one may well be inclined to conclude that the concept of dependency as a generalized trait or behavior system is untenable. One would then proceed to a functional analysis of much more narrowly defined response classes and to the stimuli which elicit or maintain them in specific behavior settings, as Bijou (in this symposium) or Gewirtz (1969) might suggest. It seems, however, that there is a possible alternative. This is to consider behaviors which have generally been grouped under the rubric of emotional dependency, affiliation, or other related terms, as developmental derivatives of the *attachment* system. The concept of "attachment" refers essentially not merely to a given class of responses, but rather to a special sort of relationship between a subject and a social object, to a particular kind of interpersonal transaction. This is, of course, implied when such dependent behaviors as "seeking attention" or "protest at separation" are recorded; judgments by observing the subject's behavior in reference to a specific social object, such as mother or teacher or peer, are always being made. Thus in making predictions about dependent behavior, the object towards whom it is directed must be just as relevant as the specific form of the behavior. In fact, the question of how to categorize a child's behavior can only be answered after the response which it elicits has been observed. Is a given bit of "acting-up" in the classroom an expression of an aggressive reaction to frustration or of negative attention-seeking? Often this cannot be determined until the teacher's response and the child's subsequent reaction to that response has been observed. And the same sequence of acts directed towards a classmate may have quite a different meaning—may be intended, for instance, to secure acceptance and approval.

In accounting for the development of dependent behavior, then, a primary task is to describe the developmental sequences in (*a*) the stimulus conditions and specific responses through which attachments are established and maintained, and (*b*) the differential choices of objects of attachment. Experimental and observational studies of infants suggest some developmental sequences of specific interactions which are important in the development of attachment in the first year of life. Of earliest significance are tactile stimuli provided by skin contact with the mother, and especially those secured through sucking; the proprioceptive stimulation provided by rocking and secure holding may be important too. By two or three months the distance receptors of audition and vision have become important avenues of stimulation, and Walters and Parke (1965) have made a very convincing case for their significance in the attachment process. In fact, they suggest that "contact comfort" may be important primarily for the development of affectional responses which are later integrated into sexual behavior, whereas psychological attachment is primarily mediated by the distance receptors. I would prefer to consider affectional responses as part of the attachment process, but this is partly a matter of the level of analysis one chooses. It may also be that sex differences are involved here. Generalizing from Mitchell's monkey data, females would seem to get more reinforcement of contact-seeking, whereas visual stimulation may be relatively more important for males. Schaffer and Emerson (1964) report somewhat distinct patterns of mothering, one involving primarily physical contact and the other involving contact through voice and facial expression, but they do not indicate if these different patterns were associated with sex of child. Clinical literature suggests that females are more likely to be sexually aroused by tactile stimulation, whereas males have a greater erotic response to visual stimuli; it remains to be seen whether these differences relate to earlier differences in affectional responses. By the end of the first year, some sort of cognitive representation of the caretaker probably becomes possible for the infant and assumes some importance in the further development of attachment. It begins to be possible for the infant to maintain "contact" with the objects of attachment over at least brief intervals of time as well as space, although almost all children show marked reactions to separation at least through their third year, with persistence of separation anxiety in many children at least until the early school years.

In a recent review of evidence bearing on the development of fear in various mammalian species, Gordon Bronson (1968) suggests some important parallels between these stages in the crucial interactions for the establishment of attachment and the emergence of unconditioned fear reactions. In the earliest developmental period, generalized distress reactions are provoked by pain, discomfort, and sharp noises, and are allayed by physical contact, rocking, and the opportunity to suck. Fear reactions to a strange person emerge clearly, on the average, at seven to nine months, and this is precisely the period at which a differential attachment to a specific person, usually the mother, is first evident (according to Schaffer and Emerson, 1964). By the end of the first year, the mere presence of the mother and the opportunity for the infant to maintain visual contact with her seems to allay the fear reaction to strangers and to other visually presented novel stimuli. Autistic children and those who have experienced abnormal or deprived patterns of mothering, according to Bronson's review, have unusually intense fear reactions to visual novelty and are likely to engage in stereotyped, self-stimulating behavior when exposed to novel situations. For normal infants in the second year, on the other hand, the presence of the mother in a novel situation serves to support exploratory behavior. This is amply illustrated by some of the recent work of Ainsworth (1967) and others. Cox and Campbell (1968), for instance, report that babies aged 13 to 15 months, placed in a novel situation, show significant decrements in speech, movement, and play when the mother is absent as compared to when she is present, and there are a number of other studies of this age group which report very similar findings. The authors just cited carried out similar observations of another group of subjects aged 20 to 37 months, and found similar but much less marked effects of mother absence. Apparently by the third year of life, children are more able to adapt to the mother's absence and sustain exploratory and constructive activity. It is not clear, however, whether this developmental effect is a function of increasing familiarity with a range of environmental conditions, so that a "novel" situation is in fact less novel—the emergence of other means of coping with fear which do not involve contact with the mother (e.g., aggressive reactions)—or whether it is a function of the increasing ability to maintain contact by symbolic means and thus tolerate separation. It is hoped that future research focusing on the two- to three-year-old age group will clarify just which of these processes are involved. I would like to suggest, at this point, that there may well be developmental continuities between the security-giving function of the mother in novel situations, sustaining exploratory behavior, and the findings of such studies as Rowland's (1968), reported earlier, on the relation between the coping behavior of school-aged boys and a supportive mother-child interaction. Again, future research might well attempt to clarify the nature of the age-appropriate patterns of interaction by which such a supportive attachment is maintained at later ages—one is reminded of the concept of "nonpossessive warmth" currently being used in process studies of psychotherapy interaction. An observation which may be relevant here comes from Diana Baumrind's (1967) study of parent-child interactions associated with different patterns of social adjustment in nursery-school children. She found that the parents of children who showed the most mature and adaptive cluster of coping behaviors in the nursery school, as contrasted to the parents of less mature or more inhibited children, did not differ in the overall amount of praise they used as a socializing technique, but did

differ in the extent to which the praise was clearly contingent on a speci-
fiable preceeding action of the child. Thus these parents interacted positively with their children in a way which implied close attention to the
child's ongoing behavior and which also made for predictability from the
child's point of view. Similarly, Mary Ainsworth (1967) reports differences in the extent to which mothers engage in nurturant activities which
are geared to the natural rhythms of the infant and the cues which he
emits as to his current need states, and she suggests that such caretaking
may not only be more successful in alleviating the infant's current needs
but may also make for the establishment of a stronger attachment, as
evidenced by separation reactions at one year.

Although the significance of these rather scattered observations for the
development of dependency is not yet entirely clear, they do serve to
emphasize the point that was made earlier about the essentially trans-
actional or reciprocal nature of the responses of mother and infant
through which attachment develops. Experimental studies of social responsiveness suggest that in the early months of life the visual stimulus
of a smiling human face, especially a familiar one, is the most effective
elicitor of the smiling response. Similarly, babbling seems to be stimulated most effectively by hearing a familiar voice, although stimulation
across auditory and visual modalities is also effective in increasing the
rate of social responses. Moss and Robson (1968) have reported some
data on the occurrence of the "vis-à-vis" interaction between mothers and
very young infants (one month and three months of age) which suggest
that it may be a useful index of positive affective interchange in the
mother-infant relationship. The frequency of "vis-à-vis" is predicted by
positive maternal attitudes expressed during pregnancy, and at least for
girl infants was predictive of their responsiveness to other social stimuli.
That such observations may have fairly long-term developmental significance is illustrated by some of the studies (Efran, 1968; Exline and
Winters, 1965) of the function of eye-contact in interview situations with
adult subjects. These studies have been stimulated by Tomkins' (1965)
theoretical notion of the importance of eye-contact in communicating
intimacy. Results of experiments by Efran (1968), Exline and Winters
(1965), and others (e.g., Ellsworth and Carlsmith, 1968) suggest that the
occurrence of mutual visual regard and eye contact in an interview
situation both are a function of, and serve to enhance, the affective content of the interaction. Subjects are more likely to maintain eye contact
with interviewers who are approving, and Ellsworth and Carlsmith
(1968) have demonstrated that increasing eye contact accentuates the
positive or negative reaction to the interview manipulated through the
content of the experimenter's communications. Thus it appears that

mutual visual regard may well retain into the adult years some of the functions of establishing intimacy and heightening the affective import of dyadic interactions which it first acquires as an important component of the attachment process.

Imitative responses emerge most clearly at somewhat later stages of the attachment process, but may be observed during the first year of life. Earlier theoretical formulations generally assumed that attachment or dependency on a specific social object was a precondition, or at least a facilitating condition, for the occurrence of imitation. That imitation might then function as a means of coping with separation is the basic notion elaborated by psychoanalytic writers and social learning theorists in the concept of anaclitic or developmental identification. Recently Kohlberg (1967) has suggested that the functional relationship may in fact be the other way around, that imitative responses serve a very basic function in perceptual development, and that the attachments are formed to social objects which the child has occasion to imitate.

Walters and Parke (1965, p. 80) also take the view that: "The social significance of the imitative responses of early infancy resides largely in their capacity for fostering adult-child interactions." They indicate that imitative behavior clearly precedes specific attachments. In any case it is clear that there is a close correlation between certain forms of dependent behavior and generalized tendencies to imitate, especially during the preschool years. Data from an identification study (Sears *et al.*, 1965) on the close association between positive attention-seeking and adult role behavior were referred to earlier, and one view of this association is that imitative responses are one of the means by which attachment is maintained, that they are a substitutive form of contact. Findings to the effect that nurturant models are more likely to be imitated support this view. A slightly different statement would be that imitative responses are a special case of the generalization which was suggested earlier, and that attachments are established and maintained through a wide range of *reciprocal matching responses*, e.g., mutual visual regard, mutual vocalization, etc. Studies of imitation tend to focus on the child as respondent and the parent as model. It may be profitable, however, also to look at the interaction the other way around. I vividly remember an incident during my very frustrating attempts to engage in play therapy with a brain-injured, socially unresponsive child of about seven. Our sessions had gone along for some time with very little in the way of real contact between us or of change in any aspect of the child's behavior. One day I happened deliberately to imitate something the child had done and repeated my imitative response several times until she clearly noticed it. For the first time I saw her smile delightedly and show real interest in pursuing further interactions with me. I am not at all sure how to interpret this particular clinical observation, but I am convinced that my imitation of her was instrumental in establishing some sort of contact between us, which then made me slightly more able to influence her behavior. A final observation in this connection: O'Toole and Dubin (1968) report that mothers engaged in spoon-feeding babies are highly likely, as they insert the spoon in the baby's mouth, to open their own mouths, and they suggest this as an instance of Mead's concept of "taking the role of the other."

It was stated earlier that in addition to tracing the developmental continuities and changes in the reciprocal responses by which attachments are established and maintained, it is also important to account for the changes as well as the continuities in the *objects* of attachment or dependency. The general developmental shifts—the shifts from diffuse social responsiveness to specific attachments in the first year of life, and from parents and close family members to other adults and the beginnings of peer relations in early childhood, the importance of social contacts with same-sex peers in middle childhood, and finally the emergence of heterosexual object choices in adolescence—are too well known descriptively to warrant any detailed recapitulation here. This is not to say, however, that the processes which underlie these developmental transitions in object choices are by any means equally clear or well understood. Simple generalization is clearly not an adequate explanation. It has already been noted that the peak of specific attachment seems to coincide with the period when the infant shows the most intense fear reactions to strangers. Thus the growing discrimination between the familiar and the strange is an important mediator of object choice, and Bronson (1968) suggests that this is a special case of a generalized fear reaction to novel visual stimuli. The presence of the mother tends to reduce this fear reaction, and this anxiety-reducing function both strengthens attachment and supports the development of exploratory behavior and mastery over the environment. Thus the child's capacity for detachment at later ages depends in part on the strength of attachment which has been formed earlier, or at least whatever aspects of the attachment relationship mediate the object's anxiety-reducing functions. What then controls the transitions to other social objects of attachment and affiliation? Certainly anxiety continues to be an important variable. The kindergarten child who is generally fearful is likely to resist separation from the mother and cling to other adults, and is unlikely to make successful contacts with peers. In a study of interpersonal characteristics associated with differential patterns of ability (Ferguson and Maccoby, 1966), it was initially predicted that differential verbal ability would be associated with emotional dependency, assuming a generalized trait of dependence on both adults and peers. The prediction proved to be true as far as dependence on adults was concerned, but our data indicated clearly that the high-verbal child who shows continued dependence on adults is *less* likely to be involved with peers.

Perhaps the balance between the fear-arousing properties of strangeness and the anxiety-reducing functions of the familiar, and of the child's own coping abilities in particular situations, will serve in large part to account for transitions in attachment and reactions to new social objects. It can be suggested that in each new personal relationship which is formed in later childhood and adult life, the object presents a complex combination of familiar and novel characteristics and thus evokes a mixture of positive and aversive responses. Both the effectiveness of the social object as a source of influence and the long-term fate of the relationship will depend on the balance between these competing tendencies. The process of "falling in love" among adolescents and adults is a good illustration. The novelty of the new object and the unpredictability of his or her responses is both exciting and somewhat anxiety arousing, although some dimensions of similarity with past objects of attachment also provide some of the attraction. As familiarity develops in the course of acquaintance, anxiety lessens, attachment may strengthen, but excitement also tends to subside.

The differential effectiveness of different sources of social reinforcement in influencing the behavior of young children, as summarized by Stevenson (1965) in his review of the experimental literature in this area, may be explained on similar grounds. It would appear that those agents of reinforcement who are most effective in sharing the child's behavior, through attention and approval, are not those most familiar to him or most often associated with positive reinforcement in the past. In general a strange experimenter seems to be more effective than the parent, and the child seems to be less responsive if the parents have been consistently supportive in the past. These findings suggest that approval or positive attention, in the context of the social reinforcement experiment, may be especially effective if it serves to allay the child's anxiety as to what the response of the strange adult, or of the parent who has sometimes been restrictive or inattentive in the past, is going to be.

A somewhat more puzzling, although quite reliable, finding of the social reinforcement studies is the so-called cross-sex effect: attention or approval from a male experimenter is relatively more effective in influencing the performance of girls, whereas a female is more effective with boys. This finding is reminiscent of the Oedipus complex in psychoanalytic theory, or more simply, of the general observation that during the preschool years children form a strong preferential attachment to the parent of the opposite sex. It was also found in the identification study that the affectional relationship with the parent of the opposite sex seemed most influential on the child's reactions in a deviation situation— it is especially the threatened loss of approval from that parent which seems to underlie the anxiety aroused by such situations. It is perhaps stretching the argument offered above a bit far to suggest that once the child becomes aware of his own sexual identity, he recognizes the parent of the opposite sex to be somewhat more different from himself than the same-sex parent, and this perceived difference operates in somewhat the same way as the novelty of a strange person. However, a more plausible explanation of this "cross-sex" effect is not readily available.

The data from longitudinal studies and from studies of adolescents (e.g., Kagan and Moss, 1962; Douvan and Adelson, 1966) indicate that the shift to extrafamilial objects of attachment, especially to peers, is more complete for boys than for girls and has a greater developmental significance for them. While it is usual for girls to remain quite strongly attached to their families and identified with parental values even into adult life, a shift in allegiance to peers seems to predict greater self-reliance and generally positive adjustment in boys. This is only one of the many sex differences in the development of attachment and its relations to other behavior systems. It is certainly an oversimplification, but still a fair fit with the overall trend of the data, to suggest that the development of attachment and the generalization of affiliative behavior in girls is more purely a matter of positive reinforcement than it is for boys. In boys, the detachment process is normally facilitated by the more vigorous emergence of exploratory and assertive behavior, and there is a more marked shift in middle childhood away from the primary object of attachment, the mother, and towards affiliative response to peers. Overtly "dependent" behavior in boys may thus be more a function of interference with the development of exploratory and assertive behavior than of the strength of the attachment system. These speculations will hopefully gain some confirmation as the data from current studies of attachment beyond the first year of life, by Ainsworth, Maccoby and others, become available.

In summary we have questioned the usefulness of the concept of "dependency" as currently used to refer both to a motivational construct and to a great variety of interpersonal behaviors. If the main interest is in accounting for the capacity of parents and other agents of socialization to exert influence over the child, then it is primarily those responses which have been considered manifestations of "emotional dependence" which are of interest. Individual differences in emotional dependence, or in the nurturance of the socializing agent, have been found to relate to susceptibility to social reinforcement, to imitation, to manifestations of conscience, to achievement motivation, and to many other aspects of socialization. It has been suggested that the specific behaviors which have been used as measures of emotional dependence are either identical with or developmentally derived from those responses which have been considered indices of attachment. I am thus in agreement with the view expressed by Walters and Parke (1965) that it would be well to substitute the term "attachment" for the concept of dependency in future discussions of social development. This is taken to mean that the focus will be on the developmental continuities in social interactions which derive from the attachment system, rather than on the concept of "dependency" as a generalized trait or motive.

Specific attachments are formed in the course of a series of interactions between infant and caretaker, or between any two individuals, which are characterized by the occurrence of a number of reciprocal matching responses, such as mutual physical contact, mutual visual regard, and mutual vocalization. Another important source of reinforcement for the development of attachment is the capacity of the familiar person to allay distress reactions and the fear elicited by strange persons and situations. Kessen and Mandler (1961) suggest that physical contact and other stimuli provided by the caretaker are "specific inhibitors" of distress reactions. This anxiety-reducing function of the object of attachment then serves to support exploratory behavior and the emergence of autonomous coping skills or "mastery." Thus, rather than assuming that "instrumental" and "emotional" dependency are positively related, as has sometimes been assumed, it would seem that the establishment of secure attachments are a precondition for autonomous and self-directed behavior.

At a number of points we have seen that there appear to be significant sex differences in the development of the attachment process and its significance for later social development. These differences may originate in congenital differences in patterns of activity and of responsivity to various dimensions of stimulation provided by the mother. Thus boy and girl infants may tend to elicit somewhat different chains of reciprocal matching responses. Undoubtedly sex is only one of the variables which will prove important in indexing the different ways in which the attachment process becomes patterned, but it is an obvious one at this point because of the relatively voluminous literature on the differential significance of dependency in the later social development of the two sexes.

Finally, it has been suggested that transitions in the *objects* of attachment may be of equal significance for social development as stages in patterns of response. The processes which underlie developmental changes in affectional and affiliative object choices are much less clear than the descriptive nature of these changes. It has been suggested that the functional balance between the security provided by familiar persons and the fear-arousing and attractive properties of strange or novel persons, embedded in either familiar or strange situational contexts, may serve to account for these transitions of objects. Their importance for socialization is attested by the data on the relative effectiveness of various agents of social reinforcement as well as on the growing influence of peers in middle childhood and adolescence. Current research on the vicissitudes of attachment and exploratory behavior in early childhood, especially during the third year of life, should prove very important in clarifying the nature of these processes.

REFERENCES

Ainsworth, M. D. Salter, and Bell, S. M. (1967). Some contemporary patterns of mother-infant interaction in the feeding situation. Paper presented at the inaugural meeting of the Centre for Advanced Study in the Developmental Sciences, London.

Baumrind, D. (1967). Child care practices anteceding three patterns of preschool behavior. *Genet. Psychol. Monographs*, **75**, 43–88.

Bayley, N., and Schafer, E. S. (1964). Correlations of maternal and child behaviors with the development of mental abilities: Data from the Berkeley Growth Study. *Child Development Monographs*, **29**, No. 6.

Bell, R. Q. (1968). A reinterpretation of the direction of effects in studies of socialization. *Psychol. Rev.*, **75**, 81–95.

Beller, E. K. (1959). Exploratory studies of dependency. *Trans. N.Y. Acad. Sci.*, Ser. II, **21**, No. 5, 414–425.

Bowlby, J. (1951). Maternal care and mental health. Monograph Series, No. 2, World Health Organization, Geneva.

Bronson, G. W. (1968). The development of fear in man and other animals. *Child Development*, **39**, 409–431.

Caldwell, B. M. (1964). The effects of infant care. In M. L. Hoffman and L. W. Hoffman (Eds.), *Review of child development research*, Vol. 2. Russell Sage Foundation, New York.

Cox, F. N., and Campbell, D. (1968). Young children in a new situation with and without their mothers. *Child Development*, **39**, 123–131.

Davis, H. V., Sears, R. R., Miller, H. C., and Brodbeck, A. J. (1948). Effects of cup, bottle and breast-feeding on oral activities of new born infants. *Pediatrics*, **2**, 549–558.

Douvan, E., and Adelson, J. (1966). *The adolescent experience*. Wiley, New York.

Efran, J. S. (1968). Looking for approval: Effects on visual behavior of approbation from persons differing in importance. *J. Personality and Social Psychol.*, **10**, 21–25.

Ellsworth, P. C., and Carlsmith, J. M. (1968). Effects of eye contact and verbal content on affective response to a dyadic interaction. *J. Personality and Social Psychol.*, **10**, 15–20.

Exline, R., and Winters, L. C. (1965). Affective relations and mutual glances in dyads. In S. Tomkins and C. Izard (Eds.), *Affect, cognition and personality*. Springer, New York.

Ferguson, L. R., and Maccoby, E. (1966). Interpersonal correlates of differential abilities. *Child Development*, 37, 549–571.

Gewirtz, J. L. (1969). A distinction between dependence and attachment in terms of stimulus control. Paper presented at the biennial meeting of the Society for Research in Child Development.

Goldman-Eisler, F. (1953). Breastfeeding and character formation. In C. Kluckhohn and H. A. Murray (Eds.), *Personality in nature, society and culture*. Knopf, New York.

Harlow, H. F. (1961). The development of affectional patterns in infant monkeys. In Foss, B. M. (Ed.), *Determinants of infant behavior*, Vol. I. Wiley, New York.

Heathers, G. (1955). Acquiring dependence and independence: A theoretical orientation. *J. Genet. Psychol.*, 87, 277–291.

Kagan, J. and Moss, H. A. (1962). *Birth to maturity: A study in psychological development*. Wiley, New York.

Kessen, W., and Mandler, G. (1961). Anxiety, pain and the inhibition of distress. *Psychol. Rev.*, 68, 396–404.

Kohlberg, L. (1967). A cognitive-developmental view of imitation and identification. Paper presented at the biennial meeting of the Society for Research in Child Development.

Levy, D. (1943). *Maternal overprotection*. Columbia Univ. Press, New York.

Mitchell, G. D. (1968). Attachment differences in male and female infant monkeys. *Child Development*, 39, 611–620.

Moss, H. A. and Robson, K. S. (1968). Maternal influences in early social visual behavior. *Child Development*, 39, 401–408.

O'Toole, R. and Dubin, R. (1968). Babyfeeding and body sway: An experiment in George Herbert Mead's "Taking the role of the other." *J. Personality and Social Psychol.*, 10, 59–65.

Radke-Yarrow, M., Campbell, J. D., and Burton, R. V. (1968). *Child-rearing: An inquiry into research methods*. Jossey-Bass, San Francisco.

Rau, L., Anastasiow, N., and Mlodnosky, L. B. (1964). Child-rearing antecedents of achievement behaviors in second grade boys. Final report on U.S.O.E. Cooperative Research Project No. 1838, Stanford University.

Rheingold, H. L., Gewirtz, J. L., and Ross, H. W. (1959). Social conditioning of vocalizations in the infant. *J. Comp. Physiol. Psychol.*, 52, 68–73.

Rowland, T. S. (1968). Mother-son interaction and the coping behavior of young boys. Unpublished doctoral dissertation, Michigan State University.

Schacter, S. (1959). *The psychology of affiliation*. Stanford Univ. Press, Stanford, California.

Schaffer, H. R., and Emerson, P. E. (1964). The development of social attachments in infancy. *Monographs Soc. Res. Child Development*, 29 e, Serial No. 94.

Sears, R. R., and Wise, G. W. (1950). Relation of cup-feeding in infancy to thumbsucking and the oral drive. *Am. J. Orthopsychiat.*, 20, 123–138.

Sears, R. R., Maccoby, E. E., and Levin, H. (1957). *Patterns of child rearing*. Row, Peterson, Evanston, Ill.

Sears, R. R., Rau, L., and Alpert, R. (1965). *Identification and child rearing*. Stanford Univ. Press, Stanford, California.

Stendler, C. B. (1954). Possible causes of overdependency in young children. *Child Development*, 25, 125–146.

Stevenson, H. W. (1965). Social reinforcement of children's behavior. In L. P. Lipsitt and C. C. Spiker (Eds.), *Advances in child development and behavior,* Vol. 2. Academic Press, New York.

Thomas, A., Chess, S., Birch, H. G., Hertzig, M. E., and Korn, S. (1963). *Behavioral individuality in early childhood.* N.Y. Univ. Press, New York.

Tomkins, S. S. (1965). The biopsychosociality of the family. In Coale, A. J., Fallers, L. A., Levy, M. J., Schneider, D. M. and Tomkins, S. S. (Eds.), *Aspects of the analysis of family structure.* Princeton Univ. Press, Princeton, New Jersey.

Walters, R. H., and Parke, R. D. (1965). The role of distance receptors in the development of social responsiveness. In L. Lipsitt and C. C. Spiker (Eds.), *Advances in child development and behavior,* Vol. 2. Academic Press, New York.

Winder, C. L., and Rau, L. (1962). Parental attitudes associated with social deviance in preadolescent boys. *J. Abnormal and Social Psychol.,* 64, 418–424.

Yarrow, L. J. (1964). Separation from parents during early childhood. In M. L. Hoffman, and L. W. Hoffman (Eds.), *Review of child development research,* Vol. I. Russell Sage Foundation, New York.

5

THE ROLE OF PUNISHMENT
IN THE SOCIALIZATION PROCESS*

Ross D. Parke†

According to a large scale study of child-rearing, 98 percent of the parents interviewed occasionally used physical punishment to control their children (Sears *et al.*, 1957). This is an interesting statistic in light of our current belief that this is a permissive era and in light of current child-rearing recommendations. Possibly parents have been wiser than the "experts" who for many years assumed that punishment was an extremely ineffective means of controlling human behavior. Due to ethical and practical reasons, little research was executed with children or even human adults to dispel this "legend" as Solomon (1964) has termed it. However, the professional zeitgeist has shifted as evidenced by the more cautious approaches taken in recent theoretical discussions of punishment (e.g., Church, 1963; Solomon, 1964). In fact, according to these reviews, punishment may be an extremely effective means of controlling behavior.

Socialization involves the teaching of discriminations concerning appropriate and inappropriate responses through inhibiting undesirable behaviors and strengthening prosocial responses. Clearly in socialization contexts reward and punishment often work in concert aiding the child in acquiring acceptable behaviors. The usefulness of punishment lies in its suppressive power, and the primary practical value of studies of punishment is to determine the conditions under which suppression will most readily occur. Punishment will probably be particularly effective as a socializing technique if at the same time socialization agents provide

* The preparation of this paper and some of the studies that are reported here were supported in part by Research Grant GS 1847, National Science Foundation.

† University of Wisconsin.

information concerning alternative prosocial responses (Walters and Parke, 1967).

The main purpose of this paper will be to review and assess the current status of punishment as a means of inhibiting unacceptable behavior in children. The available research strongly suggests that punishment, especially physical punishment, may have diverse effects and that these effects are dependent on such parameters as the timing, the intensity of punishment, the nature of the relationship between the agent and the recipient of punishment, and the consistency with which punishment is administered. The evidence pertaining to the operation of each of these punishment parameters will be examined in order to illustrate the potential role that punishment plays in the socialization process.

TIMING OF PUNISHMENT

A factor of considerable importance in naturalistic socialization contexts is the timing of punishment. In home situations, punishment is often delayed beyond the completion of the deviant behavior. Does the timing of the administration of a punisher affect its effectiveness as a means of inhibiting undesirable behavior? Mowrer (1960) has provided a theoretical framework for predicting the effects of timing of punishment. According to Mowrer, each component of a response sequence provides sensory feedback in the form of response-produced kinesthetic and proprioceptive cues. Punishment may be administered at any point during the sequence of responses and result in a relatively direct association of a fear-motivated avoidance response with the response-produced cues occurring at the temporal locus of punishment. If the punishment is administered at the initiation of the deviant response sequence, the maximal degree of fear is attached to the cues produced by the instrumental acts involved in initiating the sequence. In this case, subsequent initiation of the sequence will arouse anxiety that activates incompatible avoidance responses, which are reinforced by anxiety reduction if they are sufficiently strong to forestall the deviant behavior.

In contrast, punishment occurring only when a transgression has been completed attaches maximal anxiety to stimuli associated with the goal response or to the immediately subsequent responses and less strong anxiety to stimuli associated with the instrumental acts. Under these circumstances the deviation is more likely to be initiated on future occasions than it is when punishment is associated with instrumental acts occurring early in the response sequence. Once an act has been initiated, secondary positive reinforcers associated with the instrumental behavior involved in the commission of the sequence may serve to maintain and facilitate it and thus to some degree to counteract the inhibitory effect of punishment (Walters and Demkow, 1963). Moreover, once a transgression is completed, response inhibition cannot serve to forestall or mitigate punishment (Aronfreed and Reber, 1965). Consequently, response inhibition should be more effectively achieved by punishment that is delivered early in the deviant response sequence than by punishment that is delivered only when the sequence is completed.

Mowrer's account undoubtedly overemphasizes the role of kinesthetic-proprioceptive feedback and the emotion of fear, and underemphasizes the part played by perceptual-cognitive factors that are associated with the functioning of the distance receptors (Bandura and Walters, 1963; Walters and Parke, 1967). Visual and auditory cues accompanying the commission of a deviant act can become as closely associated with the experience of punishment as kinesthetic-proprioceptive feedback; since such cues tend to be far more distinct and readily discriminable, they probably play a more important part in the maintenance of behavioral control. This consideration does not, however, vitiate the argument leading to the timing-of-punishment hypothesis.

The timing-of-punishment hypothesis has been tested with children in a number of recently reported experiments. All of the studies reported to date have employed resistance to deviation as the dependent measure. A study by Walters et al. (1965) will serve to illustrate the timing of punishment effect that has been found with children and will introduce the methodology typically employed in the punishment studies that will be discussed in this presentation. On each of nine training trials, the five- and six-year-old boys used in the study were presented with pairs of toys —one attractive and one unattractive. Each time the boy selected the attractive toy, the experimenter verbally punished him by saying, "No, that's for the other boy." For subjects in the early punishment condition, the experimenter administered the punishment just before the subject touched the attractive toy. Late punishment subjects were punished after picking up and holding the attractive but prohibited toy for 2 to 3 seconds. On all trials, subjects were given the opportunity to choose and describe the unattractive toy. Subjects are then, usually seated before a display of three rows of toys similar to the toys used in the punishment training session—and told not to touch the toys. In this particular study, some subjects were shown a film of a boy playing with the prohibited toys and experiencing different consequences for his deviant behavior. The resistance-to-deviation test is a 15-minute period during which the subject is left alone with a German-English dictionary and the prohibited toys. An observer seated behind a one-way screen recorded the latency, number and duration of the subjects' deviant activity. A deviation was defined, simply, as touching a toy. Weighted deviation scores were calculated as follows: a deviation involving one of the three most accessible toys was scored one; a deviation involving toys in the second row of toys was assigned a value of two; the subject touching a toy in the third row, three. The combined data for all film conditions indicated that early-punished subjects deviated less quickly, less often, and for shorter periods of time than late punished subjects; moreover differences between early-punished subjects were also apparent under the no-film condition. This timing of punishment effect has been reported by a number of investigators (Aronfreed and Reber, 1965; Parke and Walters, 1967; Parke, 1969; Cheyne and Walters, 1969).

Recent extensions of this timing paradigm indicate that this finding is merely one aspect of a general relationship: the longer the delay between the initiation of the act and the onset of punishment, the less effective the punishment for producing response inhibition. This proposition is based on a study in which the effects of four delay-of-punishment positions were examined (Aronfreed, 1965). Using a paradigm similar to Walters *et al.* (1965), Aronfreed punished one group of children as they reached for the attractive toy; under a second condition they were permitted to pick up the attractive toy and were punished at the apex of the lifting movement. Under a third condition, six seconds elapsed after picking the toy up before punishment was delivered. In the final group, six seconds following picking up the toy, the children were asked to describe the toy and only then was punishment administered. The latency of deviation in the experimenter's absence steadily decreased as the time between the initiation of the act and the delivery of punishment increased. In fact, highly reliable differences between each of the adjacent points on the timing-of-punishment effects held for both boys and girls with both male and female experimenters.

In these studies, a verbal rebuke has been used as the punishing stimulus; in other studies either a noxious noise or a noise accompanied by a verbal rebuke have been used (Cheyne and Walters, 1969; Parke, 1969; Parke and Walters, 1967). Although there have been some inconsistencies, and some complex interactions with other punishment parameters, the timing-of-punishment relationships reported tend to hold across a number of types of punishing stimuli.

However, is the timing of punishment an important determinant in producing response inhibition in naturalistic socialization contexts? The reason for raising this issue stems from the observation that effective suppression is often achieved with punishment delivered for a completed transgression; in fact, generally there are few opportunities in real life disciplinary contexts to punish the child in the approach phase of his transgression sequence. However, naturalistic socialization has a number of features which tend to dilute the significance of timing and to facilitate response inhibition even when punishment follows well beyond the completion of the act. For example, as Aronfreed (1968, p. 95) has noted "parents often punish in the midst of a committed or sustained transgression or after a discrete repeatable act that the child has completed but is about to initiate again. Anxiety may, therefore, become attached to the intrinsic cues associated with an incipient transgression, even though the punishment is originally contingent on visible commission of the act."

In addition, there may be other factors associated with punishment administration that can clearly increase the effectiveness of a late-timed punishment and so make the timing less crucial for successful inhibition. In this presentation, some of the other factors which affect the operation of punishment—such as intensity, the nature of the relationship between agent and recipient of punishment and cognitive variables—will be discussed and, where the data allow, the modifying impact of these variables on the timing-of-punishment effect will be noted.

INTENSITY OF PUNISHMENT

A second factor that may alter the effectiveness of punishment is, of course, the intensity of the punishing stimulus. A large number of animal studies indicate that intensity of punishment may have a variety of effects that unfold as intensity increases. At low levels of intensity, punishment may be used as a cue, as a discriminative stimulus, as a response intensifier, or even a secondary reinforcer. As intensity increases, temporary suppression of the punished response may result, followed by complete recovery; at increasingly higher levels enduring partial suppression, and finally complete suppression, may ensue (Church, 1963). Since there have been few studies of punishment intensity with human subjects, these conclusions have been based almost entirely on studies involving infrahuman organisms. This paucity of information is, in part, the result of the ethical consideration that high intensities of punishment should not be employed with humans (Bandura and Walters, 1963).

In fact, until recently most of the evidence concerning the effects of varying intensities of punishment on children's behavior was derived from field studies of child-rearing practices (e.g., Sears et al., 1953; Sears et al., 1957). However, little reliable information concerning the operation of specific punishment parameters, such as intensity, has been gained from these projects. The main problem involves the use of rating scales of parent behavior which confound several aspects of punishment such as frequency, intensity, and consistency (Walters and Parke, 1967). Laboratory experimental studies are clearly necessary to demonstrate the effects of variations in intensity of punishment on children's behavior.

A number of laboratory studies using children as subjects have varied intensity and examined its effects on resistance to deviation (Aronfreed and Leff, 1963; Parke, 1969; Parke and Walters, 1967).

Parke and Walters (1967) investigated the effects of differing levels of intensity of punishment using a procedure similar to that employed in the Walters *et al.* (1965) study of timing of punishment. In the first of a series of three studies, two levels of prior interaction between the agent and recipient of punishment, and two levels of timing (early vs. late) as well as two levels of intensity of punishment were employed. High-intensity punishment consisted of a verbal rebuke, "No, that's for the other boy," combined with a 96 db tone; the tone was reduced to 65 db for the low intensity condition. Subjects who had received high-intensity punishment deviated less quickly, less often, and for shorter periods of time than did children who had been punished mildly. There were no interactions among the experimental variables.

The results of the second study, which involved the same two levels of intensity as were employed in the first study and two levels of timing, were in the predicted direction, but failed to reach statistical significance. The third study—again employing a 2x2 factorial design with two levels of intensity and timing—yielded a rather complex interaction effect. However, later studies (e.g., Parke, 1969) have clearly confirmed the intensity of punishment effect and suggest that this effect will be most clearly observed when verbal cues accompanying a punishing stimulus are minimized. A fuller discussion of this issue will be presented when the role of cognitive variables is elaborated.

In spite of some discrepancies, the overall findings from field and laboratory studies generally support the expectation that high-intensity physical punishment in most circumstances more effectively inhibits the punished behavior than does punishment that is less intense. This is probably true even for the data on aggression (e.g., Bandura and Walters, 1959) since severe punishment for aggression in the home, characteristic of the child-training practices of parents of aggressive children, is associated with a relatively low incidence of aggression within the home on the part of these children in comparison to the frequent aggression that they display elsewhere (Walters and Parke, 1967).

A question of particular importance for socialization theories is the manner in which intensity modifies or attenuates the operation of other parameters, such as timing of punishment. Is timing as critical for pro-

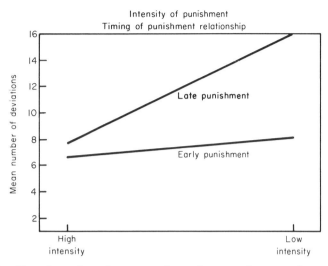

Figure 1. The relationship of intensity of punishment and timing of punishment.

ducing response inhibition when the intensity of punishment is high? Some data from studies of delay of punishment with rats suggest that the delay gradient is most marked under conditions of low-intensity punishment; under high-intensity punishment Renner (1964) did not find the delay of punishment gradient. In a recent study Parke (1969) found a similar relationship. The timing-of-punishment effect was present under low-intensity conditions; under high intensity, children punished early in a response sequence and children punished late in this sequence did not differ (see Fig. 1). However, this finding is only suggestive in light of the failure to find this relationship in previous studies. Methodological and procedural differences across the series of studies may account for the inconsistencies. To determine more precisely the nature of this interaction, a study varying a number of intensity levels and a number of timing of punishment positions is clearly required.

NATURE OF THE RELATIONSHIP BETWEEN THE AGENT AND RECIPIENT OF PUNISHMENT

The nature of the relationship between the agent and the recipient of punishment has received considerable attention in discussions of the effects of disciplinary techniques (e.g., Aronfreed, 1968; Bandura and Walters, 1963; Becker, 1964; Hoffman, 1963). In general, these viewpoints assume that adequate socialization requires that a child form a positive attachment with the disciplinarian if this agent is to be an effective socializing force.

The assumption that the administration of sanctions by a normally nurturant agent will be more effective than a neutral agent has been explicitly suggested by Sears *et al.* (1953) and by Whiting (1954). This hypothesis is based on the assumption that parents acquire the capacity to generate positive and negative affective reactions in their children. For example, the affection bestowed on a child by a nurturant socializing agent is assumed to be a source of positively valued affect for the child recipient. Similarly, the withdrawal or threat of withdrawal of affection is assumed to be affectively aversive for the child. Threats of affectional withdrawal possess power for inducing aversive states in the child, and hence they become important means for producing behavioral control. In fact, a certain degree of positive interaction and affection between a parent and a child is necessary if social punishment is to be an effective means of producing response inhibition. This argument rests on the assumption that withdrawal of affection is an effective component of all forms of social punishment. A similar view has been expressed by Bandura and Walters (1963), who noted that any disciplinary act may involve in varying degrees at least two operations, the presentation of a negative reinforcer and the withdrawal or withholding of positive reinforcement. In an affectionless parent-child relationship, or one in which the parents are indiscriminatively punitive towards the child, the child does not develop a strong positive attachment to the socializing agent and may become adapted to a high level of aversive stimulation in their presence (Aronfreed, 1968). In such a relationship, the threat of disruption of the affection-based tie would be of little import to the child being disciplined, and consequently the disciplinary action might not induce sufficient anxiety to motivate the child to conform to the disciplinarian's demands or to adopt the disciplinarian's standards of conduct. On this basis, it is assumed that a nurturant punishing agent arouses a greater degree of anxiety than a neutral agent and that consequently the former agent is more effective in producing response inhibition in the child.

Some support for the preceding analysis comes from field studies of social development and from recent experimental investigations. For example, Sears *et al.* (1957) have presented some evidence which is consistent with this hypothesis. Mothers who were rated as warm and affectionate and made relatively frequent use of physical punishment were more likely to say that they found spanking to be an effective means of discipline. In contrast, cold hostile mothers who made equally frequent use of physical punishment were more likely to report that spanking was ineffective. Moreover, according to mothers, spanking was more likely to be effective if it was administered by the warmer of the parents.

These findings are consistent with evidence obtained by Freedman (1958) who reported that pups who had received "indulgence" training were more likely to refrain from executing a punished act in the absence of the experimenter than were pups who were reared under conditions of severe discipline. However, an alternative interpretation of the Freedman data would suggest that the dogs raised under severe punishment conditions became insensitive to or adapted to high levels of physical punishment, thus making the levels of punishment used in the experimental situation relatively ineffective.

Employing a controlled laboratory situation, Parke and Walters (1967) investigated the influence of the relationship between the agent and recipient of punishment on the effectiveness of punishment for producing response inhibition in children. In this study the nature of the experimenter-child relationship was varied in two interaction sessions prior to the administration of punishment. Forty boys experienced a ten-minute period of positive interaction with the experimenter on two successive days. Attractive construction materials were provided for the children, and as they played with them, the experimenter provided encouragement, help, and warmly expressed approval of their efforts. A second group of forty boys played, in two ten-minute sessions, with relatively unattractive materials while the experimenter sat in the room without interacting with the children. An equal number of children from each interaction condition were assigned to one of four punishment conditions, involving two levels of intensity and two levels of timing. Regardless of punishment conditions, children who had experienced positive interaction with the agent of punishment showed significantly greater resistance to deviation than subjects who had had only impersonal contact.

The results of the nurturance manipulation perhaps provide support for theories of behavior that stress the importance of the sequencing of reinforcement events. These theories (e.g., Helson, 1964; Rotter, 1954) suggest that the reinforcement value of a stimulus is dependent on the events that precede it or, more generally, on the context in which it occurs. Recent studies with children (Crandall, 1963; Crandall et al., 1964) have demonstrated that nonreward (adult silence) that followed reward (adult approval) functioned analogously to a negative reinforcer, whereas nonreward following punishment functioned analogously to a positive reinforcer. Extending these results to the sequencing of two kinds of reinforcing events, positive and negative, it follows that the effects of a negative event may be enhanced if it follows a positive one, and vice versa.

One implication of the outcome of the nurturance manipulation is that the suppressing effect of a given amount of punishment depends upon the experiences of the recipient preceding the introduction of punishment.

In a recent discussion of punishment, Solomon (1964, p. 242) has expressed a similar viewpoint: "A punishment is not just a punishment. It is an event in the temporal and spatial flow of stimulation and behavior, and its effects will be produced by its temporal and spatial point of insertion in that flow."

However, a problem of interpretation still remains. In the present study the procedure involved the presentation of noxious stimulation by a nurturant agent, and the effectiveness of this procedure may derive either from the "withdrawal of affection" implied in the punitive operation or from both the withdrawal component and the presentation of aversive stimulation.

In the case of the present study, it is impossible to determine which aspect of the punishment procedure was the significant one, nor is it possible to assess the relative contributions of these separate components to the greater inhibition of the high-nurturance subjects. Probably it was the combination of these two sources of anxiety which led the high-nurturance subjects to engage in less deviant activity than their low-nurturance counterparts.

The nurturance manipulations paralleled, in some respects, those that have been used in studies of the effects of nurturance withdrawal. Generally speaking, these latter studies have indicated that withdrawal of affection may motivate the previously nurtured subject to engage in behavior that is likely to reinstate the affectional relationship (e.g., Hartup, 1958; Rosenblith, 1959, 1961). In the present study, subjects under the high-nurturance condition have nurturance withdrawn after two intensive nurturance conditions, with the experimenter switching roles and acting in a punitive, rather than a nurturant manner. The greater resistance to deviation of subjects under the high-nurturance condition may thus reflect an attempt to win back the experimenter's approval through conformity to his prohibition.

This hypothesis of greater resistance-to-deviation following nurturance-withdrawal has recently been experimentally tested (Parke, 1967). Two experimental treatments were employed. In the continuous nurturance condition the subjects, 6- to 8-year-old boys and girls, experienced ten minutes of friendly and nurturant interaction with either a male or female experimenter. Subjects in the nurturance withdrawal group experienced five minutes of nurturant interaction, followed by five minutes of nurturance withdrawal during which the experimenter turned away from the subject, appeared to be busy, and refused to respond to any bid for attention. Following these manipulations, all subjects were placed in a resistance-to-deviation situation, involving a display of attractive, but forbidden toys. In the instructions to the subject, it was made clear that if the subject conformed to the experimenter's prohibition, the experimenter would play with him upon returning. In this way the link between resistance-to-deviation and nurturance was established. As in previous experiments, a hidden observer recorded the subject's deviant activity during the fifteen minutes that the experimenter was absent from the room.

The results provided some support for the hypothesis, with subjects in the nurturance-withdrawal group deviating significantly less often than subjects in the continuous-nurturance condition. However, interaction effects indicated that nurturance withdrawal influenced girls to a greater degree than boys, and that the effect was most marked with girls experiencing withdrawal of a female experimenter's nurturance.

COGNITIVE VARIABLES

In most analyses of the effects of punishment on response inhibition (e.g., Bandura and Walters, 1959; Hill, 1960; Mowrer, 1960), the role of anxiety arousal and reduction has been emphasized, and little attention has been paid to the role of cognitive factors. While it is undoubtedly correct that much of the learning of response inhibition is due to anxiety arousal and reduction, a good deal of inhibition in humans is probably due to reliance on cognitive, rather than emotionally-based factors (Parke and Walters, 1967; Walters and Parke, 1967). An adequate theory of response inhibition in humans requires that both cognitive and emotional factors be taken into consideration.

In field studies of socialization practices, the modifying impact of cognitive variables on punishment has received some recognition. For example, in the Sears *et al.* (1957) study, mothers who combined physical punishment with extensive use of reasoning reported more often that punishment was effective than mothers who tended to use punishment alone. However, these field investigations yield little information concerning the relative effectiveness of different aspects of reasoning. In the child-training literature, reasoning may include not only descriptions of untoward consequences that the child's behavior may have for others, but also the provision of examples of incompatible socially acceptable behaviors, explicit instructions on how to behave in specific situations, and explanations of motives for placing restraints on a child's behavior (Bandura and Walters, 1963). Moreover, these studies do not indicate the manner in which the provision of reasons in combination with punishment can alter the operation of specific punishment parameters such as timing, intensity, and the nature of the agent-child relationship.

The effect of providing a rationale in conjunction with punishment, both in increasing the effectiveness of the punisher and in modifying the impact of other punishment parameters, is illustrated in a recent study by Parke (1969). A 2x2x2x2 factorial design involving two timing-of-punishment conditions (early vs. late), two intensity-of-punishment conditions (high vs. low), two nurturance conditions (high vs. low), and two levels of cognitive structure was employed. Since the apparatus and procedures were similar to the earlier studies, only the cognitive structuring manipulations need be described. Subjects in the low-cognitive structure condition were informed that they should not touch or play with some of the toys, and that if they picked an incorrect one, a buzzer would sound. On punished trials, subjects heard only the buzzer—no verbal remark accompanied the noise. Subjects in the high-cognitive structure conditions received a much more elaborate rationale for having restrictions placed on their behavior. In addition to the statement "some of these toys you should not touch or play with"—which subjects in both the high- and low-cognitive structure conditions heard—the experimenter added the following for the high-cognitive structure subjects: "Because I don't have any others like them. And if they were to get broken or worn out from boys playing with them, I wouldn't be able to use them anymore. So for that reason I don't want you to touch or play with some of these toys. And if you pick one of the toys you're not supposed to touch or play with, I'll tell you and you'll hear a buzzer." For the high-cogni-

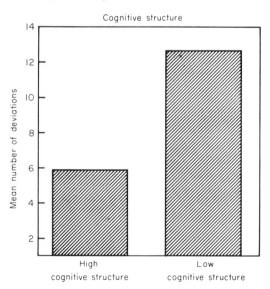

Figure 2. Mean deviations of low- and high-cognitive structure conditions.

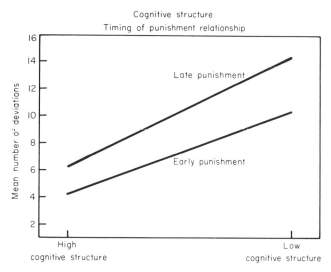

Figure 3. The relationship of cognitive structure and timing of punishment.

tive structure subjects, the experimenter sounded the buzzer and said, "No, that one might get broken" on each punishment trial. Following the punishment training session, the boys were left alone with the toys that they had been punished for choosing.

The provision of a rationale increased the effectiveness of the punisher for producing response inhibition. Subjects in the high-cognitive structure group deviated significantly less frequently than boys in the low-cognitive structure group who heard the buzzer unaccompanied by a rationale. This result is illustrated in Fig. 2. These data are consistent with the child-rearing findings of Sears *et al.* (1957).

As Fig. 3 indicates, the predicted relationship between timing and cognitive structure was confirmed: early punishment was more effective than late punishment under conditions of low-cognitive structure; under conditions of high-cognitive structure, a significant superiority of early- over late-timed punishment was absent. Although this effect held only for the frequency of deviation index in this study, other investigators using similar procedures (Cheyne and Walters, 1969) have reported this effect for both duration and frequency indices of response inhibition.

In both the Cheyne and Walters (1969) study and the Parke experiment, the reasoning procedures that were presented in conjunction with punishment stressed the consequences of violation of the experimenter's prohibition. Aronfreed (1965), in a series of pioneering studies in this area, found a similar relationship between cognitive structuring and timing of punishment when the rationale focused on the child's intentions. Using a variation on the basic timing of punishment paradigm, the subjects heard: "No, you should *not* have *wanted* to pick up that thing" in conjunction with the punishment. Again, the addition of cognitive structure to a late-timed punishment made this temporal position equal to an early-timed punishment in its effectiveness.

Before the modifying impact of cognitive structure on the intensity and nurturance effects is examined, this timing-of-punishment cognitive-structure relationship merits discussion. In conjunction with the earlier findings, these results suggest that the timing of punishment may be less important for producing response inhibition under two conditions—if cognitive structure is provided or if the agent employs punishment of high intensity. However, it is unlikely that both increasing intensity and providing a rationale are equally effective in naturalistic situations as means of overcoming delay of punishment effects. Punishment in real life settings is often delivered after the deviant response is terminated and also at a time when the child is engaging in another activity. Punishment in this case is both delayed and not contingent on the response that the agent is attempting to inhibit. Probably if the punishment is accompanied by a verbal explanation which symbolically reinstates the nature of the deviant act, the ineffectiveness of the delayed and noncontingent punishment may be overcome. However, in the absence of some kind of verbal restructuring or reinstatement, it is highly improbable that merely increasing the intensity of punishment when the child is engaged in an unrelated behavior will help in reducing the detrimental effect of the delayed punisher. In the Parke (1969) study, it was probably of greater importance for the timing-intensity relationship than for the timing-cognitive structure effect that the child was holding the toy when punishment was administered. In naturalistic situations the provision of cognitive structure rather than increasing the intensity of punishment will probably be a more effective means of overcoming delay of punishment effects.

An experiment recently reported by Walters and Andres (1967) addresses itself directly to this issue. In an initial session the subjects were left alone with an attractive truck which, when rolled forward, broke in half. To assess the effects of reinstatement of relevant cues associated with the deviant act in increasing the effect of a delayed punisher, all subjects returned four hours later. One group was seated at the table on which they had committed their earlier deviation and a 104 db buzzer was sounded. A second group was lured into breaking a similar truck after which the buzzer sounded, while a third group heard a buzzer after reviewing a video recording of themselves breaking a truck. Of central interest was the fourth group, which was provided with a detailed de-

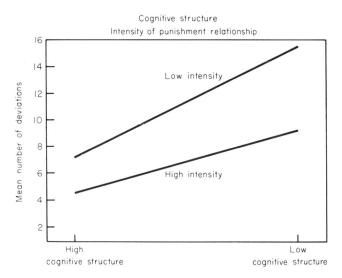

Figure 4. The relationship of cognitive structure and intensity of punishment.

scription of their earlier deviation before being punished. In a subsequent test for resistance to deviation, the subjects in the video recording and the verbal reinstatement conditions deviated less than the other two groups of subjects. The reinstatement—even after a four-hour lapse— was clearly effective in overcoming the delay in the administration of punishment. Probably the pairing of the punisher with the verbal description resulted in the successful association of anxiety with the cognitive representation of the motor act.

This is an ingenious study which bears replication, since the act of reinstatement or of showing the video recording may suggest to the subjects that their behavior is being monitored in the experimenter's absence. It is possible that punishment was unnecessary since the fear of detection in future similar situations may have been the critical factor in their procedure.

Other results from the Parke (1969) study are of interest. The factorial nature of the experimental design permitted an evaluation of the modifying impact of cognitive structure on the intensity and nurturance manipulations. As Fig. 4 shows, when cognitive structure was low, high-intensity punishment produced significantly greater inhibition than low-intensity punishment but under high-cognitive structure the difference between intensity levels was not significant.

As Fig. 5 indicates, these reasoning procedures had a modifying effect on the nurturance variable as well. When cognitive structure was low,

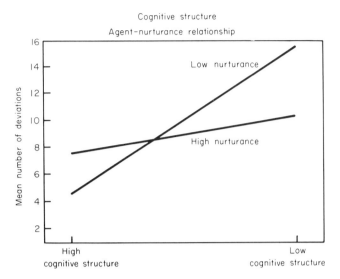

Figure 5. The relationship of cognitive structure and agent-nurturance.

subjects in the high-nurturance condition deviated less often than subjects in the low-nurturance condition. No significant differences between high- and low-nurturance treatments were found when cognitive structure was high.

Together, these experiments constitute impressive evidence of the important role played by cognitive variables in modifying the operation of punishment.

A question that has received only very limited attention is the stability of inhibition produced by various punishment procedures. To investigate this issue, the degree of deviant activity for each of the three five-minute periods of the resistance-to-deviation test session was calculated. As Fig. 6 indicates, the low-cognitive structure subjects increased their degree of deviant activity over the three blocks while the degree of deviation over the three time periods did not significantly change for the high-cognitive structure subjects. Cheyne and Walters (1969) have reported a similar finding.

These data clearly indicate that the stability of inhibition over time was affected by the reasoning or cognitive structuring procedures. The interesting implication of this finding is that fear-producing procedures may serve to secure short-term inhibition, but long-term inhibition—or internalization to use a less neutral term—may require the use of cognitively-oriented training procedures. To further assess the stability of cognitively-based punishment procedures, current studies are including follow-up tests one week after training.

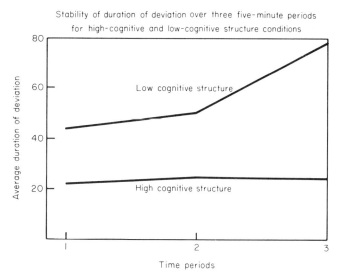

Figure 6. The stability of the duration of deviation over three 5-minute periods for high- and low-cognitive structure conditions.

These experimental studies not only point to the importance of cognitive factors in response inhibition, but bring into question models derived mainly from research with lower organisms that attempt to account for response inhibition solely in terms of acquired emotional reactions, such as fear or anxiety.

However, there are a variety of problems that require further attention if the role of cognitive factors in punishment is to be understood. The specific nature of the cognitive structuring procedure clearly requires further examination. For example, in Aronfreed's research the focus has been on the subject's intention, while in our research, consequences have been the major focus. Comparative studies in which these two types of cognitive structuring are examined are clearly in order. Similarly, within the consequences paradigm, is an object-oriented appeal as effective as person-oriented appeals? Person-oriented rationales may take a variety of forms and probably are an important facet of love-withdrawal disciplinary techniques. For example, the child is informed that an adult, parent, or peer may be upset or in some way adversely affected by his failure to conform to the prohibition. As Sears *et al.* (1957) found, such appeals are most effective in a warm-nurturant agent-child relationship. Experimental investigations of these variables would clearly be of interest due to the difficulty of determining from the child-rearing studies which aspect of the complex disciplinary maneuver is in fact operating to produce the effect.

Other types of studies might involve assessing the interaction between the level of the child's understanding of moral rules—as assessed, for example, by the Kohlberg (1963) scheme—and the effectiveness of different types of moral rules or appeals. Possibly, closer attention to the compatibility of the child's cognitive level and the kind of rationales used for imposing restraints on his behavior will yield stronger evidence for the seemingly elusive relationship between levels of moral thought and behavioral indices of morality, such as resistance to deviation.

Similarly, the manner in which verbal rationales gain their effectiveness requires investigation. Cheyne and Walters (1969) argue that these rationales—which often are stated in the form of general rules—may gain their potency to modify behavior because they have, through past learning, become transsituational cues; thus a prohibition may be very effective for producing response inhibition because noncompliance with rules has previously been associated with anxiety induction, often through punishment. However, once a rule has been learned, it may function to produce inhibition with little or no accompanying anxiety. According to this position, anxiety arousal may be necessary for efficient rule learning but after sufficient training in rule observation, the anxiety component plays a less important role. If it is further assumed that the child's ability to use verbal behavior to control nonverbal responses increases with age, a developmental prediction is possible. (Luria, 1961, has provided some support for this assumption.) As the child increases in age, the relative contributions of emotional and cognitive components to response inhibition will shift. With younger children, response inhibition will be most successfully achieved by a reliance on physical punishment techniques which stress the production of anxiety. With older children, punishment techniques which diminish the role of anxiety and stress the role of verbal control of motor behavior, through the appeal to general rules, will be more effective in producing response inhibition. Information concerning the relative effectiveness of different kinds of punishments and the modifying impact of cognitive variables at different age levels is clearly necessary for a clearer understanding of the role of punishment in naturalistic socialization.

CONSISTENCY OF PUNISHMENT

Another facet of punishment which clearly deserves increased attention is the consistency with which punishment is employed. In naturalistic socialization contexts, consistency assumes a variety of forms. For example, consistency between parents concerning the kind or severity of punishment and the occasions on which it should be used, constitutes one classification. Consistency may also refer to the extent to which a single agent treats violations in the same manner each time they occur or to the extent to which a parent or other socializing agent follows through on their threats of punishment (Walters and Parke, 1967).

Data from field studies of delinquency have yielded some clues concerning the consequences of inconsistency of discipline. Glueck and Glueck (1950) found that parents of delinquent boys were more "erratic" in their disciplinary practices than were parents of nondelinquent boys. Similarly, McCord et al. (1959 and 1961) have found that erratic disciplinary procedures were correlated with high degrees of criminality. Inconsistent patterns involving combinations of either love-oriented techniques, laxity, and punitiveness—or mixtures of punitiveness and laxity alone—were particularly likely to be found in the background of their delinquent sample. However, the definition of inconsistency has shifted from study to study in this delinquency research, making evaluation and meaningful conclusions difficult (Walters and Parke, 1967).

The well-known study by Fisher (1955) provides an interesting laboratory analogue of inconsistent punishment in the home situation. One group of pups was consistently rewarded by petting and fondling for approaching the experimenter. The remaining pups received training, but in addition were handled roughly and occasionally shocked for making approach responses. Tests conducted toward the end of, and following, the training showed that pups that had received both reward and punishment training exhibited greater dependency in the form of remaining close to the experimenter than did pups in the 100 percent-reward group.

The implications of the Fisher findings are provocative. Punishing rather than inhibiting the dogs approach responses actually strengthened these behaviors compared to the nonpunished pups. Recent theorizing by Martin (1963) and by Banks (1966) has formally elaborated the effects of punishment and reward being associated with the same behavior. By extending Amsel's (1958, 1962) theory of frustrative nonreward to punishment situations, Martin suggested that pairing reward and punishment with the same goal would lead to greater resistance to extinction. Briefly it was argued that reinforcing a response, while providing intermittent punishment of this same response, results in the classical conditioning of anticipatory punishment responses to the approach response, thus resulting in greater resistance during extinction. Studies using both animal (Brown and Wagner, 1964) and adult human (Deur and Parke, 1968) subjects have supported this prediction.

Of equal interest for socialization are the effects of intermittently punishing a response on subsequent persistence in the face of continuous punishment. Banks (1966), in a further theoretical extension of Amselian theory which closely parallels Martin's, has argued that an intermittent reward and punishment schedule produces a response that is highly resistant to regular or consistent punishment. Due to the conditioning of anticipatory punishment during training to approach responses, subjects given intermittent punishment training will continue to exhibit approach tendencies when continuous punishment begins; in comparison to non-punished subjects for whom punishment elicits avoidance behavior, the intermittently punished subjects will persist longer under consistent punishment conditions. Again both animal (Banks, 1966) and adult human (Deur and Parke, 1968; Parke et al., 1969) research findings are consistent with the prediction.

In a recently completed study, Deur and Parke (1970) investigated the effects of inconsistent punishment on aggression in young children. Aggression was chosen as the response measure in order to relate the findings to the previous field studies of inconsistent discipline and aggressive-delinquent behavior. The effects of inconsistent punishment training on both resistance to extinction and to continuous punishment were examined in this study.

An automated Bobo doll similar to that previously employed by Walters and his colleagues (e.g., Cowan and Walters, 1963), was used to measure aggression. Following a two-minute baseline, six- to nine-year-old boys were exposed to one of three training conditions. In one case, the boys received marbles each time they punched the Bobo doll for 18 trials. In a second group the subjects received the marble reward on 9 trials, while on the remaining trials punching behavior was not rewarded. The remaining boys were rewarded on half of the punching trials but heard a noxious 84 db buzzer on the other nine occasions of the training period.

In the next part of the study, the effects of these training procedures on resistance to extinction and resistance to continuous punishment were assessed. Half of the children in each of the three groups were neither rewarded nor punished for their hitting behavior. The other subjects heard the noxious buzzer each time they punched the Bobo doll. Subjects had been informed at the onset of the training session that they could terminate the punching game whenever they wished. The main index of persistence was the number of hitting responses before the child voluntarily ended the session. The results are shown in Fig. 7. It can be seen that punished subjects made fewer hitting responses than subjects in the extinction condition, which suggests that the buzzer was effective in inhibiting the aggressive behavior. Of greater interest is the effect of the training schedules. In comparison with the 100% reward group, the

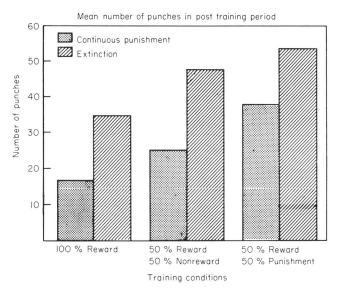

Figure 7.   Mean number of punches in the post-training period as related to the type of training.

inconsistently punished subjects showed greater resistance to extinction; moreover these previously punished children tended to persist significantly longer than the 100% reward boys under continuous punishment conditions. The persistence scores of the 50% reward group fell between the 100% reward and the 50% punishment subjects. The difference in resistance to extinction scores of the 50% reward and 100% reward subjects reached statistical significance; none of the other comparisons between the 50% reward subjects and the other groups were statistically reliable.

The similarity of the pattern of these findings and the data of a study (Deur and Parke, 1968) employing adult subjects provides further confidence in the intermittent punishment effect. In this study, subjects solved a simple three button problem solving task in which a particular combination (e.g., 3-1-2, 1-3-2) was designated as the correct response. The design paralleled the aggression study with children. On 20 training trials, the correct sequence was either rewarded on a 100% reward schedule, a 50% reward, 50% nonreward schedule, or a 50% reward, 50% punishment schedule. The data shown in Fig. 8 represent the number of correct responses the subjects gave before quitting, under either extinction or continuous punishment conditions. Both 50% nonreward and 50% punishment training led to greater resistance to extinction than continuous

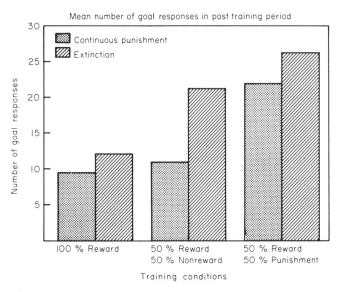

Figure 8.   Mean number of goal responses in the post-training period as related to the type of training.

reward. As in the aggression study, partial punishment training increased persistence under continuous punishment in comparison with the continuous reward group.

Although the heightened resistance to continuous punishment, exhibited by the intermittently punished subjects in these two experiments, is consistent with extensions of frustration theory to punishment situations, (Banks, 1966; Martin, 1963) other interpretations are possible. According to an adaptation-to-punishment explanation, the subjects in the 50% reward, 50% punishment training condition may have adapted to the noise while it was being presented intermittently. These competing interpretations were experimentally evaluated in a recent study by Parke *et al.* (1969). Adult subjects were exposed to either contingent or noncontingent intermittent punishment in a button-pressing task before being continuously punished. If the adaptation interpretation is correct, all groups exposed to the punisher, regardless of whether or not punishment is contingent on the button-pressing response, should show greater resistance to continuous punishment than will groups having no prior exposure to the punishment. On the other hand, the conditioning interpretation derived from frustration theory predicts that only the subjects receiving contingent punishment training will show the intermittent punishment effect.

The data were consistent with frustration theory: only the contingent punishment group showed increased resistance to continuous punishment. The opportunity for adaptation by exposure to the punishment on a non-contingent basis was not sufficient to produce the effect.

The paradigm of inconsistency employed in these studies represents only one of a variety of possibilities. In a current study we are examining the effects of inconsistent intensities of punishment on subsequent resistance to continuous high-intensity punishment. Will the parent who gradually increases the intensity of punishment over a series of occasions have more difficulty achieving control of the child's behavior with a punisher of consistently high intensity? Data from rat studies, such as Miller (1960) and Azrin (1959, 1960), suggest that gradual introduction of the punishing stimulus will reduce its effectiveness for inhibiting behavior.

Probably of equal importance for socialization would be studies of interparent inconsistency. What effect will mother-rewarding and father-punishing the same class of behaviors have on the persistence of these response patterns? Will the child merely learn to discriminate the occasions on which the behavior is acceptable or will the behavior, in addition, become stronger and more difficult to inhibit? Finally, the impact of reward following punishment deserves investigation. The parent who follows the administration of punishment with a display of affection directed toward the errant child may counteract the impact of the punishment and will probably strengthen the response as well.

CONCLUSIONS AND FUTURE DIRECTIONS

These research findings provide a partial and incomplete answer to only one question that requires consideration in a discussion of punishment's role in socialization, namely, what variables influence the effectiveness of punishment for inhibiting children's behavior? This is the issue that we have dealt with but other questions warrant consideration.

The issue of the ecological validity of these findings requires examination. Baldwin (1967) has recently charged social learning theorists with building a "mythology of childhood" in which a set of effects demonstrated in the laboratory are assumed to actually take place in naturalistic socialization contexts and, in fact, to be an accurate account of how the child does develop. As a result, there has been a confusion between necessary and sufficient causality; the laboratory experiments tell us *only* that punishment is a *possible* contributor to childhood learning of inhibition of deviant behaviors. The extent to which punishment is, in fact, a necessary technique for adequate socialization is clearly left unanswered.

Specifically, if we are to achieve an understanding of the "role" of punishment, we need information concerning such simple dimensions as the frequency with which parents use punishment. What kinds of punishments are usually employed? How often is punishment used relative to other techniques available to the parent for controlling the child's behavior?

Are some kinds of "punishment" more effective than others? *Or*, stated slightly differently, what kinds of events act as punishers? And how do these events acquire their aversive properties? Investigations of this kind are particularly necessary in light of recent studies such as Harris *et al.* (1967) on the role of attention in shaping and maintaining children's social behavior. Many of the events, such as social disapproval, which have been found to be such potent inhibitors in laboratory studies, appear to function quite differently in natural settings—and in some cases in a paradoxically opposite manner—by increasing rather than decreasing the probability of occurrence of the behavior.

Another set of questions concerns eliciting stimulus conditions for the use of punishment, rather than another disciplinary technique. Are there certain classes of behavior, such as aggression, that are likely to elicit punishment? Or are high-intensity versions of an undesirable response more likely to be punished?

What role does the child play in determining the choice of disciplinary technique? For example, what characteristics of the child—such as age and sex—predict the use of punishment? Systematic data on the relative frequency of the use of verbal punishment and physical punishment as a function of age and sex of the child would be of interest. Does the frequency of use of punishment decrease with age, or does the form shift with age? Casual observation clearly suggests that both frequency and form of punishment do change with age, but systematic documentation of these shifts are clearly necessary. Similarly, are different kinds of punishers differentially effective either as a function of sex or age?

Another issue concerns the manner in which children learn to control parental choices of disciplinary techniques through reactions to punishment. Generally, what role does recipient reaction have in controlling parental choice of technique and in determining parental behavior following punishment? Is the intensity of the child's emotional response a factor? For example, does the child who gives a marked emotional reaction deter the parent from using punishment on the next occasion of a similar misbehavior? Recent studies of the effects of victim feedback on aggressive behavior (e.g., Buss, 1966) suggest that a child's reactions may indeed play an important role in shaping parental disciplinary patterns.

A related issue concerns the role of cultural value judgments regarding the appropriateness of punishment for different types of misbehaviors and for children of different ages and sexes. An understanding of these judgmental processes would be important for predicting parental reactions to their own use of various disciplinary techniques. Do parents, for example, respond differently following the administration of punishment when they feel that the punishment was justified? Or, when a parent views their use of punishment as unjustified, are they likely to compensate by showing affection and warmth? Therefore, information concerning the defining characteristics and circumstances of justified and unjustified punishment would be of interest not only for its own sake, but as a prediction of parental behavior in disciplinary contexts.

Is the parent's current emotional state an important predictor? For example, is punishment more likely to occur when anger level is high or when a recent frustration has occurred? Generally, how useful is the aggression literature in providing a guide concerning the conditions under which punishment is likely to be employed?

Finally to what extent do structural factors such as family organization and size, and physical characteristics of the home (such as the amount of living space) contribute to choice of technique? Cross-cultural data (Whiting, 1961) suggest a strong association between severity of aggression training and household type, with extended families being much more severe than nuclear households. Similarly Roy (1950) found a direct increase in the permissiveness of child-rearing attitudes as the number of rooms in the house increased.

Answers to these questions are unlikely to come from merely following the common field-study approach of interviewing and questioning parents about child-rearing practices. Probably detailed and extensive home observational studies of parent-child interaction are necessary. Such investigations will provide descriptive data concerning the utilization of punishment as a socializing technique. Moreover, information concerning the eliciting conditions can be derived from such studies, and finally sequential analyses of parent-child interactions will yield interesting data concerning the child's role in shaping parental choice of disciplinary techniques. This emphasis does not argue for a rejection of experimental studies of punishment. Rather, observational studies can provide valuable guides concerning the kinds of experiments and experimental analogues that will be relevant to the issue of punishment and socialization. In any case, the issues raised clearly require examination if the role of punishment in the socialization process is to be more fully understood.

REFERENCES

Amsel, A. (1958). The role of frustrative nonreward in noncontinuous reward situations. *Psychol. Bull.*, **55**, 102–119.

Amsel, A. (1962). Frustrative nonreward in partial reinforcement and discrimination learning. *Psychol. Rev.*, **69**, 306–328.

Aronfreed, J. (1965). Punishment learning and internalization: Some parameters of reinforcement and cognition. Paper presented at the Biennial Meeting of the Society for Research in Child Development. Minneapolis, March.

Aronfreed, J. (1968). *Conduct and conscience.* Academic Press, New York.

Aronfreed, J., and Leff, R. (1963). The effects of intensity of punishment and complexity of discrimination upon the learning of an internalized inhibition. Unpublished manuscript, Univ. of Pennsylvania.

Aronfreed, J., and Reber, A. (1965). Internalized behavioral suppression and the timing of social punishment. *J. Personality and Social Psychol.*, **1**, 3–16.

Azrin, N. H. (1959). A technique for delivering shock to pigeons. *J. Exp. Analysis of Behavior*, **2**, 161–163.

Azrin, N. H. (1960). Effects of punishment intensity during variable-interval reinforcement. *J. Exp. Analysis of Behavior*, **3**, 123–142.

Baldwin, A. L. (1967). *Theories of child development.* Wiley, New York.

Bandura, A. and Walters, R. H. (1959). *Adolescent aggression.* Ronald Press, New York.

Bandura, A., and Walters, R. H. (1963). *Social learning and personality development.* Holt, New York.

Banks, R. K. (1966). Persistence to continuous punishment following intermittent punishment training. *J. Exp. Psychol.*, **71**, 373–377.

Becker, W. C. (1964). Consequences of different kinds of parental discipline. In M. L. Hoffman and L. W. Hoffman (Eds.), *Review of child development research,* Vol. 1. Russell Sage Foundation, New York.

Brown, R. R., and Wagner, A. R. (1964). Resistance to punishment and extinction following training with shock and nonreinforcement. *J. Exp. Psychol.*, **68**, 503–507.

Buss, A. H. (1966). Instrumentality of aggression, feedback, and frustration as determinants of physical aggression. *J. Personality and Social Psychol.*, **3**, 153–162.

Cheyne, J. A., and Walters, R. H. (1969). Intensity of punishment, timing of punishment, and cognitive structure as determinants of response inhibition. *J. Exp. Child Psychol.*, **7**, 231–244.

Church, R. M. (1963). The varied effects of punishment on behavior. *Psychol. Rev.*, **70**, 369–402.

Cowan, P. A., and Walters, R. H. (1963). Studies of reinforcement of aggression: I. Effects of scheduling. *Child Development*, **34**, 543–551.

Crandall, V. C. (1963). The reinforcement effects of adult reactions and nonreactions on children's achievement expectations. *Child Development*, **34**, 335–354.

Crandall, V. C., Good, S. and Crandall, V. J. (1964). The reinforcement effects of adult reactions and nonreactions on achievement expectations. A replication. *Child Development*, **35**, 485–497.

Deur, J. L., and Parke, R. D. (1968). Resistance to extinction and continuous punishment in humans as a function of partial reward and partial punishment training. *Psychonom. Sci.*, **13**, 91–92.

Deur, J. L., and Parke, R. D. (1970). The effects of inconsistent punishment on aggression in children. *Developmental Psychol.*, in press.

Fisher, A. E. (1955). The effects of differential early treatment on the social and exploratory behavior of puppies. Unpublished doctoral dissertation. Pennsylvania State University.

Freedman, D. G. (1958). Constitutional and environmental interactions in rearing of four breeds of dogs. *Science*, 127, 585–586.

Glueck, S., and Glueck, E. (1950). *Unraveling juvenile delinquency.* Harvard Univ. Press, Cambridge, Mass.

Harris, F., Wolf, M., and Baer, D. M. (1967). Effects of adult social reinforcement on child behavior. In W. W. Hartup and N. L. Smothergill (Eds.), *The young child.* Nat. Assoc. for the Education of Young Children, Washington.

Hartup, W. W. (1958). Nurturance and nurturance-withdrawal in relation to the dependency behavior of preschool children. *Child Development*, 29, 191–201.

Helson, H. (1964). *Adaptation level theory.* Harper and Row, New York.

Hill, W. F. (1960). Learning theory and the acquisition of values. *Psychol. Rev.*, 67, 317–331.

Hoffman, M. L. (1963). Childrearing practices and moral development: generalization from empirical research. *Child Development*, 34, 295–318.

Kohlberg, L. (1963). Moral development and identification. In H. W. Stevenson (Ed.), *Child Psychology:* Yearbook No. 62, Part I, pp. 383–431. Nat. Society for the Study of Education, Chicago.

Luria, A. R. (1961). *The role of speech in the regulation of normal and abnormal behavior.* Liveright, New York.

Martin, B. (1963). Reward and punishment associated with the same goal response: A factor in the learning of motives. *Psychol. Bull.*, 60, 441–451.

McCord, W., McCord, J., and Zola, I. K. (1959). *Origins of crime.* Columbia Univ. Press, New York.

McCord, W., McCord, J. and Howard, A. (1961). Familial correlates of aggression in non-delinquent male children. *J. Abnormal and Social Psychol.*, 62, 79–93.

Miller, N. E. (1960). Learning resistance to pain and fear: Effects of overlearning, exposure and rewarded exposure in context. *J. Exp. Psychol.*, 60, 137–145.

Mowrer, O. H. (1960). *Learning theory and the symbolic processes.* Wiley, New York.

Parke, R. D. (1967). Nurturance, nurturance withdrawal, and resistance to deviation. *Child Development*, 38, 1101–1110.

Parke, R. D. (1969). Effectiveness of punishment as an interaction of intensity, timing, agent nurturance and cognitive structuring. *Child Development*, 40, 213–235.

Parke, R. D., Deur, J. L. and Sawin, D. B. (1969). The intermittent punishment effect in humans: conditioning or adaptation. *Psychonom. Sci.*, in press.

Parke, R. D., and Walters, R. H. (1967). Some factors determining the efficacy of punishment for inducing response inhibition. *Monographs of the Soc. for Res. in Child Development*, 32, No. 109.

Renner, E. K. (1964). Conflict resolution and the process of temporal integration. *Psychol. Rep.*, 15, 432–438.

Rosenblith, J. F. (1959). Learning by imitation in kindergarten children. *Child Development*, 30, 69–80.

Rosenblith, J. F. (1961). Imitative color choices in kindergarten children. *Child Development*, 32, 211–223.

Rotter, J. B. (1954). *Social learning and clinical psychology.* Prentice-Hall, Englewood Cliffs, N.J.

Roy, K. (1950). Parent's attitudes toward their children. *J. Home Economics,* **42,** 652–653.

Sears, R. R., Whiting, J. W. M., Nowlis, V., and Sears, P. S. (1953). Some child-rearing antecedents of aggression and dependency in young children. *Genet. Psychol. Monographs,* **57,** 135–234.

Sears, R. R., Maccoby, E. E., and Levin, H. (1957). *Patterns of child rearing.* Row, Peterson, Evanston, Ill.

Solomon, R. L. (1964). Punishment. *Am. Psychologist,* **19,** 239–253.

Walters, R. H., and Andres, D. (1967). Punishment procedures and self-control. Paper read at the Annual Meeting of the American Psychological Association, Washington, D.C. September.

Walters, R. H., and Demkow, L. (1963). Timing of punishment as a determinant of response inhibition. *Child Development,* **34,** 207–214.

Walters, R. H., and Parke, R. D. (1967). The influence of punishment and related disciplinary techniques on the social behavior of children: theory and empirical findings. In B. A. Maher (Ed.), *Progress in experimental personality research.* Vol. 4, pp. 179–228.

Walters, R. H., Parke, R. D., and Cane, V. A. (1965). Timing of punishment and the observation of consequences to others as determinants of response inhibition. *J. Exp. Child Psychol.,* **2,** 10–30.

Whiting, J. W. M. (1954). Fourth presentation. In J. M. Tanner and B. Inhelder (Eds.), *Discussions on child development:* II. Tavistock, London.

Whiting, J. W. M. (1961). Socialization process and personality. In F. L. K. Usu (Ed.), *Psychological anthropology: Approaches to culture and personality.* Dorsey, Homewood, Illinois.

6

THE ROLE OF IMITATION
IN CHILDHOOD SOCIALIZATION

Willard W. Hartup*
and Brian Coates†

Developmental psychology has profited greatly from the recent surge of research interest in imitation. First, a clearer conception has been gained of certain variables that influence children's observational learning and imitative performance. Well-replicated findings show that children imitate the behavior of other persons as a consequence of: (*a*) contingent reinforcement given to the subject (Baer *et al.*, 1967; Lovaas *et al.*, 1966; McDavid, 1959); (*b*) contingent reinforcement delivered to the model and observed by the subject (Bandura, 1965; Clark, 1965); (*c*) the subject's awareness that the model is particularly competent or prestigeful (Miller and Dollard, 1941); (*d*) a history of positively reinforcing interaction with the model (Bandura and Huston, 1961; Hetherington and Frankie, 1967); (*e*) the power or dominance of the model (Hetherington, 1965; Mischel and Grusec, 1966); and (*f*) the observer's verbalizations about the model's behavior during observation of the model (Bandura *et al.*, 1966; Coates and Hartup, 1969).

Second, it has been shown that an extensive range of children's behaviors is susceptible to modeling influences. These include problem-solving, speech, conditionability in Taffel-type tasks, self-rewarding behavior, delay of gratification, moral judgments, aggression, altruism and other charitable actions, phobic behavior, and so forth. This list will be lengthened if present research trends continue even though it may not be necessary to demonstrate further that molar segments of social behav-

---

* University of Minnesota.

† University of North Carolina. When this paper was written, Brian Coates held a National Institute of Mental Health Predoctoral Fellowship (MHO-6668) at the Institute of Child Development, University of Minnesota.

ior are susceptible to the influence of models. The operation of observational learning and imitation in child behavior has been amply demonstrated and their relevance to social development amply proved.

It should be expected, then, that past research would furnish extensive information concerning the role of imitation in childhood socialization. Upon close examination, however, two lacunae in imitation research are evident. First, little is known about the developmental viscissitudes of imitation. The origin of "first imitations" is not adequately accounted for, and little information concerning age-changes in this area of behavior is available. Second, hypotheses emanating from experimental research have not been tested in long-term naturalistic studies; in other words, little is known about the factors influencing imitation in the everyday socialization of the child.

The purpose of this paper is to present an assessment of these two gaps in the literature. The few empirical studies that exist on these problems will be reviewed and directions for future research will be discussed. Specifically, the following problems will be probed: (a) the origins of imitation, i.e., "first" imitations; (b) generalized imitation; (c) developmental patterns, and (d) naturalistic research on imitation.

THE DEVELOPMENT OF IMITATION

Stimulated by Miller and Dollard's (1941) early work, an attempt was begun in the 1940s to bring imitation into the framework of general behavior theory. What has come to be called "social learning theory" is partially an outgrowth of this effort. Before evaluating the contributions of imitation research to our understanding of childhood socialization, it seems necessary to distinguish between the "psychology of development" and the "psychology of learning" as Bijou (1968) has recently done.

Bijou described these two branches of psychology as follows: The psychology of learning primarily involves the study of strengthening and weakening of stimulus and response functions. The psychology of development, on the other hand, is concerned with progressive changes in the interactions between a physiologically changing organism and environmental events with these interactions involving genetic factors, present circumstances, and historical occurrences. Bijou's distinction, and others like it, define the field of developmental psychology far more broadly than the simple study of correlations between chronological age and patterns of child behavior. Such distinctions imply, however, that variable-oriented studies—whether they involve organismic variables or stimulus variables—must make some reference to age in order to be regarded as developmental investigations. When developmental studies are defined in this way, it can be argued that a developmental psychology of imitation scarcely exists.

Most of the contemporary research on children's imitation has been devoted to the study of situational variables that influence the functional relation between a given set of stimuli (including the behavior of a social model) and matching responses in children at one selected age level. These studies assist greatly in the analysis of such developmental problems as socialization but in themselves do not represent developmental analysis of the socialization problem. Some investigators, including Robert Sears (1957), have approached the problem of childhood imitation from a social learning view which is, simultaneously, a developmental view. But the bulk of research on children's imitation, from Miller and Dollard (1941) to Bandura and Walters (1963), has been primarily concerned with the "strengthening and weakening of stimulus-response functions." The yield from this effort consists of principles that undoubtedly have considerable trans-age applicability, but it is becoming increasingly apparent that qualifications must be placed on virtually every one of them.

Take, for example, the well-documented finding that reward, contingent upon the subject's emission of a matching response, increases the frequency of such responding. Flanders (1968) cites 28 studies, the results of which demonstrate that this is so. Joan Grusec (1966), however, found that increased imitation of self-critical responses in preschool children occurred under contingent reward *only for one of the two types of rewards used.* An increase in imitation was obtained when the reinforcement consisted of reinstating the experimenter's approval following a period in which this approval had been withdrawn. No increase was obtained, however, when the reinforcer consisted of reinstating token rewards. It is entirely possible (as Grusec suggests) that the hypothesis —that withdrawal of material rewards would be punishing—was incorrect (i.e., the subjects had some access to the reinforcing stimuli during the withdrawal period—the token reinforcers remained in the child's view). The possibility, however, that incentive factors in observational learning may be specific to the age of the subject cannot be dismissed. Unfortunately, information concerning the relation between developmental status and incentives in observational learning is completely lacking. Stevenson (1968) has deplored the same lack of developmental information concerning the role of incentives in other forms of children's learning.

Developmental factors may also necessitate qualification of some of the general principles emerging from recent research concerning vicarious reinforcement. Bandura *et al.* (1963) reported, some time ago, that observation of models who receive positive reinforcement enhances imitation. These data were based on preschool children and the findings have been replicated by Bandura and his associates, by Walters and his associates, and many others. Most of these replications, however, have involved preschoolers or young elementary school children. Other replications of the vicarious reinforcement effect have been reported with somewhat older children in studies of self-reinforcement behavior (e.g., Mischel and Liebert, 1966), but in many of these studies the manipulations designed to produce vicarious reinforcement (reward and punishment of the model) were confounded with amount of self-reinforcement displayed by the model. Two investigations which did *not* involve this confounding and which were also conducted with older children failed to reveal the conventional vicarious reinforcement effect. Barnwell and Sechrest (1965) reported that positively rewarding the model enhanced the frequency with which first graders matched the picture preferences of a peer model but did not enhance matching among third-grade subjects; Rosekrans (1967) was unable to produce vicarious reinforcement effects in a group of twelve-year-old boys. Procedural differences among the studies in this area of research may have some bearing on the differences in results, but this does not rule out the possibility that the typical vicarious reinforcement procedure may have different effects on imitation by children of different ages.

Existing research contains many other indications that variance in imitation may derive from the developmental status of the subjects. Another example: the literature concerning the effects of model-rewardingness on children's imitation shows that, in general, children imitate nurturant, rewarding models to a greater extent than they imitate distant, cold, and unrewarding models. This literature also reveals, however, that a number of other variables affect the relation between model rewardingness and imitation. For example, Bandura and Huston (1961) found that model-rewardingness affected preschool children's imitation of incidental verbal and motor responses, but not two other response classes (aggression and solution of a discrimination problem). Thus, task characteristics seem to intrude on the relation between model-rewardingness and imitation. Next, Mischel and Grusec (1966) reported that model-rewardingness facilitated imitation, but this depended upon whether the behavior being modeled was "aversive" or "neutral" and whether imitation was measured in terms of "rehearsal" or "transmission." Rosenblith (1959) reported sex differences in responsiveness to a model's attentiveness; Stein and Wright (1964) reported that the model's nurturance affected preschool children's imitation depending on the extent to which the child manifested changes in dependency during the experiment.

Finally, Hartup and Coates (1967) showed that the rewardingness of a peer model was positively associated with imitation when the child had had a prior history of frequent positive social experiences in the nursery school peer group but, on the other hand, was negatively associated with the tendency to imitate when earlier amounts of social reinforcement from the peer group were low. These results may be seen in Fig. 1. Such findings suggest that factors in the child's prior learning history affect his influencibility by rewarding models. In short, a variety of situational, historical, and personality factors appear to be involved in determining a child's responsiveness to the factor of model rewardingness.

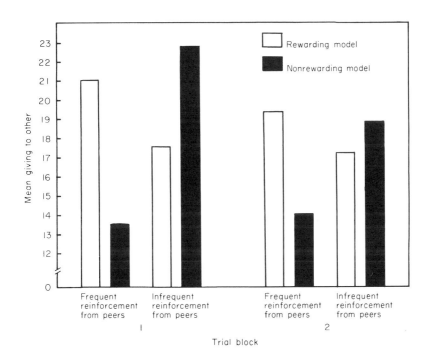

Figure 1.   Mean giving to other scores in blocks of five trials by reinforcement condition and type of peer model. (From Hartup and Coates, 1967.)

It is difficult to incorporate the disorderly findings concerning model rewardingness into existing theories. For example, the secondary reinforcement theory of imitation proposed by Mowrer (1950) does not adequately encompass the findings since that theory simply points to a positive linear relation between model rewardingness and imitation. It is also difficult to ascribe the diverse experimental findings to procedural differences. On the other hand, it is possible that some of these variations represent interactions between the experimental requirements and the developmental status of the preschool child, upon whom most of the findings are based. More extensive developmental study of the history and operation of social responsiveness during early childhood would add considerably to our present theoretical capacity for handling the data concerning model-rewardingness and imitation.

Why has there been such a paucity of research concerning the development of imitation? In the first place, such research is hard to do. However, this is probably not the major reason for the lack of developmental research in this area. Rather, this research gap is most likely due to the historical domination over imitation research by the various theories of social learning.

As was said earlier, learning theories are not really developmental theories even though learning principles can be applied developmentally. Why, then, have learning principles not been used more frequently in developmental studies of imitation? Part of the problem may be that the direction of research on imitation was fixed early by individuals who were not trained in developmental psychology (e.g., Miller and Dollard, 1941). On the other hand, the nature of research on children's imitation has probably been shaped for more sanguine reasons. For one thing, variable-oriented learning research on imitation is needed as a prerequisite for research on developmental problems in this area. Further, learning theory has a certain theoretical elegance; it has been associated with a concern for experimental methodologies and a cathexis for parametric study of the variables relating to behavior change. These characteristics have probably lured investigators away from the study of complicated developmental interactions that undoubtedly characterize children's imitation.

Let us be clear: the concentration on nondevelopmental problems in contemporary imitation research has not been a strategic mistake. However, our functional analyses of observational learning and imitation are sufficiently sophisticated to begin in earnest the study of their development in children. The lack of developmental studies in this area is a serious problem. First, developmental psychology needs this type of research. The question that is before us here (the role of imitation in childhood socialization) is a terribly pertinent question and cannot be discussed on the basis of nondevelopmental data alone. An analysis of the extent to which imitation is involved in socialization requires information concerning the interaction of temperamental viscissitudes, other individual difference factors, and historical circumstances as these change in affecting imitation over broad periods in children's lives. Finally, developmentally-oriented research would increase the practical usefulness of our knowledge concerning observational learning and imitative performance as these may be involved in child-rearing, education, and psychotherapy.

To summarize: (*a*) The domination of social learning theory in recent research on children's imitation has been sanguine; no other theory has had the precision nor the elegance required to push the study of children's observational learning and imitation so far, so fast. (*b*) A developmental psychology of observational learning and imitation has not yet been created. (*c*) Until it is, many of the present research areas in imitation (e.g., rewardingness of the model, vicarious reinforcement) will remain uninterpretable. (*d*) Without developmental research, the role of imitation in childhood socialization cannot be clearly delineated.

Developmental Theories

The fact that the present psychology of imitation is not a developmental psychology of imitation is a fascinating quirk of history since the two Olympian developmental theorists of the century—Freud and Piaget —both posited that imitation occupies a central position in the psychological development of the child. Freud introduced the construct of *identification* which subsumes the child's attempts to emulate the parental ideal along with other aspects of the child's feelings toward his parents. Piaget, on the other hand, was more interested in simple imitation. Both of these theorists, however, hypothesized that imitative behavior emerges in the child's repertoire in an epigenetic fashion. That is, they hypothesized that there are precursors and primitive forms of behavior which precede the emergence of what might be called "true" imitation. Further, each formulated hypotheses concerning those factors that play a role in producing the phenomenon of imitation itself and, finally, each had something to say about the outcomes of imitation in children's development (e.g., sex-typing and moral values in the case of Freud; symbolic skills in the case of Piaget).

Freud. Freud's ideas concerning the development of identification are difficult to pull together in a few paragraphs. As has been reported elsewhere (e.g., Bronfenbrenner, 1960), Freud's thinking on this topic was constantly in flux. He never attempted to clarify or systematize a "theory" of identification; gaps and inconsistencies in his writings are ubiquitous. Even so, several themes emerge; two are emphasized in the following commentary. First, a linkage is implied between the behavior repertoire in infancy (oral incorporation) and the identificatory repertoire of later childhood. Second, the theory of identification is linked to a conception of developmental stages. Freud consistently posited that "secondary" identification, a precipitate of the Oedipus complex, is a derivative of the "primary" identification of infancy and ambivalent cathexes that ensue during infancy and early childhood. In consequence, Freud's theory of identification is clearly a developmental one.

To elucidate, briefly: "Primary" identification refers to the initial un-differentiated state of fusion between the unformed infant ego and the early social objects with whom the infant is in contact. Of the several aspects of infant experience having importance in the history of identifi-cation, the formation of attachments to those who feed and care for the infant was stressed most consistently by Freud. These attachments are manifest in the motoric behaviors or oral incorporation, through which the infant attempts to introject the ego of the attached object and thereby sustain the attachment.

In describing the events which lead to secondary identification, Freud introduced a welter of hypotheses, some of which were incompletely formulated and some of which were inconsistent with one another. Pre-sumably, the child's earliest object choice focusses on the mother because of her primary caretaking function. Early cathexis must also be assumed to involve the father; otherwise some of Freud's speculations concerning the development of identification make very little sense. Freud was vague concerning the sources of these dual cathexes; he seems to have thought that they derive from the innate physiological bisexuality of the child. In any event, the attachments of infancy are presumed to intensify in chil-dren of both sexes as a consequence of sexual viscissitudes.

The manner in which the parents respond to these changes threatens the child's initial object-choice(s) and increases his ambivalence about them. Freud treated the role of sexual conflicts in this period differently in his analysis of superego development in boys and in girls. Later writers have actually extrapolated two distinct processes of identification from this differential treatment of development in the two sexes—namely, "anaclitic" identification and "aggressive" identification. In general, how-ever, Freud seems to have tried to build a case for the hypothesis that ambivalence in the child's object relations, created by "withdrawal of love" or "castration threats," furnishes the motivational base for the defensive activity known as secondary identification.

A necessary last step in this theorizing seemed to have been omitted. That is, what elicits the first identifications with the "loved-hated" object(s)? Fear of "loss of love" is perhaps a sufficient construct for explaining the maintenance of identification once this activity has been evoked. The oral incorporative activities of early infancy, however, do not seem continuous with the fantasized imitations of later childhood. For one thing, the "incorporative" mode, while it involves "taking-in of another ego," does not involve overt copying or matching of any kind.

This is the briefest outline that has probably ever been presented of Freud's theorizing about identification. It is sufficient for our purposes, however, since we wish only to emphasize the developmental nature of Freud's approaches to the problem. The developmental history of identification involves organismic and environmental changes that occur throughout infancy and early childhood: the theory emphasizes the formation of early attachments, the increasingly ambivalent nature of these attachments as a function of libidinal changes and parental threats, and the discovery by the child that identification (which involves matching the parent ideal) brings about psychic equilibrium.

Freud's writings are frequently cited in publications concerning the effects on imitative behavior of model "warmth," "nurturance," "reward-ingness," or "love." Experimental procedures, whereby a model interacts "warmly" with a child for 10 or 15 minutes prior to modeling, may be regarded as loose analogs of the attachment phenomena assumed by Freud to be antecedents of identification. On the other hand, this stretches Freud's conceptualizations almost beyond recognition since he conceived identification as: (a) a pervasive phenomenon, (b) a mechanism focused on the parents, and (c) a process that undergoes a history of modulations and transformations through infancy and early childhood. Most of the recent laboratory findings concerning children's imitation are, then, irrelevant to the *developmental* aspects of the theory.

Some of the recent studies of identification (e.g., Sears et al., 1965) have adhered more closely to the developmental spirit of Freud's theorizing. Many of these studies, however, have involved awkward retrospective strategies, the use of outcome measures derived from subjects only when they were preschoolers or adolescents, and behavioral measures that refer to social relations with teachers or peers rather than measures of the similarity between the child and his parents. Here, too, the research strategy has precluded the most direct test of the developmental components of Freud's theory.

It is amazing that Freud's speculations concerning the antecedents of identification have provided such a substantial base for experimental predictions about children's imitation. Of course, the theoretical reformulations by Mowrer (1950) and others have facilitated these experimental extensions and there is no inherent reason why the effects of ten minutes of model "nurturance" should not be analogous to the effects of parental "nurturance" in long-term development. If, in experimental work, parents are used as models (as they have been by Hetherington, 1967) the results are somewhat more revealing about the historical antecedents of children's imitation. They at least indicate the relevance of nurturance to children's imitation of their parents. Such experiments, however, still do not touch the developmental "stuff" of Freud's theory. It cannot be inferred from them that anaclitic identification proceeds, over time, in the way that Freud imagined (if anyone can say exactly how Freud imagined it).

To summarize this part: much fruitful experimental work concerning children's imitation has been stimulated by Freud's speculations. It should be made clear, however, what this body of literature tells us and what it does not. The experimental findings concerning model-rewarding-ness indicate that Freud did, indeed, put his finger on an aspect of interpersonal relations that is relevant to children's imitations. The research fails, however, to test Freud's notions concerning the ontogenesis of identification.

Piaget. Piaget presented his most detailed account of the development of imitation in *Play, Dreams and Imitation,* published in 1951. Extrapolations of his views, particularly concerning imitation in middle childhood, were presented in *The Moral Judgment of the Child* (1932). There are two major themes in Piaget's discussions of imitation. First, he too described certain precursors of mature imitation that appear during infancy. He did not assume that the young infant's actions constitute "true" imitation although the assumption was made that the matching behavior displayed by the infant is epigenetically related to later imitation. Second, Piaget's theory stresses a close functional relation between intellectual development and imitation. This relation is emphasized at each of the six stages used by Piaget to describe early cognitive development. It is also stressed in his descriptions of intellectual development in later childhood.

In the first three stages of the sensori-motor period (up to eight months of age), all of which may be called pre-imitative, the infant is able to duplicate only those responses of other people which are already in his own repertoire. His imitations are also limited to actions that produce clear perceptual feedback. The earliest forms of pre-imitative behavior consist of reflexive matching of others' behavior, as in crying when the crying of other infants is heard. In general, during these periods, the child merely increases the deliberateness and regularity with which he copies, as in his duplication of others' hand movements. This description of the early aspects of imitation is reminiscent of classical descriptions of iteration (Holt, 1931), and, indeed, Mowrer (1960) has interpreted Piaget in this manner.

The linkage between the child's developing intellectual competence and his imitations becomes more apparent at Stage IV (between 8 and 12 months). Here, the child's more extensive behavioral repertoire and what Piaget called the "coordination of schemas" make possible the imitation of new models utilizing actions which produce less distinct feedback to the infant himself. The coordination of schemas involves a preliminary understanding of the relation between an instrument and the goal object, in other words, the means-end relation. In Stage IV, the infant becomes capable, for the first time, of copying behaviors which are not in his own functioning repertoire. At Stage V, between 12 and 18 months, means-end coordinations become more sophisticated through active experimentation with the environment. A concomitant of this change is experimentation, trial-and-error fashion, in the copying of models. Much of the new copying is described as "groping and inefficient" but improvement in the efficiency of copying is a major characteristic of this stage.

At Stage VI (following 18 months), representational processes begin to be evident. The child shows new capacities to employ images and symbols; these capacities are accompanied by several changes in imitative behavior. First, there is more efficient copying of complex, new models. Second, the ability to copy objects as well as persons becomes evident. Third, and most important, the child displays "deferred imitation"—i.e., he can reproduce the behavior of a model who is no longer present.

Of particular concern to us here are Piaget's views concerning the relation between imitation and thought at the close of the sensori-motor period (Stage VI). In some ways, he treated the problem as a chicken-and-egg issue. That is, he addressed a major portion of his discourse to the question (Piaget, 1951, p. 62): "Does this representational capacity come to the support of imitation from the outside, as a new factor, or can we consider that the representative image is itself only the interiorised product of imitation in its final state?" As put later in his treatise, the problem is quite complex (p. 67): "Is deferred imitation in continuity with that of the earlier stages, of which it is the interiorisation . . . or must we recognize that at this sixth stage there is a new faculty (evocative memory, representation, etc.) which accounts for what occurs: deferred imitation of an absent model, or immediate directional imitation of new models?"

Piaget appears to have concluded that the relation between changes in imitation and changes in thought is reciprocal. He says (p. 77, italics ours): "At the representational levels, interiorised imitation *leads* to the formation of images *which may in their turn* give rise to new exterior imitations." The major attention in Piaget's argument, however, is given to the hypothesis that imitation is a vehicle for advancing the child's representational skills. The discussion neglects his own, softly stated, hypothesis that the child's new cognitive skills, in turn, produce changes in imitation. It seems to us that Piaget thought this latter proposition so obvious that it did not require extensive argument.

In general, Piaget's theory underscores an interplay in the mental life of the child in that imitation contributes to intellectual functioning, and the child's developing intellectual capacities also give rise to changes in imitation. To us, it is Piaget's stress on the close linkage between these types of functioning that is impressive. It suggests important empirical studies. The epigenetic aspects of the theory, which contrast so vividly with the total bulk of contemporary research on children's imitation, are also impressive.

The Piagetian analysis is weak, on the other hand, in at least one way. It gives no accounting of the factors which determine age changes in imitation during early childhood. Perhaps Piaget's analysis should not be criticized on this point since he purposely laid out a theory which did not attempt to delineate causes. It is legitimate to ask the question, nevertheless: What factors bring about the intertwined changes in thinking and in imitation during the child's development? The social learning theories of imitation offer more help in answering this question and it is precisely here that Bandura's (1969) recent statements concerning the functioning of imitation stand in sharpest contrast to Piaget's comments. Note, in the following passage, however, that Piagetian-like constructs have crept into Bandura's theory.

"Recent theoretical analyses of observational learning—which is the basic learning process underlying identification, however defined—assign a prominent role to representational mediators that are assumed to be acquired on the basis of a contiguity learning process. According to my formulation, observational learning involves two representational systems—an *imaginal* and a *verbal* one. After modeling stimuli have been coded into images or words for memory representation, they function as mediators for response retrieval and reproduction. . . . During the period of exposure, modeling stimuli elicit in observers perceptual responses that become sequentially associated and centrally integrated on the basis of temporal contiguity of stimulation. If perceptual sequences are repeatedly elicited, a constituent stimulus acquires the capacity to evoke images of the associated stimulus events even though they are no longer physically present. . . . In the course of observation, transitory perceptual phenomena produce relatively enduring, retrievable images of modeled sequences of behavior. Later, reinstatement of imaginal mediators serves as a guide for reproduction of matching responses" (Bandura, 1969, p. 220).

In this brief passage, Bandura has summarized his familiar contiguity theory of observational learning. He has, however, given cognitive processes an enhanced position in this theory. He uses them in a way that coincides neatly with a part of Piaget's analysis even though he incorporates cognitive constructs into the theory only as mediators of imitation and not *vice versa*. There is no hint, however, either in this brief passage or elsewhere in Bandura's writings, that the relation between symbolic behavior and imitation is thought to undergo developmental change. In short, Bandura's theory is weak with respect to some issues on which Piaget is strong; simultaneously, Piaget is weak with respect to certain issues on which Bandura is strong.

The developmental question is crucial. Does the relation between representational behavior and observational learning hold across all ages from infancy through adulthood? A minimum level of perceptual-representational capacity would seem necessary in order for deferred imitation to occur. This possibility is not recognized, however, either in Bandura's current theorizing or in most of the research now being generated by this theory.

For example, recent research with preschool and elementary school children has shown that verbalizing about the actions of the model enhances reproduction of the model's behavior (Bandura *et al.*, 1966; Coates and Hartup, 1969); in other words, representational activity facilitates imitation. At the same time, it is becoming clear that the relation between verbal processes and imitation changes as a function of age (Coates and Hartup, 1969). These findings will be discussed more fully at a later point but for now it may be pointed out that recent research supports the Piaget-Bandura thesis that intellectual functioning is closely linked to modeling effects.

To summarize this brief excursion into cognitive theory: this theory furnishes several examples of descriptive and explanatory problems in the analysis of children's imitation that are also *developmental* problems. We belabor this point because developmental issues in the psychology of imitation have not been the focus of much research and because there has been so little recognition that the theory proposed by Bandura concerning the role of representational processes in observational learning is essentially a nondevelopmental theory.

The Origins of Imitation

"First imitations" were of primary interest to a number of psychologists in the early years of this century. Holt's (1931) "echo principle" constituted an early theoretical attempt to account for infant imitations, and the origins of imitation were of major interest to McDougall (1908) and to Baldwin (1895), as well as to many others. Nevertheless, research on this topic has languished. Virtually all that is known about first imitations is based on the study of older, partially-socialized children.

Within the past two or three years, reinforcement psychologists have become interested in this problem. One account, from this viewpoint, of the acquisition and maintenance of imitation is provided by Gewirtz and Stingle (1968, p. 379):

"The first imitative responses must occur by chance, through direct physical assistance, or through direct training (with shaping or fading procedures applied by a reinforcing agent to occurring responses). When such responses occur, they are strengthened and maintained by direct extrinsic reinforcement from environmental agents. After several imitative responses become established in this manner, a class of diverse but *functionally equivalent* behaviors is acquired and maintained by extrinsic reinforcement on an intermittent schedule. Differences in response content of the imitative behaviors are thought to play a minimal role as long as the responses are members of the imitative response class as defined functionally by *reinforcing agents*."

Thus, Gewirtz and Stingle hypothesize that matching responses first occur by chance; response strength (rate of occurrence) of matching responses increases as a function of intermittent reinforcement, and eventually a sufficient number of reinforced responses occurs so that a generalized imitative repertoire (relatively free of reinforcement) is built up.

The analysis of the origins problem by Baer and his associates (1967) is slightly different from the preceding approach. Baer emphasizes that similarity between the behavior of the model and the subject becomes *both* a discriminative stimulus for imitative behavior and a conditioned reinforcer. In other words, if the child receives positive reinforcement for imitating the behavior of the model, the quality of *similarity* between the model's behavior and the child's behavior functions as a discriminative stimulus. In addition, as a discriminative stimulus for positive reinforcement, it eventually acquires a conditioned reinforcing function. As Baer *et al.* (1967, p. 411) note, "as a positive reinforcer, it (similarity) should strengthen any new behavior that produced or achieved it. Behaviors that achieve similarity between one's self and a model are, of course, imitative behaviors; furthermore, they are imitative by function and not by coincidence."

There are a number of experiments (Baer, *et al.*, 1967; Hewett, 1965; Hingtgen *et al.*, 1967; Lovaas *et al.*, 1966 and 1967; Metz, 1965) which have been based on a reinforcement analysis of the problem of first imitations. This literature possesses several characteristics which differentiate it from other research on children's imitation. First, and perhaps most obviously, the experiments have been carried out with children who evidence little or no imitative behavior. This initial failure to imitate social models is usually assessed before the experiment begins. Baseline rates of imitative responding have involved simple pretreatment imitation measures in the laboratory (Metz, 1965) and ratings of imitative behavior made in institutional ward settings (Baer, *et al.*, 1967). Assessment of baselines is rare, indeed, in other imitation research.

Another characteristic of this literature is that the subjects have been unusual children. They have been retarded (Baer, *et al.*, 1967) or schizophrenic (Hewett, 1965; Hingtgen, *et al.*, 1967; Lovass *et al.*, 1966 and 1967; Metz, 1965), and have ranged in age from 4 to 13 years.

A final characteristic of these studies of first imitations is the use of very small samples of subjects. Hewett, Metz, and Baer *et al.* employed 1, 2, and 3 subjects in their respective investigations. Lovaas, who has completed the most extensive work in this area, has published data on 13 subjects. All of these investigations have involved within-subject experimental designs consisting of three phases: (*a*) a pre-experimental phase in which the operant level of the subject's imitative behavior is determined; (*b*) an experimental phase in which the subject is reinforced (usually with food) for matching the behavior of the model; and (*c*) an extinction period in which reinforcement for imitative behavior is completely withdrawn or reinforcement is made noncontingent with respect to the imitative behavior of the subject. A fourth phase, reinstatement of the experimental procedure, has been employed in some of these studies. Prompting and fading techniques have been commonly used. A prompt consists of the experimenter's guiding the subject through the motor aspects of the desired behavior during the beginning of the experimental phase.

These experiments have consistently shown that children having little or no imitative behavior in their initial repertoires emit frequent imitations when reinforcement is made contingent on responses which match those of the model. This has been demonstrated using three different dependent measures: (*a*) the rate at which new imitations (as opposed to imitations involved in the early phases of training) are mastered; (*b*) the number of new imitations elicited on a first test trial, and (*c*) the rate with which behaviors that are never reinforced are imitated.

A number of questions may be raised concerning the relation of this literature to the problem of imitative origins. First, the small samples limit the generality of the findings. This presumably will be remedied as time goes on. There are several problems, however, when we attempt to generalize the results to normal children particularly to infants. First, there are obvious differences between infancy, the period in which matching behavior is first manifested, and the psychological status of the older retarded or psychotic child. Contingencies of reinforcement may well be related to the emergence of first imitations in normal infancy, but it may also be necessary to bring other variables into our analysis in order to account for the generalized imitations that babies develop. Attentional processes, conceptual abilities, and motivational factors may be involved, in important ways, in the infant's first imitations that differ from the ways in which these processes impinge on the first imitations of the retarded or schizophrenic child.

Second, there needs to be an assessment of the role of prompts in first imitations. Prompts of the kind used in experimental work may play a relatively unimportant role in the infant's first imitations. In fact, the first instances of matched behavior in infancy are likely to be outcomes of the deliberate matching of the child *by the parent*, rather than the parent's manipulations of the child's motor responses in such a way as to produce a match. Parents occasionally may use prompting, but this is probably not practiced extensively. Consequently, there is reason to study *parental* matching as a concomitant of first imitations in the *child*. The phylogentic properties of parental behavior, as well as parental learning histories, may both be relevant antecedents of the child's first imitations. One sees immediately why the problem of first imitations is so complex.

Reinforcement theory may effectively account for the strengthening of imitative stimulus-response functions in infancy but infant studies—particularly studies involving parent-infant interaction—are needed to test this assertion. Present research on the first imitations of disturbed, nonimitating older children constitutes a promising base from which to pursue the origins of imitation in typical child development. Infants must be studied directly, however, since the imitations that can be produced in retarded and schizophrenic children may not, even with extensive training, be similar to the imitations which one observes in normal one- or two-year-olds (Piaget, 1951; Valentine, 1930). As Lovaas (1967, pp. 151–52) says: "It is apparent at this stage that the variables we have isolated to produce imitative behavior. . . . We are, however, dissatisfied with the limited extent of such imitation. In the verbal area, the previously mute children show little feeling for language; they do not play with or explore speech the way normal children do. In the nonverbal area, we do not observe the extensive kind of imitative behavior described as identification or incorporation."

Generalized Imitation

Naturalistic observation of children reveals that they readily imitate new models (i.e., models that are not involved in the precipitation of first imitations) and also, that they imitate old models in new situations. These phenomena bring to mind the concepts of stimulus and response generalization. Both concepts have been used in theories of imitation (e.g., Mowrer, 1950, 1960) and it is surprising that there are very few systematic studies of "generalized imitation." There has actually been more concern with the conditions giving rise to first imitations than to the generalization of these response tendencies.

First, consider those experiments focussing on the generalization of imitation to new models. Baer et al. (1967) exposed one of the three retarded subjects involved in their study to new models after the initial imitation training had been completed. These models, who displayed the same behaviors that were used in the training phase, were of both the opposite and the same sex as the original model. During the generalization sessions, reinforcement was given for each correct matching response. The subject matched most of the new models' behaviors during a series of reinforced trials. It should be pointed out that if reinforcement is given for imitative responses during a series of generalization trials, as was done in this study, a well-known methodological problem is presented: the subject may imitate as a consequence of the reinforcement rather than the past training. On the other hand, testing for generalization without reinforcement being given for imitation constitutes an extinction procedure.

Earlier studies of stimulus generalization in imitation were reported by Miller and Dollard (Experiments 7 and 8, 1941). These studies minimize the methodological problem cited above since testing for generalization was confined to one or two trials at the most. Fourth-grade boys were trained, using contingent reinforcement, to: (a) imitate an adult and nonimitate a third-grade peer; or (b) nonimitate the adult and imitate the peer. Following the training, the subjects were tested for the frequency with which they imitated new adult and peer models. Considerable stimulus generalization was found; the subjects responded to the new peer and adult models in the same way (imitation or nonimitation) as they had been trained to do in the preceding experiment.

In still another experiment, Miller and Dollard (Experiment 5) trained first graders to imitate or nonimitate a peer model. During training, the subjects were exposed to the model's choices between two boxes. Following this training (Experiment 6) the subjects observed the model choose from among four boxes. Once again, the percentage of subjects who did or did not imitate indicated the occurrence of stimulus generalization, this time across situations rather than across models.

Other research on generalization in children's modeling has been rather indirect. The tests for observational learning used by Bandura et al.

(1963) and by Mischel and Grusec (1966) have usually involved removing the child from the modeling situation and testing for imitation in a slightly different, but very similar, physical setting. Since observational learning was not first measured in the original modeling situation, these studies lack the comparisons needed in order to constitute a test for generalization. The fact that imitation occurred in the test situations, however, may be *prima facie* evidence of such generalization.

Chittenden (1942) reported transfer from a quasi-modeling training situation to behavior in the nursery school. Her training procedures, which were directed at assertive behavior, did not rely exclusively on modeling since direct tuition was also involved. Consequently, the degree to which these data reflect a generalization phenomenon is unknown. Siegel (1956) failed to find transfer when the modeling involved aggressive cartoon characters and the tests involved peer interaction. The evidence regarding the operation of stimulus generalization in recent studies of children's observational learning is, then, not very extensive.

There is a small, but generally convincing, literature on response generalization in children's imitation. Baer and Sherman (1965) reinforced preschool children for imitating head nodding, mouthing, and a variety of nonsense verbalizations (e.g., "glub," "flub," "gub"). During the presentation of these responses, the model (a puppet) pressed a bar at varying rates. The subject was never reinforced for *his* bar-pressing. Despite this lack of reinforcement, the frequency of bar-pressing by the subjects was found to increase as reinforcement was given for the other three imitative responses.

Lovaas (Lovaas *et al.*, 1966; Lovaas *et al.*, 1967), established imitative verbal and nonverbal repertoires in schizophrenic children. Two of the children in one of these experiments (Lovaas *et al.*, 1966) were tested for response generalization by presenting them with Norwegian words. One subject was exposed to three Norwegian words, the other to two. Each word was presented 300 times; one word was presented each day. There was no reinforcement for imitation of the Norwegian words. As in the experiment by Baer and Sherman (1965), however, other imitative behaviors were reinforced. In this case, three to five English words were presented after, on the average, every seventh presentation of a Norwegian word. If the child imitated the English word, he was reinforced. Both subjects showed response generalization in that there was an increase over trials in the number of imitations of the Norwegian words.

Miller and Dollard (1941) reported two experiments on response generalization. In one experiment (Experiment 9) the same subjects were used that had been used in Experiments 7 and 8, discussed above. The earlier imitation training had involved depressing or rotating a handle. In the first part of Experiment 9, the model now exhibited choices between two boxes; in the second part, the model pulled one of two rings. The subjects were again exposed to both peer and adult models. Response generalization was demonstrated with the ring task but not with the box task.

The research reviewed in this section supports the hypothesis that generalized imitation is a functional characteristic of children's social behavior. Little is known, however, except that stimulus and response generalization are demonstrable. There are a number of questions that need to be answered at this time. What conditions affect the extent to which imitation generalizes? Would training of imitation on partial reinforcement schedules result in different generalization gradients from training with continuous reinforcement? What are the stimulus dimensions which govern generalized imitation in natural settings? Is generalization similar at different age levels? Recent studies of generalization in other forms of children's learning suggest that generalization may vary as a function of the developmental status of the child. In addition, the range of models to which the child is exposed obviously increases during early and middle childhood and this may broaden the operation of generalized imitation.

One widespread assumption in naturalistic studies of identification is that propensities to imitate parents generalize to teachers and peers, but there are no data concerning this hypothesis. In fact, the range of stimuli used in experiments on the generalization of children's imitation has been extremely narrow. Obviously, much research is needed, both experimental and naturalistic, concerning the generalization of imitation. Whether children simply evidence generalized imitation across models, across situations, across responses, across time, and across motives, is perhaps not the major issue, however, since it is obvious that generalized imitation characterizes both child and adult behavior. Casual observation firmly supports this conclusion. But the complex developmental interactions modulating the generalization of imitation in children are unknown. In particular, we know little concerning those factors that lead to the discriminations resulting in the imitation of some models and some behaviors, but not others.

Developmental Patterns During Childhood

Age differences have been analyzed in nine studies of children's imitation. The youngest children involved in these studies were 3-year-olds and the oldest subjects were 18 years of age. Modeling involved the following behaviors: (a) use of the passive voice in speech; (b) simple positional discriminations; (c) hand movements; (d) picture and toy preferences; (e) avoidance of inappropriate-sex toys; (f) solutions to a maze problem; and (g) novel styles of playing with toys. These studies have little relevance to the developmental propositions of Freud and Piaget. They do not concern the ontogenesis of imitative behavior in infancy and early childhood nor do they concern the precursors of imitation in parent-child relations.

On the other hand, the nine studies can be examined with respect to three broad questions. First, do the results show a strengthening of "generalized imitation" during childhood? That is, does susceptibility to social models increase with age? The answer to this question is, "We cannot tell." The studies indicate that the occurrence of significant age differences in children's imitation depends on the task involved. With age, there seem to be increases in imitation in complex tasks, but few increases on relatively simple tasks. This state of affairs suggests that "generalized imitation" (i.e., imitative "habit strength") has not been measured in these investigations.

Second, do age differences in children's imitations reveal changes in developmental status? Nine studies do not cover much behavioral territory, but the results suggest that age differences in children's imitations do, indeed, reflect changes in developmental status.

Third, do various types of stimulus input differentially affect imitation at different age-levels? Are there interactions between age and input factors in determining children's imitation? The answer to this question appears to be "Yes."

Age differences in imitation on easy tasks involving no explicit instructions to imitate. Hetherington (1965) examined age differences in the modeling of picture preferences. The children were four- to five-, six- to eight-, and nine- to eleven-year-olds. The models consisted of the children's parents. Imitation of each parent was measured in sessions that were separated by a one-month interval. The parent model indicated his preferences on 20 pairs of pictures and the child then indicated his. This task was not difficult and the instructions made no reference to imitation. No significant age differences were found. In another study of preference modeling, which was mentioned earlier, Barnwell and Sechrest (1965) arranged for first and third graders to observe an age-mate express preferences between one of two toys. Here again, no significant age differences were obtained.

Two investigators have examined age-differences in the acquisition of imitative responses using the Miller-Dollard two-choice discrimination task. In both of these studies, reinforcers were delivered contingent upon the emission of a matching response by the subject but the subjects were not actually instructed to imitate. McDavid (1959) reported no age differences between one group of children who ranged from 45 to 56 months of age and a second group who ranged from 57 to 67 months. There was a significant age by sex interaction, however, indicating that younger males showed greater imitation than did older males while the opposite was true for girls. May (1966), who studied three-, five-, and seven-year-olds, found no age differences in imitation on a similar discrimination problem.

There has been one study of age differences with respect to "incidental imitation." In May's study, the model exhibited a number of incidental behaviors in addition to exhibiting his solutions to the discrimination problem. The five-year-olds imitated the "incidental" behaviors of the model significantly more than did the seven-year-olds who, in turn, imitated more than did the three-year-olds. Here we have results that can be interpreted as reflecting changes in the developmental status of the child. It can be hypothesized, for example, that three-year-olds (who have had limited experience with nonparental models) have not developed widely generalized tendencies to imitate social models and that their limited attentional and representational skills may limit such imitation. On the other hand, the seven-year-olds (whose school experiences probably reinforce a high degree of task-orientation) may have attended primarily to the model's solutions of the discrimination problem thereby missing, or dismissing as irrelevant, the incidental behaviors of the model. Thus, the five-year-old may be more susceptible to the "incidental" behaviors of social models than either his older or younger peer.

These results suggest future studies of incidental imitation that resemble existing developmental work on other forms of children's incidental learning. Siegel and Stevenson (1966) reported a curvilinear relation between age and incidental learning in school children, with the peak occurring in late-middle childhood. The May data concerning incidental imitation do not fit easily into this pattern of results, but then they were not acquired in the usual incidental learning paradigm. Nevertheless, it is clearly time for investigators to recognize that children's imitation of behaviors that are distal to the central task of the experiment may well be different (and the relations of such imitation to age may well be different) from imitation on the salient experimental task. Ross's (1966) findings underscore this point since she found different relations between children's dependency and "incidental"—as contrasted to "intentional"—imitation.

One additional study of age differences in imitation also involved a simple task and nondirective instructions. In an unpublished study by Hartup and Eichensehr (1968), subjects were presented with toys of two different kinds: (a) toys that were inappropriate for the child's sex (e.g., dolls in the case of a male subject); and (b) toys defined by the culture as appropriate for either sex. The subjects consisted of four- and five-year-olds and six-and seven-year-olds of both sexes. The between-subjects experimental conditions were as follows: (a) a control condition in which the child was not exposed to a model; (b) a condition in which the child observed a same-sex adult model who silently enacted the temptation to play with the toys, but did not; (c) exposure to a model who verbalized both his temptation and his resistance, but who gave no reasons for his behavior; and (d) exposure to a verbalizing model who also explained his resistance to deviation (i.e., he said that the experimenter "wouldn't like it"). The data shown in Fig. 2 consist of mean percentages of the children's play which involved contact with the inappropriate toys.

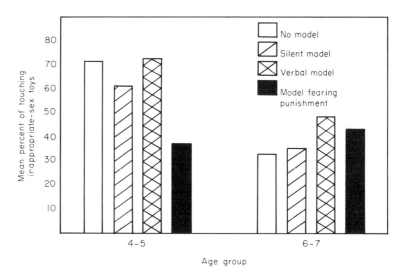

Figure 2. Mean percent of touching inappropriate sex toys by age and model condition. (From Hartup and Eichensehr, 1968.)

First, note that there is a significant difference between the two age groups in the control condition; the first graders resisted playing with the "wrong-sex" toys more than did the preschoolers. This is not a striking finding, but it suggests that the first-grade child is more securely sex-typed than the preschooler; i.e., there appears to be a difference in the developmental status of children at these two age-levels. Now notice the modeling effects. The interaction between age and modeling conditions is significant. The younger children proved relatively impervious to modeling that was either silent or unexplained; that is, when no clear basis was established for the model's behavior, no transmission of the model's values occurred. On the other hand, when punishment for deviation was brought into the picture, the model's influence is clearly apparent—significantly less inappropriate sex-typed behavior occurred than in the other conditions.

Next, consider the older children. Here, no significant modeling effects were found in any of the experimental groups. The results do not seem accountable by a floor effect, since 32 percent of the control subjects' behavior involved contact with the inappropriate toys. There are two other interpretations of these data, both of which suggest that the developmental status of the older children attenuated the effectiveness of the model who "feared" the experimenter's disapproval. First, the mild punishment anticipated by the model may have been interpreted by the older child as not relevant to himself. (God punishes silly adults who play with opposite-sex toys, but not children.) Such a discrimination is distinctly more probable among older children than among younger children. Second, the lack of modeling effects shown among the older subjects may reflect their more secure sex-typing. There may be sufficient solidity of values in this area among first-graders so that modeled resistance to deviation has relatively little effect upon them. Unfortunately, the ancillary data needed to validate either of these interpretations of the age difference in modeling effects were not obtained.

To summarize: in easy, unstructured tasks, age differences in children's imitation are seldom found; actually, less responsiveness to models has sometimes occurred on such tasks among older than among younger children.

Modeling in more complex tasks under explicit instructions to imitate. Age differences are more uniformly found when complex problems are used which are accompanied by direct instructions to imitate. Rosenbaum (1967) asked seven- to eight-, nine- to ten-, and eleven- to twelve-year-old children to observe an age-mate trace a multiple-choice maze. Each subject was then tested for his retention of the maze solution. It was found that nine- to ten- and eleven- to twelve-year-olds showed significantly greater observational learning than did the seven- to eight-year-olds. Next, in a recent study of our own (Coates and Hartup, 1969), four- to five- and seven- to eight-year-olds were asked to watch a movie. The subjects were also told that after the movie they would be asked "to show what the man in the movie did." The children then watched a film showing a man performing a number of relatively novel behaviors which included among others: building a tower of blocks in a unique way, putting a toy on the tower, hitting a Bobo clown, and throwing a bean bag between his legs at a target. The seven- to eight-year-olds showed greater amounts of observational learning than did the four- to five-year-olds.

Next, in studies of language development, greater amounts of imitation have been reported for older than for younger children when they are asked to imitate the experimenter's use of the passive voice. Cazden (1965) reported that none of the twelve children she studied, who were between 28 and 38 months of age, was able to imitate the passive sentence, "His hair has been cut." On the other hand, Fraser *et al.* (1963) found that three-year-olds were correct half of the time in their imitation of reversible passive sentences. Finally, Menyuk (1963) found that all of her fourteen nursery school-age subjects were able to imitate passive-voice sentences. On the basis of Menyuk's findings, one would expect no further changes, after four-years of age, in the imitation of this aspect of grammatical usage. This expectation has been confirmed by Turner and Rommetveit (1967). They investigated imitation of both active and passive voices in both reversible sentences ("the girl hit the boy") and non-reversible sentences ("the car hit the tree"). Children of five age levels were studied: four, six, seven, eight, and nine years. There were no age differences in the children's imitation of these sentence-types. All age groups gave perfect imitation of the model on 90 percent to 100 percent of the sentences.

The foregoing studies show that, in tasks which require a relatively high degree of skill and which the child is instructed to imitate, older children tend to imitate more frequently than younger children. The shape of the age gradient seems to be asymptotic, however. It is possible, then, that it is the low level of cognitive skill required by very simple tasks, such as the Miller-Dollard imitative discrimination, that is associated with the lack of age differences found on such tasks. The findings of Bandura *et al.* (1966), showing no differences in observational learning as a function of the presence or absence of an instructional set, also buttress this conclusion. That is, task difficulty, rather than instructional set, seems to differentiate the studies showing age differences in imitation from those showing no differences.

A recent study by Wapner and Cirillo (1968) vividly indicates how imitation of social models reflects the nature of the cognitive skills required in the experimental task. This study shows more clearly than any of the preceding studies that social imitations depend on the cognitive requirements of the task. The subjects, who ranged in age from 8 to 18 years, were instructed to imitate the hand movements of the experimenter. Although the model completed three series of items, the results of only one series will be discussed here. In this particular series, the model touched his hand to his ear. There were four imitation measures.

These can be illustrated by referring to the instance in which the model touched his *right* ear with his *left* hand: (*a*) transposition—the subject touches his *right* ear with his *left* hand; (*b*) mirroring—the subject touches his *left* ear with his *right* hand; (*c*) object mirroring—the subject touches his *left* ear with his *left* hand; and (*d*) hand mirroring—the subject touches his *right* ear with his *right* hand.

There was significantly greater transposition across age. This represents an increase in "exact" or "correct" imitations. Correspondingly, there was significantly less mirroring and object-mirroring across the age range studied; this decrease applies to behaviors which might be called "inexact" or "wrong" imitations. The results for hand-mirroring (also an "inexact" imitation) were inconsistently related to age.

These results, based on imitative responding, can be interpreted as revealing developmental changes in the child's understanding of left-right relations. Such understanding involves that particular capacity, described by Piaget and Inhelder (1956), as the ability: (*a*) to represent to oneself the left-right relations between objects as they appear from viewpoints other than one's own, and (*b*) to coordinate these perspectives with one's own. The findings of Wapner and Cirillo support the contention that age differences in imitation are interactive functions of organismic changes and the particular modeling situation to which the child is exposed. These findings probably reveal very little concerning the *strengthening or weakening of imitative stimulus-response functions themselves*. Rather, it is our belief that the data reflect the changing capacity of the child to imitate *these particular actions* as he becomes older and do not represent acquisition or extinction of imitative tendencies. They reveal, however, a set of cognitive constraints that developmental change places upon imitative behavior.

Perhaps, then, one can only study the strengthening or weakening of imitative stimulus-response functions in "task-free" or "subject-free" environments. However, the conflicting evidence that is contained in the age-difference studies of imitation is cause for excitement rather than despair. First, this conflicting evidence indicates that children acquire a complex group of discriminations, involving distinctive cues within the task or setting, which govern imitative performance, and perhaps observational learning as well. Second, such differences may be correlated with other developmental changes, notably in cognitive skill. In other words, the disorderly age changes contained in the present literature may have considerable psychological significance rather than reflect mere "situational variance." Indeed, such an assumption has been the basis for the inclusion of items on intelligence tests that require copying the verbal or motoric behavior of the examiner. Thus, imitation appears to be intertwined with a variety of cognitive and motivational changes taking place during childhood. Perhaps imitation contributes to some of these cor-related behavior changes and perhaps these behavior changes lead to changes in imitation. For the moment, however, it is known only that "generalized" imitation appears to be an operant whose elicitation is related to a variety of age-related changes in the child.

Age differences in the determinants of observational learning. One study shows that manipulation of mediational activity differentially affects children's imitation at different age levels (Coates and Hartup, 1969). In this study, we were interested in whether or not symbolic rep-resentational processes (i.e., verbalization) might account for age differ-ences in observational learning between four- and seven-year-olds. In order to test this hypothesis, the children watched a movie, described previously, under one of three conditions: (*a*) induced verbalization, in which the subject was told how to describe the model's actions during exposure (i.e., the subject repeated the experimenter's verbalizations about the model's behavior); (*b*) free verbalization, in which the subject was asked to describe the model's actions in his own words during ex-posure; and (*c*) passive observation, in which no instructions related to verbalizing were given to the subject.

Predictions for the study were based on the production deficiency hypothesis (Flavell *et al.*, 1966). According to this hypothesis, younger children do not spontaneously produce relevant verbalizations in problem-solving situations whereas older children spontaneously produce and effectively employ such verbalizations. In addition, the hypothesis stipu-lates that if younger children are helped to produce relevant verbaliza-tions, task performance will be enhanced. On the basis of this hypothesis, the following predictions were generated: (*a*) four-year-olds would show greater observational learning in the induced verbalization condition than in the passive observation condition; (*b*) four-year-olds in the free ver-balization condition (who would presumably make fewer relevant verbal-izations than the induced verbalization subjects) would perform at an intermediate level between four-year-old induced verbalization and pas-sive observation subjects; and (*c*) there would be no differences in observational learning among seven-year-olds in the three conditions—they presumably produce relevant verbalizations spontaneously.

The results are shown in Fig. 3. All of the predictions were confirmed except for the finding that free verbalization older subjects showed less observational learning than *both* older induced verbalization and passive observation subjects. Thus, the study suggests that the production of rele-vant verbalizations is one of the mechanisms which may account for the greater observational learning among seven-year-olds than among four-year-olds.

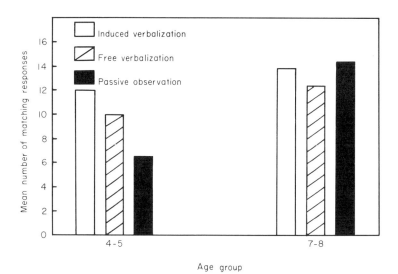

Figure 3.   Mean number of matching responses by age and verbalization condition. (From Coates and Hartup, 1969.)

Rosenbaum's (1967) results support our own, within the limits of the design he used. In this study, as noted above, seven-to-eight-, nine-to-ten-, and eleven-to-twelve-year-olds observed a peer model complete a multiple-choice maze. Although Rosenbaum was interested in the effects of verbalization by both the model and observer on observational learning, two of his subgroups are similar to the induced verbalization and passive observation groups of our study. In one subgroup, the observers called out the number of the correct maze-choice after the silent model had made the correct response. In accordance with our results, there was no difference between the verbalization and no verbalization subgroups for these elementary school children. Preschool-aged children were not employed in this study, however, so full comparison between the studies mentioned is not possible.

In a recent study of six- to eight-year-olds, Bandura *et al.* (1966) utilized only a free verbalization condition and a passive observation condition. Free verbalization of the model's behavior increased observational learning. This finding is not in agreement with the Coates and Hartup results. As can be seen in Fig. 3, free verbalization of the model's behavior in our study *reduced* observational learning among the older subjects. These results are surprising because we made an attempt to replicate the Bandura *et al.* experiment by using essentially the same procedure that they did. Further, our older subjects were essentially of the same age as those studied by Bandura *et al.*, the model displayed the same behaviors, and we used basically the same test for observational learning. Therefore, the reasons for the discrepancy in the results of the two studies are unclear.

In general, the findings from the foregoing studies indicate that changing verbal capacities function as determinants of age changes in observational learning in children. The extant studies represent a small start toward an understanding of the interactions between stimulus inputs, developmental status, and observational learning in children. Such studies can serve as the beginning, however, of an intensive effort to examine the relation between changes in attentional, motivational, and cognitive processes and imitation in childhood.

THE NATURALISTIC STUDY OF CHILDREN'S IMITATION

One final gap in research on children's imitation is the lack of naturalistic studies. Naturalistic data, as opposed to data derived from laboratory work, are needed for several reasons. First, we have virtually no information concerning the extent to which brief modeling experiences transfer to behavior in other settings. If observational learning is as powerful a determinant of behavior change as has been thought, the effects of brief modeling experiences should be explored in settings other than the one in which the training took place. At present, research contains only a few instances in which the effects of brief exposure to models have been examined in other settings. We have already referred to relevant studies by Chittenden (1942), Seigel (1956), and Bandura et al. (1966), but the evidence showing extensive transfer from such modeling experiences is meager, indeed. Unless this particular aspect of the "generalized imitation" problem is explored more fully, the significance of imitation for children's socialization cannot be adequately assessed.

Next, naturalistic studies are needed to verify the applicability of principles emanating from experiments. Research on children's imitation has been dominated by the use of contrived procedures and models that are unfamiliar to the child. The tasks and the interpersonal aspects of these procedures have been life-like, but it must be said that some of the "novel" actions displayed by experimental models have been extremely bizarre. Current research in "behavior modification" could well serve as a model for students of children's imitation since both observational (e.g., Patterson et al., 1967) and manipulative studies (e.g., Harris et al., 1967) have been conducted to show that basic learning principles provide a sound basis for explaining behavior in nonlaboratory settings. Similar outcomes could be expected of naturalistic research on children's imitation.

Finally, naturalistic research is needed that is also developmentally-oriented. Freud's theories and Piaget's notions constitute good guesses concerning the manner in which imitation functions in children's development. The need for developmental studies was defended earlier; hence, we wish only to add here that the usefulness of such studies depends heavily on the generalizability of the results to children's behavior in natural environments. Unless naturalistic verification of developmental principles is assured, the role of imitation in children's development can only be conjectured. Our present knowledge concerning the role of imitation in childhood socialization is not really knowledge at all, but extrapolations from short-term experiments. There has been a proclivity among social-learning psychologists in general to construct a picture of child development from such extrapolations, but only direct observation of children's social behavior in natural settings can validate such analyses. We are far from an empirically based description of the manner in which imitation is involved in the natural development of children's behavior.

Present research contains a small amount of information concerning children's imitation that involves naturalistic referents. There are three general types of such research. First, a small number of investigators have employed parents or peers as models. Second, a well-known group of studies has concerned the child-rearing antecedents of identification (Sears *et al.*, 1965). Third, a number of investigations have employed measures of parent-child similarity. Each of these types of research involves some real-life referent for children's imitations. On the other hand, each of these research endeavors is associated with methodological problems that have restricted their usefulness in describing the role that imitation plays in child development.

The studies of parent or peer modeling have already been commented upon. For example, Hetherington (1967) found that parental dominance, measured in a standard test situation, was positively associated with imitation of the parent by his child, suggesting that dominance is one factor in parent-child relations that has an historical influence on the child's imitation of his parents. This finding, verifying the relevance of parental dominance to children's imitation does not reveal, however, the changes that the relation between dominance and imitation may have undergone in the course of early experience. Developmental theories, as we have indicated, suggest that the relation of a factor, such as parental dominance to imitation, fluctuates or changes over time. Therefore, Hetherington's cross-sectional laboratory work is an important first step in the study of the natural history of children's imitation, but a first step only.

Most of the child-rearing studies of identification (e.g., Sears, *et al.*, 1965) have related variations in parental child-rearing practices to behavioral measures of conscience. Implicit in these studies is the assumption that relations between child-rearing practices and conscience measures indicate the operation of mechanisms of identification such as those conceived by Freud. Such an inference is dubious unless the research design also supplies measures of the child's disposition to imitate the parental models—covertly, if not directly. Typically, imitation measures have not been included in child rearing studies of identification, and it is more proper to describe these as studies in conscience development than as studies in identification. It is certainly true that, if the patterns of antecedent-consequent relations in such data are consistent with Freud's notions about identification, these same patterns constitute presumptive evidence that the child's emulation of the parental ideal is a mechanism in conscience development. But the results of this research have been relatively thin, possibly due to the sampling and measurement strategies chosen by the investigators. Further, the use of outcome measures based on preschool or older children gives a cloudy picture of the early viscissitudes that identificatory processes may undergo in the child's development. Thus, it is apparent that prospective research, involving measurement of imitative tendencies in infancy and early childhood, is required for full tests of the classic accountings of conscience development in children.

Another type of imitation research which involves naturalistic referents centers upon the measurement of "real" or "assumed" similarity between parents and children. The typical strategy in studies of "real" similarity is to assess the behavior of a model (e.g., the parent) and look for similar behaviors in the child. Measures of "assumed" similarity typically involve either the child's own assessment of his resemblance to the parent or the congruence between the child's perceptions of his parent and his perceptions of himself. Interpreting such data involves problems that have been discussed by Bronfenbrenner (1958), and others. Briefly: it cannot be assumed from such measures that parent-child similarity, measured at some arbitrary point in time, has been brought about by modeling; other influences on the child, including exposure to nonparental models and direct tuition, could be responsible for such similarity. Even if one agrees with Heilbrun (1965) that the literature concerning the correlates of parent-child similarity supports the major theories of identification, this literature still does not reflect upon the functioning of imitation as a process in childhood socialization.

In general, then, present research that refers to natural factors in children's imitation yields little good information concerning the functional contribution of imitative learning to children's development. How, then, can we obtain the direct knowledge needed with respect to this problem? Although no easy solution is in sight, we suggest that the following strategies should be exploited. (*a*) Short-term *prospective* longitudinal studies should be launched, in which direct assessment of both child-rearing factors and imitative behavior is employed. Such research will need to rely heavily upon observational techniques, but such observations should involve standardized testing situations as well as extensive observations in home or school settings. (*b*) Cross-sectional analyses of the factors in the home and in the peer group which appear to maintain or change the frequency of children's imitations should be conducted. Such studies would supplement those longitudinal investigations that focus on longer-term antecedents of imitation. (*c*) Longitudinal research should focus on several special problems including the emergence of first imitations in infancy and the generalization of imitation.

There is considerable gain to be derived from studies in which the independent variables consist both of historical data about the child and experimental manipulations. Such studies would be useful, for example, in investigating the interactions between various conditions of attachment to parental objects and the characteristics of strange models, as these may interact in affecting the child's imitation.

Future research on the development of imitation must be as process-oriented as past research. Descriptive data are needed but we do not advocate the laborious collection of age norms. The overriding goal should consist of furthering our understanding concerning the functional role that imitation plays in the child's development. Changes in imitative behavior must be studied over relatively long periods, however, in order that the fluctuating developmental interactions affecting the imitative process may come to light. We realize that the research described here is difficult. Even if one were to begin such research tomorrow, none could be completed without the limiting constraints of current methodologies; all of the strategies we have outlined are time-consuming. We contend, however, that some effort must be directed toward these kinds of research if, even in the foreseeable future, we are to give an adequate accounting of the "role of imitation in childhood socialization."

REFERENCES

Baer, D. M., and Sherman, J. A. (1965). Reinforcement control of generalized imitation in young children. *J. Exp. Child Psychology*, **1**, 37–49.

Baer, D. M., Peterson, R. F., and Sherman, J. A. (1967). The development of imitation by reinforcing behavioral similarity to a model. *J. Exp. Analysis of Behavior,* **10,** 405–417.

Baldwin, J. M. (1895). *Mental development in the child and the race.* Macmillan, New York.

Bandura, A. (1965). Influence of model's reinforcement contingencies on the acquisition of imitative responses. *J. Personality and Social Psychol.,* **1,** 589–595.

Bandura, A. (1969). Social-learning theory of identificatory processes. In D. A. Goslin (Ed.) *Handbook of socialization theory and research.* Rand McNally, Chicago, Illinois.

Bandura, A., and Huston, A. C. (1961). Identification as a process of incidental learning. *J. Abnormal and Social Psychol.,* **63,** 311–318.

Bandura, A., and Walters, R. H. (1963). *Social learning and personality development.* Holt, New York.

Bandura, A., Ross, D., and Ross, S. A. (1963). Vicarious reinforcement and imitative learning. *J. Abnormal and Social Psychol.,* **67,** 601–607.

Bandura, A., Grusec, J., and Menlove, F. (1966). Observational learning as a function of symbolization and incentive set. *Child Development,* **37,** 499–507.

Barnwell, A., and Sechrest, L. (1965). Vicarious reinforcement in children at two age levels. *J. Educational Psychol.,* **56,** 100–106.

Bijou, S. W. (1968). Ages, stages, and the naturalization of human development. *Am. Psychologist,* **23,** 419–427.

Bronfenbrenner, U. (1958). The study of identification through interpersonal perception. In R. Tagiuri and L. Petrullo (Eds.), *Person perception and interpersonal behavior.* Stanford Univ. Press, Stanford, Calif.

Bronfenbrenner, U. (1960). Freudian theories of identification and their derivatives. *Child Development,* **31,** 15–40.

Cazden, C. B. (1965). Environmental assistance to the child's acquisition of grammar. Unpublished doctoral dissertation, Harvard University.

Chittenden, G. E. (1942). An experimental study in measuring and modifying assertive behavior in young children. *Monographs Soc. for Res. in Child Development,* **7,** 1 (Serial No. 31).

Clark, B. S. (1965). The acquisition and extinction of peer imitation in children. *Psychonom. Sci.,* **2,** 147–148.

Coates, B., and Hartup, W. W. (1969). Age and verbalization in observational learning. *Developmental Psychol.,* **1,** 556–562.

Flanders, J. P. (1968). A review of research on imitative behavior. *Psychol. Bull.,* **69,** 316–337.

Flavell, J. H., Beach, D. R., and Chinsky, J. M. (1966). Spontaneous verbal rehearsal in a memory task as a function of age. *Child Development,* **37,** 283–299.

Fraser, C., Bellugi, U., and Brown, R. (1963). Control of grammar in imitation, comprehension, and production. *J. Verbal Learning and Verbal Behavior,* **2,** 121–135.

Gewirtz, J. L., and Stingle, K. G. (1968). Learning of generalized imitation as the basis for identification. *Psychol. Rev.,* **75,** 374–397.

Grusec, J. (1966). Some antecedents of self-criticism. *J. Personality and Social Psychol.,* **4,** 244–253.

Harris, F. R., Wolf, M. M., and Baer, D. M. (1967). Effects of adult social reinforcement on child behavior. In W. W. Hartup and N. L. Smothergill (Eds.), *The young child.* Nat. Assoc. for the Study of Young Children, Washington.

Hartup, W. W., and Coates, B. (1967). Imitation of a peer as a function of reinforcement from the peer group and rewardingness of the model. *Child Development,* 38, 1003–1016.

Hartup, W. W., and Eichensehr, F. (1968). Age and modeling influences on sex-typed behavior in children. Unpublished manuscript, University of Minnesota.

Heilbrun, A. B. Jr. (1965). The measurement of identification. *Child Development,* 36, 111–127.

Hetherington, E. M. (1965). A developmental study of the effects of sex of the dominant parent on sex role preference, identification and imitation in children. *J. Personality and Social Psychol.,* 2, 188–194.

Hetherington, E. M. (1967). The effects of familial variables on sex typing, on parent-child similarity, and on imitation in children. In J. P. Hill (Ed.), *Minnesota symposia on child psychology.* Vol. I. Univ. of Minnesota Press, Minneapolis, Minn.

Hetherington, E. M., and Frankie, G. (1967). Effects of dominance, warmth, and conflict on imitation in children. *J. Personality and Social Psychol.,* 6, 119–125.

Hewett, F. M. (1965). Teaching speech to an autistic child through operant conditioning. *Am. J. Orthopsychiat.,* 927–936.

Hingtgen, J. N., Coulter, S. K., and Churchill, D. W. (1967). Intensive reinforcement of imitative behavior in mute autistic children. *Arch. Gen. Psychiat.,* 17, 36–43.

Holt, E. B. (1931). *Animal drive and the learning process.* Vol. I. Holt, New York.

Lovaas, O. I. (1967). A behavior therapy approach to the treatment of childhood schizophrenia. In J. P. Hill (Ed.), *Minnesota symposia on child psychology.* Vol. I. Univ. of Minnesota Press, Minneapolis, Minn.

Lovaas, O. I., Berberich, J. P., Perloff, B. F., and Schaeffer, B. (1966). Acquisition of imitative speech in schizophrenic children. *Science,* 151, 705–707.

Lovaas, O. I., Freitas, L., Nelson, K., and Whalen, C. (1967). The establishment of imitation and its use for the development of complex behavior in schizophrenic children. *Behavior Res. and Therapy,* 5, 171–181.

McDavid, J. W. (1959). Imitative behavior in preschool children. *Psychol. Monographs,* 73, Whole No. 486.

McDougall, W. (1908). *An introduction to social psychology.* Methuen, London.

May, J. G. Jr. (1966). A developmental study of imitation. *Dissertation Abstracts,* 26, (6), 6852–6853.

Menyuk, P. (1963). Syntactic structures in the language of children. *Child Development,* 34, 407–422.

Metz, R. J. (1965). Conditioning generalized imitation in autistic children. *J. Exp. Child Psychol.,* 2, 389–399.

Miller, N. E., and Dollard, J. (1941). *Social learning and imitation.* Yale Univ. Press, New Haven, Conn.

Mischel, W., and Grusec, J. (1966). Determinants of the rehearsal and transmission of neutral and aversive behaviors. *J. Personality and Social Psychol.,* 3, 197–206.

Mischel, W., and Liebert, R. M. (1966). Effects of discrepancies between observed and imposed reward criteria on their acquisition and transmission. *J. Personality and Social Psychol.,* 3, 45–53.

Mowrer, O. H. (1950). Identification: a link between learning theory and psychotherapy. In O. H. Mowrer, *Learning theory and personality dynamics.* Ronald Press, New York.

Mowrer, O. H. (1960). *Learning theory and the symbolic processes.* Wiley, New York.

Patterson, G. R., Littman, R. S., and Bricker, W. (1967). Assertive behavior in children: A step toward a theory of aggression. *Monographs of the Soc. for Res. in Child Development,* 32, Whole No. 5.

Piaget, J. (1932). *The moral judgment of the child.* Kegan Paul, London.

Piaget, J. (1951). *Play, dreams and imitation in childhood.* Norton, New York.

Piaget, J., and Inhelder, B. (1956). *The child's conception of space.* Routledge and Kegan Paul, London.

Rosekrans, M. A. (1967). Imitation in children as a function of perceived similarity to a social model and vicarious reinforcement. *J. Personality and Social Psychol.,* 7, 307–316.

Rosenbaum, M. E. (1967). The effect of verbalization of correct responses by performers and observers on retention. *Child Development,* 38, 615–622.

Rosenblith, J. F. (1959). Learning by imitation in kindergarten children. *Child Development,* 30, 69–80.

Ross, D. (1966). Relationship between dependency, intentional learning, and incidental learning in preschool children. *J. Personality and Social Psychol.,* 4, 374–381.

Sears, R. R. (1957). Identification as a form of behavior development. In D. B. Harris (Ed), *The concept of development.* Univ. of Minnesota Press, Minneapolis, Minn.

Sears, R. R., Rau, L., and Alpert, R. (1965). *Identification and child rearing.* Stanford Univ. Press, Stanford, Calif.

Siegel, A. E. (1956). Film-mediated fantasy aggression and strength of aggressive drive. *Child Development,* 27, 365–378.

Siegel, A. W., and Stevenson, H. W. (1966). Incidental learning: a developmental study. *Child Development,* 37, 811–818.

Stein, A. H., and Wright, J. C. (1964). Imitative learning under conditions of nurturance and nurturance withdrawal. *Child Development,* 927–937.

Stevenson, H. W. (1968). Children's learning: Crossroad of developmental and educational psychology. Paper presented at the annual meetings of the American Psychological Association, San Francisco, September.

Turner, E. A., and Rommetveit, R. (1967). The acquisition of sentence voice and reversibility. *Child Development,* 38, 649–660.

Valentine, C. W. (1930). The psychology of imitation with special reference to early childhood. *Brit. J. Pschol.,* 21, 105–132.

Wapner, S., and Cirillo, L. (1968). Imitation of a model's hand movements: Age changes in transposition of left-right relations. *Child Development,* 39, 887–894.

PART III

ADULT CHARACTERISTICS AND CHILDHOOD SOCIALIZATION

The Socialization of Adult Cognition

*G. Alexander Milton**

In the process of becoming socialized the child develops patterns of belief about his behavior and the behaviors of others. These filtered codifications of adult reality are conceptions about his environment maintained and communicated in the language of his culture. The social development of these language systems and these systems of belief as they exist in the adult are the focus of the following two chapters.

Although the chapters share the mutual focus upon the socialization of cognitive processes, it is the difference in both method and theory which requires attention.

In tracing the development of language and conceptual systems, the authors use two quite different research strategies which are prototypic of two traditions in research on socialization. Krauss and Glucksberg have, primarily, focused upon the experimental method and analysis. By com-

---

* University of Victoria.

paring the actual communications of children under standardized conditions at cross-sectional age levels, and by multi-dimensional scale analysis of the communications of young adults, they trace a developmental sequence of competence in language which is both the result of socialization and basic to the process of socialization. The authors argue for the superiority of their method over other strategies in that it provides for a higher degree of control over the content of messages to be communicated, and it permits an effective way of numerically scoring the adequacy of communication.

Harvey and Felknor have used the method of retrospective reporting of parent-child relationships to study predicted antecedents of the development of systems of conceptual organization, particularly the four systems essential to Harvey's theory. They provide an interesting argument in support of the use of retrospective reports, while at the same time acknowledging the limitations of the method. They freely admit that the reported parent-child interactions will reflect not only what has actually occurred in the past but also the subject's interpretation of the meaning of these interactions in light of his current feelings and beliefs. They point out, however, that it is precisely this current conceptual functioning of the individual which is the main focus of their research and they go on to predict the kinds and directions of possible distortion in retrospective reporting which would characterize people representing the different personality organizations or systems of belief which they are investigating. In large part their predictions appear to be psychologically consistent with the theory and empirically consistent with the results of the investigation which they report.

In both chapters developmental hierarchies are assumed which place concrete, simplistic, inflexible, nonadaptive cognitive organizations at the low end of the scale and abstract, complex, modifiable, competent behavior at the top of the hierarchy. Both papers report evidence supporting their hierarchies. Krauss and Glucksberg attribute much of the development of this hierarchy to changing age and accompanying social feedback as the child approaches adulthood or as the young adult learns the rules of the society to which he is exposed. This is in a sense a theoretical position even though they carefully label their position as descriptive at this point. Harvey and Felknor, on the other hand, adopt a deliberately theoretical stance in their attribution of development along their hierarchy to specific experiences which are differentiated among the levels of their hierarchy. At this point it may be appropriate to ask is the Harvey-Felknor theory premature; is the Krauss and Glucksberg empiricism an illusion masking commitment to developmental theory; are both statements adequate reflections of the current evidence on the socialization of cognition?

Although rough parallels exist between the systems represented by the following chapters, the differences in theory and research strategy are the more intriguing. The adaptation of Krauss' very ingenious communication game to the study of differences among representatives of Harvey's systems of belief leads to directly testable hypotheses. The exploration of individual differences in cognitive functioning among adult communicators and the parent child interactions antecedent to these differences could lead to a better understanding of the socialization of competence in language and thought.

7

SOCIALIZATION OF
COMMUNICATION SKILLS*

*Robert M. Krauss†
and Sam Glucksberg††*

INTRODUCTION

In some fashion, a newborn infant is transformed from a mixed bag of biological potentialities into a socialized participant in a particular culture. Underlying any theory which purports to describe this process, there must be some notion about the organism's ability to exchange information with other social objects—in short, to communicate. Whether communication is viewed as the central mechanism of the socialization process (as in Mead's theory of the development of the self) or simply as one of the necessary "givens" of the organism, it is difficult to imagine how the socialization of the human infant might proceed in its absence.

For humans beyond infancy, when we think about communication we tend also to think of language. This is not to minimize the significance of such nonverbal forms of communication as facial expression, gesture, etc., but rather to underscore the extent to which human social behavior (including socialization, which is but one aspect of it) is predicated upon the capacity of the organism to communicate verbally.

Over the past decade or so, children's language behavior has become an increasingly important focus of inquiry for psychologists interested in human development. The reasons for this are not particularly obscure. To begin with, there has been a growing awareness among psychologists that language functions are significant factors in several important psy-

* Much of the research reported here was supported by Public Health Service Grant HD-MH-01910 01.

† Rutgers University.

‡ Princeton University.

chological processes, among them learning, memory, and concept formation. Part of the impetus for this realization has been the marked inability of traditional single-unit S-R approaches to deal satisfactorily with developmental differences in such relatively simple tasks as transposition, generalization, and the learning of reversal shifts. This is not to say that developmental differences in these processes can be explained simply by invoking the notion that children of different ages differ in their level of language development. Rather, it seems clear that there is a relation between language and other sorts of behavior and that this relation is something other than epiphenomenal.

In addition, the burgeoning field of psycholinguistics has provided another set of reasons for the investigation of language development. Under the impact of work in linguistics proper, notably the theory of transformational grammars put forth by Chomsky and his associates (Chomsky, 1957, 1965; Katz and Postal, 1964), researchers in psycholinguistics have begun to grapple with some of the complexities of adult language use. The central problem here is perhaps best summed up in the notion of "competence"—the complex and abstract knowledge which a language user must possess in order to comprehend and produce sentences. Given such complexity on the part of the linguistically competent adult, psychologists interested in language development have been lead to investigate the process by which a child extracts ". . . from a finite sample of speech to which he is exposed the latent structure that will generate an infinite set of sentences" (Brown, 1968, p. 49). There seems little doubt that the traditional psychological explanations of language acquisition are inadequate (Miller, 1965; Chomsky, 1959). As Roger Brown (1968, p. 49) has so pointedly put it:

"So long as psychologists did not fully apprehend the complexity of adult linguistic knowledge it was possible to believe that theory might succeed with such simple 'givens' as association by contiguity, response selection through reinforcement, and stimulus generalization. Now that the complexity of the terminal state is more fully appreciated it appears that we cannot get there by these means."

With this background in mind, it is not too surprising that relatively less attention has been paid to the child's development of the ability to communicate. In part, this neglect may be the result of a research strategy —investigators tend to focus their attention on problems that are both immediate and tractable, and language acquisition for reasons detailed above presently appears to have both these characteristics. Another factor, we believe, grows out of a confusion between an individual's competence as a language user (in the sense in which linguists use this term) and his competence as a communicator. The failure to make such a distinction appears to be based on the assumption that the ability to communicate is purely and simply a function of a speaker's knowledge of his language (Krauss and Glucksberg, 1969). It may be worthwhile, therefore, to consider briefly two experiments whose results suggest that this assumption is incorrect.

In the first (Krauss *et al.*, 1968) female college undergraduates were asked to provide names for color chips. In one experimental condition, the subject was told that at some time in the future she would be brought back to decode her names (i.e., to match the names to the colors that had elicited them). In a second condition, the subject was told that some other person would do the decoding. Actually, two weeks later all subjects were brought back and given a large number of names to decode. Some of these were the subject's own names (i.e., names she herself previously had given), some were names given by another subject under social instructions (i.e., names for another person to decode), and some were names given by another person under nonsocial instructions (to be decoded by the person who orginally had encoded them). There were large and significant differences in accuracy of decoding among these three conditions. Subjects were most accurate decoding colors from names they themselves had supplied; the next most accurate were those decoding names that had been socially encoded by some other person, and the least accurate were those decoding names which some other person had encoded nonsocially. Perhaps more important for the point we want to make is the fact that there were significant lexical differences between names which had been encoded under social and nonsocial instructions.

The second experiment (Kingsbury, 1968) makes a similar point somewhat more directly. The experimenter simply went out on the streets of Boston and Cambridge, at fixed locations, and asked randomly selected passers-by for directions to a specific destination. For some of his respondents his question was prefaced by the comment, "I'm from out of town. . . ." For others the question was delivered in a discernable nonlocal dialect. And for still others the question was asked in a standard American dialect, with nothing to indicate that the questioner was nonlocal. The subjects' replies were recorded on a concealed tape recorder. Clear differences were found in subjects' responses as a function of the experimental variations. Respondents tended to give more detailed directions, containing more units of information, in the nonlocal conditions (i.e., when the inquirer spoke in a dialect or when he announced that he was from out-of-town) than when he did not.

In both of these experiments the ostensible referents in the various experimental treatments were the same. That is to say, subjects in the different conditions were communicating about the same physical facts (colors or the route to a fixed destination). What varied were the characteristics ascribed to the listener (oneself vs. some other person in the first experiment, an unknowledgeable person vs. a presumably knowledgeable person in the second). But any message, even the simplest, can be encoded in a number of alternative ways and at least some of the time a speaker's choice from among the various encodings available to him will determine the extent to which a listener comprehends the message. Now there is nothing in linguistic theory, and certainly not in the theory of syntax, that specifies which of several "correct" alternative encodings a speaker will choose to utter. Yet clearly this choice is not an inconsequential matter. For this reason we are led to raise the question of a competence apart from linguistic competence which we term *communicative* competence.

This distinction is similar to one drawn by Cazden (1967) between what she terms "Performance A" and "Performance B." Performance A, according to Cazden, relates to the effect of *intra*personal factors such as memory and attention on linguistic performance. Performance B relates to the effect of *inter*personal factors such as setting, topic, participants, etc. What we are calling communication competence seems similar to Cazden's Performance B. But it is our feeling that if a performance-competence distinction is a useful one (and there are those who may question that it is), the sorts of knowledge incorporated into Performance B are better represented in terms of a competence model. To take a simple example, consider that the appropriate use of English address modes (Brown and Ford, 1961) requires an implicit and detailed knowledge of an abstract underlying status system. There is no reason to think that this sort of knowledge is *qualitatively* different from the abstract knowledge of the language that constitutes a speaker-hearer's linguistic competence. The former may be less complex, but this is a quantitative not a qualitative difference. Indeed, when one considers the vast amount of systematized knowledge that necessarily must underlie the distinctions a communicator can and does make among different kinds of listeners, his use of forms appropriate to different settings, etc., this apparent quantitative difference seems less impressive.

The research to be discussed here is an attempt to characterize the sorts of skills which underlie a speaker's use of language in a communication situation. Thus far, our work has been largely a descriptive enterprise. This reflects no preference for an atheoretical approach on our part; indeed our goal is to develop a model of the development of communication competence. Rather, as Moscovici (1967) has pointed out, there exists no psychological theory of communication that is even possibly adequate. In our research we have developed some hypotheses which will be presented, but it should be noted here that these are largely theoretical speculations and the supporting evidence is only a little bit stronger than our intuitions.

THE EXPERIMENTAL SITUATION

Our general strategy has been to employ for the most part a standardized and highly schematic two-person communication task. Such an approach has two substantial advantages over studying communication in natural situations or other less well-controlled settings. First, it enables the experimenter to exercise control over the content of communication. Second, it makes possible the assignment of a score to a subject or a subject's message which reflects the adequacy of communication.

Another aspect of our research strategy has been to focus on developmental differences in the ability to communicate. This is based on the assumption that adult competence is the standard which the child must eventually attain. By carefully examining the performance of children of different ages, and comparing it to that of adults in comparable circumstances, it is hoped that inferences can be drawn about the developmental processes that enable the child to move from the surprisingly poor communicator he initially is to the remarkably high standard of adult competence. We also hope that our observations will shed some light on the processes underlying the ability of adults.

In most of our experiments, subjects are given the task of communicating about a set of novel graphic designs. The set of designs is illustrated in Fig. 1. The property they have in common is their low codeability (Brown and Lenneberg, 1954). That is, they are difficult to name or characterize, each one eliciting from a group of speakers a wide variety of verbal labels. The designs are reproduced on the four vertical facets

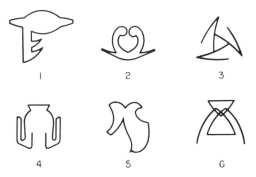

Figure 1.   The graphic designs employed.

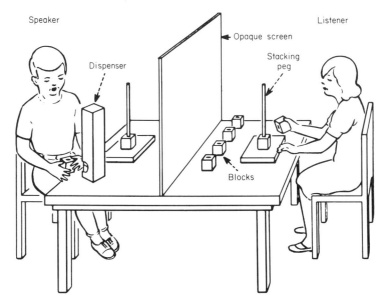

Figure 2.   Experimental situation. Although a male speaker and female listener are
shown, most of the studies employ same-sex pairs.

of a 2x2x2 inch wooden block, one design per block. Each block has a hole
drilled vertically through its center so that it can be stacked on a wooden
dowel. The experimental situation is illustrated in Fig. 2. There are two
subjects, designated the speaker and the listener, each of whom is given a
duplicate set of blocks imprinted with the novel designs. The speaker
receives his blocks in a dispenser so constructed that the blocks can only
be removed one at a time in a predetermined order. The listener receives
the six blocks spread out before her in random order. The subjects are
separated by an opaque screen so situated that they can neither see each
other nor each others' blocks.

The task is introduced to the subjects as a game called "Stack the
Blocks." The object of the game is to build two identical stacks of six
blocks. The speaker is instructed to remove the blocks from the dispenser
one at a time and stack them on his peg. At the same time, he is told, he
must instruct his partner, the listener, which block to stack on her peg.
No restrictions are placed on either subject's speech. In one set of
experimental conditions, after six blocks have been stacked, the two
stacks are compared in full view of both subjects. In such conditions, it
has generally been our practice to reward the subjects with a small plastic
charm when they completed a correct trial (i.e., stacked all six blocks
identically).

Before playing the game with the novel designs, subjects are given several pretraining trials using a set of blocks imprinted with familiar objects (animals, circus figures, etc.). Since virtually all children can identify the names of the figures depicted on the pretraining blocks, this procedure greatly simplifies teaching the rules of the game. At the same time it ensures that defective performance on the experimental task can be attributed to difficulties in dealing with the novel designs and not simply to an inability to follow the rules of the game.

In the initial pretraining trials, subjects played the game in full view of one another. If after six trials they were unable to complete a single errorless trial, the experiment was terminated. Subjects who did complete an errorless trial in the face-to-face condition were seated on opposite sides of the opaque screen and given four more trials with the pretraining materials. Subjects who met a training criterion of two consecutive errorless trials proceeded, without further explanation, to play the same with the novel figures. Subjects who did not meet this pretraining criterion were discarded.

This, then, describes the basic task. In our research we have employed it along with several variations. For example, the experimenter can play the role of the speaker and "feed" the listener-subject with standardized messages of known informative value. Or names can be elicited from a speaker on one occassion and fed back to him or to some other person on another occasion.

COMMUNICATION ABILITIES OF VERY YOUNG CHILDREN

In the first set of experiments (Glucksberg *et al.,* 1966), the subjects were from a population of children ranging in age from 33 to 63 months in two private nursery schools in Princeton, New Jersey. Virtually all of the children were from middle-class background and their parents were predominatly college educated, often beyond the undergraduate level. Conveniently, the schools were divided into two grades, a younger group with ages ranging from 33 to 49 months and an older group of 52 to 63 months.

Six randomly selected pairs from the younger group were run on the pretraining task. None were able to meet the performance criterion. For the most part these younger children were unable to follow the rules of the game using the familiar pretraining materials even when performing in full view of one another.

Accordingly, the novel designs were used only with the older group of subjects. Seven pairs of children in the 52 to 63 month-old group performed the experimental task after all had met the pretraining criterion. There were three male, three female and one male-female pair. All pairs were run for eight consecutive trials. Not one pair was able to complete a single errorless trial using the experimental materials. Indeed, none showed any systematic decrease in the number of errors over trials. However, when the pretraining materials were re-introduced, subjects performed without error, as they had previously. The subjects' difficulties, then, are attributable to the communication problem posed by the novel figures.

When we examined transcripts of these sessions, we were struck by the extent to which our subjects' messages were idiosyncratic and apparently unrelated to the stimulus figures. The imagery they employed seemed to be private, rather than socially shared or conventional. This characteristic of the speech of young children has, of course, been noted by others. It lies behind the distinction Werner and Kaplan draw between "inner" and "external" speech. As they point out (1963, p. 328), in the young child, "the distinction between inner and external speech is relatively slight, speech for the self and speech for the other are little differentiated from one another. In the older child and in the normal adult . . . the differentiation between speech for the self and speech for others becomes progressively more marked."

In a similar vein, Piaget (1926) might well have been commenting on the performance of our subjects in the following excerpt from his discussions of egocentric speech. "The main factor in rendering the explainer obscure and elliptical is his conviction that his listener understands from the outset and even knows beforehand everything that is said to him" (p. 133). "He speaks, therefore, in a language which disregards the precise shade of meaning in things and ignores the precise angle from which they are to be viewed" (p. 60).

From observations of performance in Experiment I and on the basis of these and other theoretical considerations, two related questions were raised: (a) To what extent were children in our subjects' age range capable of performing adequately as listeners, given that the messages provided them are utterances of competent communicators? (b) To what extent can messages uttered by young speakers convey information to the person who uttered them, despite the fact that they apparently convey little or no information to others?

The first question was studied in an experiment in which the experimenter played the role of speaker and provided standardized messages for a young subject-listener. Ideally, we would like to have paired a naive, competent adult with each child, but in the settings in which the experiment had to be run this was simply infeasible. Instead, we selected names for the novel figures which had been uttered by adults in an earlier experiment (Krauss and Weinheimer, 1966), and which had elicited the correct response from an adult listener. These were pretested on an independent sample of naive adults and only names which elicited correct responses with certainty were retained.

Twelve nursery school students (age 46 to 63 months), drawn from the same population as in the previous experiment, were used as subjects. They first learned the listener's role on the pretraining task, with an experimenter playing the role of speaker. All twelve met the performance criterion. The novel figures were then introduced again with an experimenter acting as a speaker. Of the twelve subjects, eight were able to meet a performance criterion of two consecutive correct trials within eight trials. These results indicate that a substantial proportion of our subjects were able to perform the listener role with some degree of adequacy, given competently formulated messages. They also suggest that to a large extent the inadequate performance of our speaker-listener dyads was attributable to deficiencies in the ability of our speakers to formulate messages that were socially adequate (i.e., were sensitive to the point of view of the listener).

The rationale for the experiment designed to investigate the second question deserves some explanation. It is clear that adult speakers distinguish sharply between messages formulated for oneself and messages formulated for others (see Werner and Kaplan, 1963; Krauss *et al.*, 1968). We have implicitly assumed that the difficulties experienced by our young subjects were due to their inability or disinclination to make such a distinction (see Flavell *et al.*, 1968 for an informed discussion of this matter). Clearly such an inference is unwarranted from our data alone. Simply because our speakers' utterances were incomprehensible to others, there is no reason to believe they necessarily were meaningful to the speakers themselves. It conceivably could have been the case that these subjects simply assigned names to the figures in a blind fashion, without any meaningful connection between the names and the figures to which they were supposed to refer. To test this, six subjects in the 47 to 59 month age-range (exhausting the available population of the nursery) were first asked to name the familiar figures used on the pretraining task. An experimenter then used these names in teaching the subject the communication task, again with the experimenter playing the role of speaker and the subject as listener. When they successfully met the pretraining criterion, as all did, the novel figures were brought out and the subjects were asked to name these. One subject, who could not or would not name these figures, was dropped from the experiment. The remaining five subjects performed at a very high level of accuracy when communicated to by the experimenter using the names they had uttered. Indeed, on the very first trial only a single error was made. The names supplied by these children were quite adequate to guide their correct identification, although, as in the experiment reported earlier, these names were short and idiosyncratic. The entire set of names, along with the figures to which they refer, are shown in Table I. Note, for example, names given by Subject 1 for figures 4 and 5, *Daddy's shirt* and *another Daddy's shirt* (it is not clear whether *another* modifies *Daddy's* or *shirt*). Neither of these names, nor anything like them, appears in our adult protocols and the likelihood of confusing the two seems great. In addition, neither name seems particularly descriptive of the figures to which they refer. Yet this subject was able to make the correct selection without error.

TABLE I

REFERENCE PHRASES GIVEN BY NURSERY SCHOOL CHILDREN

	Subject 1	Subject 2	Subject 3	Subject 4	Subject 5
Figure 1—man's legs		airplane	drapeholder	zebra	flying saucer
Figure 2—mother's hat		ring	keyhole	lion	snake
Figure 3—somebody running		eagle	throwing sticks	stip-stripe	wire
Figure 4—Daddy's shirt		milk jug	shoe hold	coffee pot	dog
Figure 5—another Daddy's shirt		bird	dress hold	dress	knife
Figure 6—Mother's dress		ideal	digger hold	caterpillar	ghost

DEVELOPMENTAL TRENDS IN COMMUNICATION ABILITY

These results indicated the advisability of broadening the age range of our sample in order to examine the sorts of developmental trends present. We did this in an experiment conducted at the Milton Hershey School in Hershey, Pennsylvania (Krauss and Glucksberg, 1969). Our subjects were 74 male students at the Hershey School—14 in kindergarten, 18 in first grade, 20 in third grade, and 22 in fifth grade. (The unequal numbers reflect the availability of subjects in the various grades.) Subjects were randomly paired within their grade and put through the pretraining procedure for the communication task described above. All met the pretraining criterion and went on to play the game with the novel figures. It was originally our intention to run all pairs for a total of 15 trials. However, the school's routine required that the entire experimental session (including pretraining) be completed in 50 minutes. For certain subjects, primarily the younger ones, it was impossible to complete 15 trials in this time. In addition, even if more time had been available, it is questionable whether it could have been utilized since subjects who were unable to communicate effectively in several trials, again primarily the younger ones, tended to become restless and uncooperative after 30 to 40 minutes. All pairs were run for at least eight trials, and only data from these eight trials will be considered.

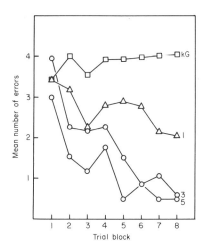

Figure 3.   Mean errors over trials for matched-age pairs in the four grades.

The mean number of errors for grade levels is plotted over trials in Fig. 3. It can be seen that initial performance differs little in the four age categories; however, the groups differ markedly in the rate at which they reduce errors. By Trial 8, third and fifth graders are making fewer than one error on the average, while the initially poor performance of kindergarteners shows no improvement whatever. First graders fall somewhere between these extremes. An analysis of variance of these data indicates significant overall differences between grades and over trials. A significant Grade X Trial interaction reflects differences in the slopes of the curves for the four groups.

These data demonstrate marked differences in communication effectiveness as a function of age, and our previous work suggested to us that such failures in communication were largely attributable to inadequacies in the speakers' encoding ability. However, this cannot be concluded from the data presented in Fig. 3 since both speaker and listener were of approximately the same age. That is, it is possible (albeit unlikely) that speakers of different ages were actually equally good and that the observed differences are attributable to age-related variation in listeners' comprehension ability.

To test this, the messages that young speakers had uttered were given to a group of college students who were asked to identify the figure each message referred to. These messages were taken from the first trial of the previous experiment, because names uttered on the first trial should be less affected by characteristics of the listener than names used later in the session. In Fig. 4 the mean number of correct identifications by adult respondents are plotted as a function of the speaker's grade. An analysis of variance reveals significant variation among these means.

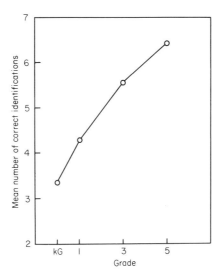

Figure 4.   Accuracy as a function of speaker's grade.

But note one interesting thing. Adult performance is ordered as an increasing function of speaker's grade. However, on Trial 1 of the previous experiment, from which the names used in this experiment were taken, no such ordering is observed. You may recall that in Fig. 3, all groups started at approximately the same level. The largest difference on Trial 1, between grades three and five, was the only one coming anywhere close to being significant ($.10 > p > .05$ by t test) and the rest clearly were not. Only on later trials did the differences between groups emerge. Clearly messages uttered by speakers of different ages contain different amounts of useful information and this undoubtedly contributes to the age-related variation in the performance of speaker-listener dyads. But it is equally the case that the youngsters in the listener role were unable to utilize all of the information present. This result suggests that, although listener proficiency may well develop earlier than speaker proficiency

(Cohen and Klein, 1968; Glucksberg *et al.*, 1966), in neither ability do our grade school subjects approach adult competence.

CHILDREN'S RESPONSES TO FEEDBACK

One aspect of younger children's behavior that we had observed in these earlier studies involved the reaction to a listener's feedback concerning message understandability. We had hypothesized earlier that in nonsocial encoding the speaker's "name" for a figure is essentially unaffected by his listener's post-message utterances. This notion is consistent with Piaget's (1926) concept of nominalism: the tendency to treat a "name" as an integral attribute of an object, an attribute which is invariant and not subject to arbitrary change. With these ideas in mind, we conducted a study (Glucksberg and Krauss, 1967) to examine speaker's responses to listener feedback as a function of age.

Kindergarten, first-, third-, and fifth-grade children, and college students, were assigned the role of speaker in our two-person communication task, with an adult experimenter playing the listener role. On the first trial with the designs, the experimenter said "OK," indicating understanding, after the description of the first, third, and sixth blocks. After the description of the second, fourth and fifth blocks, the experimenter said to 12 of the subjects in each age group, "I don't understand which one you mean." To another 12 subjects in each age group he said, "Tell me more about it." And to a third group of 12 subjects he said, "I don't understand which one you mean; tell me more about it."

Since these three different messages made no difference in the behavior of the subjects, subjects were pooled within age groups. The data indicate that younger children, in addition to displaying limited response repertoires, failed to edit, i.e., they did not modify their messages in socially appropriate ways. Figure 5 presents some of these data. Each bar represents the percentage of subjects in each age group who, on at least one occasion, displayed one or more instances of behavior falling into each category. The first category, "New description," refers to a postfeedback description which likened the figure to a different object. For example: if the initial description was, "It's like a boat," the new description might be, "It looks like a hat." A "modified description" is one which preserves the major outlines of the original description but adds or changes detail. For the example noted above, a modified description might be "a boat with a motor hanging down in back." In a "repeated description" the original description is repeated in substance, without modification. In a large number of cases such repeats were verbatim. The fourth category,

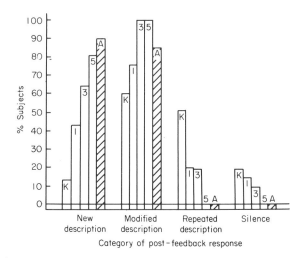

Figure 5. Response to feedback as a function of grade.

"silence," is self-explanatory. From Fig. 5 it is clear that socially appropriate behavior, as measured by these indices, increases with age. Kindergarteners seldom give entirely new descriptions, and they modify their initial descriptions considerably less often than do the older children. (Incidentally, this criterion is a relatively liberal one, and it does not consider whether the modification was any improvement over the original; often it was not.) What kindergarteners do with fair frequency is just what one should *not* do to communicate effectively: repeat the initial response. Note that this is never done by fifth graders or by our adult subjects. The data on "pointing" (not shown) are particularly revealing. Only kindergarteners and first graders "point"—that is, say things like "it goes like this" while tracing the design with a finger. The inappropriateness of such a response is particularly clear when one recalls that speaker and listener cannot see each other.

ACQUISITION OF SEMANTIC CONCEPTS

One further study concerned the socialization of college students, but its results and the method by which they were obtained have some general implications for the study of socialization in children.

An individual newly-entering a well-structured and relatively permanent subcultural group often finds himself confronted by the task of learning a specialized subcultural vocabulary. The terms of such lexicons may or may not have general currency in the language at large, but in either case their meanings within the subcultural group are specialized and frequently unfamiliar to outsiders. For example, photographers refer to hypothiosulfate of soda solution as *hypo*, graduate students refer to comprehensive examinations as *comps*, and confidence men may call their prospective victims *marks*. Often, the meanings of these new terms are relatively straightforward and easily acquired, but in certain cases their meanings are closely bound up with the group's normative and value structure. Consider the way *black* is used by certain groups of Negro militants. How could the full meaning of the term be understood, especially in its connotative aspect, apart from an understanding of the relevant ideological and attitudinal structure? The phrase *law and order*, employed by certain political candidates in the 1968 presidential campaign, had similar usages.

College students, at least on certain campuses, also develop specialized lexicons. For example, Princeton undergraduates refer to some of their number as *wonks*, *lunches*, and *punters*, and the meaning of such terms is not apparent to one who is unfamiliar with the group's dominant value and attitudinal structure. Indeed, it seems reasonable to assume that one index of an individual's membership in a subculture is his acquisition of the connotative and denotative meanings of that subculture's unique lexicon.

Friendly and Glucksberg (1968) attempted to construct a geometric representation of the space containing the traits applied by Princeton undergraduates to their fellow students, using the method of multidimensional scaling. In such a space, the similarity in meaning of terms is represented by their distance from one another. Previous research by Rosenberg *et al.* (1968) had demonstrated that multidimensional scaling provided a useful way of representing the dimensional structure of personality trait adjectives. Two separate but related questions were raised in the present study. First, do specific subcultural terms differ with respect to their location in the hypothetical geometric space as a function of the experience of groups of subjects in a particular subculture? Second, does the dimensional structure of the space also differ as a function of such experience? For example, does such experience generate one or more additional dimensions?

The study employed 60 lexical items. Of these, 40 were common personality-trait adjectives (taken from Rosenberg *et al.*, 1968), such as *industrious, cold, modest,* and *popular*. The remaining 20 were unique terms used by Princeton students. Gathered with the aid of undergraduate informants, they include such terms as *meatball, 'ceptsman,* and *gut hopper*. Thirty volunteer subjects—15 freshman and 15 seniors— sorted the terms into an arbitrary number of categories. Following a technique developed by Rosenberg *et al.* (1968), subjects were told that each category should represent the combination of traits found in some real person whom they knew. Each term could be placed in only one category, and the subjects were permitted to use a miscellaneous category for terms which could not appropriately be placed in any other category.

From these data, a disassociation measure was derived for use as a dissimilarity measure in the multidimensional scaling analysis. Essentially, the disassociation measure takes into account (*a*) the number of times any pair of terms are not put in the same category (i.e., not assigned to the same person) and (*b*) the indirect association of the terms (i.e., the extent to which they do not co-occur with the other terms in the group data). As a rough analogy which may be helpful for an intuitive understanding of the disassociation measure, consider a hypothetical social distance measure between two persons which is inversely related both to how often they interact directly with each other *and* how often they interact with the same other individuals. (Details of the derivation of the disassociation measure may be found in Rosenberg *et al.*, 1968).

Separate multidimensional scaling solutions were computed for the data provided by freshmen and seniors. Two rather different configurations of points were obtained. One way of expressing this difference is in terms of the dimensionality of the space necessary to represent the 60 terms. The space derived from the freshman data is well-represented by a two-dimensional solution, and the addition of further dimensions appears to account for little of the remaining variance. For seniors, however, the addition of a third dimension is necessary to represent the data in an adequate fashion.

Inspection of the data obtained from the freshmen suggests two dimensions. Along one dimension, words such as *warm, sociable, happy,* and *popular* were opposed to words such as *unsociable, boring, unpopular,* and *humorless.* This was interpreted as a *social desirability* dimension. Another dimension was characterized by the polarization of words such as *industrious, scientific, persistent,* and *serious* versus *irresponsible, foolish,* and *unreliable.* This dimension was interpreted as *academic-intellectual desirability.* These two dimensions are analogous to the two denotative dimensions suggested by Rosenberg *et al.* (1968) for their scaling solution of personality-trait adjectives.

The configuration of the items obtained from the senior data led to similar interpretations, but with the addition of a third dimension. With respect to this third dimension, items like *faceman, stud, sociable,* and *popular* were contrasted with *lunch, Wilcox type,* and *Key and Seal type.* This suggested a specific *Princeton Social Desirability* dimension, similar to, but not identical with, general social desirability.

These interpretations are consistent with ratings of the 60 terms performed by an independent group of undergraduates and also with a set of definitions of the 20 specialized Princeton terms obtained from knowledgeable student informants. But regardless of the specific nature of the coordinates of the space, it seems fairly clear from these data that the semantic space containing these terms is more complexly differentiated for seniors than it is for freshman, enabling the former to express more precisely differences among their classmates. For example, although freshmen recognize that the terms *wonk* and *meatball* are pejorative on the social desirability dimension, they do not acknowledge the distinction honored by seniors that the former is positive on the academic-intellectual scale. Nor do they seem to recognize that terms which are socially desirable or undesirable in a general sense may be more or less so in terms of the values of the Princeton undergraduate subculture. It should be noted, however, that the distinction here is relatively subtle and that the two social desirability dimensions are rather highly correlated.

It seems to us that the task faced by undergraduates in learning the lexicon of their newly acquired membership group is closely analogous to one faced by all entrants into a culture, including, of course, children. We believe that the technique discussed above is one useful way to study this process and we are presently attempting to adapt it for use with youngsters.

SUMMARY

To summarize, in this presentation we have attempted to stress the fundamental importance of the ability to communicate for the socialization process. In our view, this ability is comprised of a number of acquired competences which are at least analytically separable. At a minimum, to communicate adequately the child must learn to regard the world from the points of view of others—when and how to elicit information, how to respond to such information-eliciting inquiries, and the nature of the semantic structures which underlie verbal concepts. Perhaps one's appreciation of this feat should be expressed by an aphorism originally applied to a dog who managed to walk upright on his hind legs: "The remarkable thing is not that he does it poorly, but rather that he does it at all."

REFERENCES

Brown, R. (1968). In the beginning was the grammar, *Contemp. Psychol.*, **13**, 49–52.
Brown, R., and Ford, M. (1961). Address in American English. *J. Abnormal and Social Psychol.*, **62**, 375–385.

Brown, R., and Lenneberg, E. H. (1954). A study in language and communication. *J. Abnormal and Social Psychol.*, 49, 454–462.

Cazden, C. B. (1967). On individual differences in language competence and performance. *J. Special Education*, 1, 135–150.

Chomsky, N. (1957). *Syntactic structures.* Mouton, The Hague.

Chomsky, N. (1959). Review of Skinner, "Verbal behavior," *Language*, 35, 26–58.

Chomsky, N. (1965). *Aspects of the theory of syntax.* The M.I.T. Press, Cambridge.

Cohen, B. D. and Klein, J. F. (1968). Referent communication in school age children. *Child Development*, 39, 597–609.

Flavell, J. H., Botkin, P. T., Fry, C. L. Jr., Wright, J. W., and Jarvis, P. E. (1968). *The development of role-taking and communication skills in children.* Wiley, New York.

Friendly, M. L. and Glucksberg, S. (1968). A multidimensional approach to the assessment of semantic change. *J. Personality and Social Psychol.* (in press).

Glucksberg, S. and Krauss, R. M. (1967). What do people say after they have learned how to talk? Studies of the development of referential communication. *Merrill-Palmer Q.*, 13, 309–316.

Glucksberg, S., Krauss, R. M., and Weisberg, R. (1966). Referential communication in nursery school children: Method and some preliminary findings. *J. Exp. Child Psychol.*, 3, 333–342.

Katz, J. J. and Postal, T. M. (1964). *An integrated theory of linguistic descriptions.* The M.I.T. Press, Cambridge.

Kingsbury, D. (1968). *Manipulating the amount of information obtained by a person giving directions.* Senior honors thesis, Dept. Social Relations, Harvard University.

Krauss, R. M. and Glucksberg, S. (1969). The development of communication: Competence as a function of age. *Child Development*, 40, 255–266.

Krauss, R. M., Vivekananthan, P. S., and Weinheimer, S. (1968). "Inner speech" and "external speech": Characteristics and communication effectiveness of socially and non-socially encoded messages. *J. Personality and Social Psychol.*, 9, 295–300.

Krauss, R. M. and Weinheimer, S. (1966). Concurrent feedback, confirmation, and the encoding of referents in verbal communication. *J. Personality and Social Psychol.*, 4, 343–346.

Miller, G. A. (1965). Some preliminaries to psycholinguistics, *Am. Psychologist*, 20, 15–20.

Moscovici, S. (1967). Communication processes and the properties of language. In L. Berkowitz (Ed.), *Advances in experimental social psychology*, Vol. 3. Academic Press, New York.

Piaget, J. (1926). *The language and thought of the child.* Harcourt, Brace, New York.

Rosenberg, S., Nelson, C., and Vivekananthan, P. S. (1968). A multidimensional approach to the structure of personality impressions. *J. Personality and Social Psychol.*, 9, 283–294.

Werner, H. and Kaplan, B. (1963). *Symbol formation.* Wiley, New York.

8

PARENT-CHILD RELATIONS AS AN ANTECEDENT TO CONCEPTUAL FUNCTIONING

O. J. Harvey*
and Catherine Felknor*

In their theory of personality organization, Harvey *et al.* (1961) posited four basic systems of conceptual functioning or belief systems believed to arise from different developmental antecedents and to be manifest in different patterns of behavior and attitudes. A number of studies have investigated the four systems as they function at the time of assessment, but little effort has been devoted to research on developmental differences among representatives of the four systems. That is the concern of this paper.

The focus of this paper will be on the effects of parent-child relationships, *as recalled by college students*, on the development of belief systems. A summary will be presented of the function of belief systems in general, these four specific systems, and some empirical findings regarding current functioning. Based upon these analyses, predictions will be made about the developmental antecedents of the systems and an examination of the results of research based upon these predictions will be presented. Although it is acknowledged that a variety of interpersonal relationships and situation experiences (e.g., peers, school, etc.) could contribute to the development of conceptual systems, this paper is based upon the assumption that for most developing individuals, their relationship with their parents is the most pervasive and most significant aspect of their early experience.

* University of Colorado.

GENERAL NATURE AND FUNCTION
OF BELIEF SYSTEMS

A belief system represents a set of predispositions within an individual to construe or interpret *highly ego-involving* stimuli and events in consistent ways. As such, it operates as a kind of psychological filter that renders the individual selective in his sensitivity to available cues and consequently in how he interprets, feels toward, and responds to them.

The stress on ego-involving stimuli should be noted. On the basis of a great deal of evidence, it appears that belief systems mainly exert differential influence on the detection, processing, and responding to stimuli and events *in which the person is involved affectively, but that their influence is minimal on stimuli of affective neutrality to the respondent.* This position bears directly on the historical argument over whether or not the influence of personality, attitudes, and other predisposing sets are restricted to given situations or may be generalized across situations. It is our position that for an individual of a given belief system *certain generalizable statements may be made about his behavior toward stimuli of high involvement irrespective of the content domain represented by those stimuli, but that his behavior toward neutral stimuli is more situationally specific and thus subject to much less trans-situational generalization.*

This position is unlike that of certain personality and life-style theorists who maintain that personality and/or coping-style exert a consistent influence in *all* situations. Similarly, it takes issue with the position of other writers that the influence of cognitive structure and other set factors is completely situationally specific.

ATTRIBUTES OF THE FOUR SPECIFIC
BELIEF SYSTEMS

The four belief systems considered in this paper differ both in structure and content, each representing a particular *intersect* of content with a given structure. As a consequence, each is characterized by a unique pattern or syndrome of interpretive, affective, and behavioral tendencies toward concept domains of high involvement.

Of the many structural properties on which the systems are assumed to differ, our concentration has been on *concreteness-abstractness*, a quality of how the individual articulates and organizes his concepts of the ego-involving domains of his environment (Harvey, 1967; Harvey *et al.,*

1961). Concreteness-abstractness, as we have characterized the construct, refers to a superordinate conceptual dimension which encompasses a number of more molecular organizational attributes, such as degree of differentiation, extent and complexity of integration, centrality of the cognitive elements, openness to new information and the capacity to modify the existing organization. Thus variation in concreteness-abstractness rests upon differences in patterning and organization and not merely on differences in the algebraic sum of these subordinate characteristics.

At the behavioral level concreteness is manifested in high stimulus-response requiredness while more abstract functioning (because of a more complex and enriched mediational system) permits the individual to transcend the immediate characteristics of stimuli and to display greater relativism in thought and action. From a wide variety of studies it has been found that concreteness is manifested in numerous ways, such as those described below, while greater abstractness has been found to accompany reversed quantities on these dimensions:

1. A simpler cognitive structure, comprised of fewer differentiations and more incomplete integrations within domains of high ego-involvement (Harvey, 1966; Harvey *et al.*, 1968b; Harvey and Ware, 1967; White *et al.*, 1965; White and Harvey, 1965).

2. A greater tendency toward more evaluative, more extreme, and more polarized judgments (Adams *et al.*, 1966; Ware and Harvey, 1967; White and Harvey, 1965).

3. A greater dependence on social cues relating to role, status, and formal authority as guidelines to judgments (Harvey, 1964; Harvey, 1966; Harvey and Ware, 1967; Kritzberg, 1965; Tiemann, 1965).

4. A greater intolerance of ambiguity, expressed in higher scores on such measures as the California F Scale and Rokeach's Dogmatism Scale and in the tendency to form judgments of novel situations more quickly (Harvey, 1966; Reich, 1966; Ware and Harvey, 1967).

5. A greater need for or tendency toward cognitive consistency and a greater arousal and subsequent change from the experience of cognitive dissonance (Harvey, 1965; Harvey, 1967; Ware and Harvey, 1967).

6. A greater inability to change set and hence greater stereotypy in the solution of more complex and changing problems of high involvement (Felknor and Harvey, 1963; Harvey, 1966; Reich, 1966).

7. A poorer delineation between means and ends and thus less ability to think superordinately and in terms of multiple routes to solving a problem or achieving a goal (Harvey, 1966).

8. A greater insensitivity to subtle and minimal cues and hence a greater susceptibility to false but obtrusive cues (Harvey, 1966).

9. A poorer capacity to "act as if," to assume the role of the other, or to

think and act in terms of a hypothetical situation (Harvey, 1963a; Harvey and Kline, 1965).

10. The holding of opinions with greater strength and certainty that the opinions will not change with time (Hoffmeister, 1965).

11. A higher score on the factor of dictatorialness as reflected in such behavior as high need for structure, low flexibility, high rule orientation, high dictation of procedure, high frequency of the usage of unexplained rules, low diversity of activities, and low encouragement of individual responsibility and orginality (Harvey et al., 1966; Harvey, et al., 1968a; Coates et al., 1969).

12. A greater tendency toward trite and normative behavior and thus a lower tendency toward innovative and creative responses (Harvey, 1966; Brown and Harvey, 1968).

13. A greater tendency to form and generalize impressions of other people from highly incomplete information (Ware and Harvey, 1967).

Representatives of the four belief systems differ not only in level of concreteness-abstractness but also with regard to the content that is most personally relevant and affectively significant for them. Thus for an individual to be classified as representing a particular belief system, his responses must indicate *both* a given level of concreteness-abstractness *and* a particular content in which he is affectively involved.

From the intersection of ego-involving content with levels of concreteness-abstractness, a number of belief systems may be deduced; however, the major focus has been on the four systems summarized below.

System 1

This mode of construing the world and relating to it best fits the description of concrete functioning presented earlier. The cognitive structure remains fairly undifferentiated and poorly integrated. The representatives of System 1 are easily distracted by salient cues, even if they are false, and there is a strong tendency for them to make snap judgments and bifurcated evaluations. These individuals show great dependence on external authority, relying on extrapersonal forces as God, norms of society, institutionalized authority, and tradition. They prefer highly structured situations and display an intolerance for ambiguity. Their poor delineation between means and ends is accompanied by a strong commitment to "*the* right way" to do a given task. Thus the search for multiple or alternative paths and the willingness to consider new information are highly limited if not prevented completely. This situation results in stereotypy in approaching problems, insensitivity, and resistance to environmental inputs, which are not congruent with the existing cognitive organization, and low ability to change set. In addition System 1 individuals tend to show ritualistic adherence to rules without understanding, high religiosity, high absolutism, high evaluativeness, high identification with social roles and status positions, high conventionality, and high ethnocentrism (Harvey, 1966).

System 2

This style of functioning is characterized by negativism and an anti-rule, anti-authority orientation. The cognitive structure is somewhat more differentiated than in System 1, perhaps exemplified by the ability of System 2 individuals to see themselves as separate from society and to question many of the values and practices of society. However, the cognitive organization remains poorly integrated and thinking still tends to be fairly compartmentalized, as indicated by the inability of the System 2 individuals to envision the implications and possible effects of their rejection of some aspect of their environment on other aspects. Perhaps because of the ambiguity, vacillation, and inconsistency that they perceive in their environment, they associate unstructuredness with distrust, loss of security, fear of rejection, and/or a feeling of loss of control over their situation. Thus the need for structure and intolerance of ambiguity remain high but are likely to be manifested in suspiciousness and avoidance of commitment. Individuals from System 2, more than from any other system, are in a psychological void, rebelling against structure and authority on the one hand and rendered fearful and anxious by the absence of authority guidelines on the other. The rebelliousness of the System 2 individual appears more manifest while the seeking of structure and the attempt to find security in stable authority is more latent. Thus outwardly the representatives of this system tend to display negative valence toward the same referents that are of high positive relevance to representatives of System 1; it is important to note, however, that *both use these same external sources as points of reference.* Similar to System 1 individuals, high involvement among System 2 representatives appears to eventuate in high arousal, high autonomic activity, conceptual closedness and an inability to differentiate among cognitive and behavioral alternatives (Harvey *et al.*, 1968b).

System 3

This mode of functioning, next to the highest level of abstractness treated by Harvey, *et al.* (1961), is characterized by a desire to be liked and by attempts to establish and maintain relationships that foster mutual dependency and allow for manipulation of others. In fact, System 3 representatives have come to rely upon dependency and manipulation of others as their primary technique of controlling their environment. This type of interpersonal experience results in the conception of self as a causal agent, sometimes an exaggerated one, and facilitates the development of a conceptual organization which is more differentiated and better integrated than that found in either System 1 or 2. System 3 individuals are much less categorical in their evaluations and tend to base their decisions on the implications or effects they will have for themselves and/or other people. Because of their ability to exercise control over others, representatives of this system are less deferential toward authority than representatives of System 1, less negative than individuals of System 2, and in general less concerned with extrapersonal forces and institutionalized authority. They are, however, very concerned with attitudes of peers, social acceptance, and the standards of behavior prescribed by their particular reference group. Since they do not develop clearly delineated personal standards, they are in constant need of feedback from significant people in their environment in order to regulate their behavior and attain the acceptance and mutual dependency that they need. System 3 representatives manifest the need both to be dependent on others and to have others dependent on them. Their dependency apparently is directed toward individuals of power and status while those whom they would have dependent upon them appear to be persons low in status, power, and expertise possibly because such persons would be easier to manipulate under the guise of helpfulness (Ware and Harvey, 1968; Alter and Harvey, 1968). Fearful of facing a situation alone, where success would depend upon individual performance and/or personally derived criteria, System 3 individuals are extremely vulnerable to the threat of rejection, social isolation and other social conditions that might prevent the existence or use of dependency relationships.

System 4

This style of functioning, the most abstract of the four systems, is characterized by high task orientation, information seeking, exploratory behavior, risk taking, independence without negativism, internal standards of conduct, personally derived criteria of evaluation, and relativism in thought and action. The conceptual structure is more highly differentiated and integrated than the other systems. These individuals are able to consider a given concept domain from many points of view, to evaluate the concept with regard to several dimensions, and to see multiple relationships both among the several aspects which they are able to articulate within a given concept and between that concept and other elements of their cognitive organization. These individuals are open to new information and are capable of integrating such information into their existing cognitive organization, making appropriate modifications in that organization if necessary. In addition to being able to integrate apparently opposing characteristics of the same referent, (e.g., the same person may simultaneously possess "good" and "bad" characteristics) they are less likely than individuals from other systems to generalize impressions based on incomplete information (Ware and Harvey, 1967). In general their ideas and attitudes appear to have been derived pragmatically from direct experience of environmental feedback and are not oriented toward adhering to externally defined "truths" or conforming to inviolable social norms. They, more than representatives of any other system, work for intrinsic rather than extrinsic rewards (Harvey et al., 1969). Unlike individuals of the other systems who associate unstructuredness with uncertainty, insecurity, fear of reprisal, fear of rejection etc., representatives of System 4 interpret these conditions as indications of trust and respect and they welcome the opportunity to exercise their independence and behave in accordance with their own inclinations. Thus System 4 individuals display a low need for structure, a relatively high tolerance for ambiguity, an ability to differentiate between means and ends, an ability to articulate several ways of attaining the same goal, a capacity to "act as if," a high ability to change set, and a tendency to avoid stereotypy in solving problems (Harvey, 1966).

ASSUMED DEVELOPMENTAL ANTECEDENTS
OF THE FOUR SYSTEMS

In the original work of Harvey et al. (1961) a number of etiological differences among the systems were deduced, most of which were concerned with childhood independence, freedom of exploration, and the locus and consistency of rewards and punishments. The present paper shall attempt a more detailed description of the parent-child relationships which are assumed to foster the development of the four modes of conceptual functioning.

Antecedents of System 1 Functioning

This type of functioning is assumed to evolve from a developmental history in which the individual is restricted in the exploration of that part of his social world having to do with religious and moral values, power, status relations, and social casualty. Rewards and punishments are made contingent upon his ideas and approaches to problems involving these referents that conform to the omnipotently and omnisciently imposed standards of the parent or other authority. The socialization techniques experienced by System 1 representatives, more than any other system, are thought to parallel the characteristics of operant conditioning in which the behavior of the respondent must approximate the criterion held in mind by the controlling agent, before any reward is received by the former from the latter.

Because of a concern with public presentation of self and living up to role and status definitions, the parents of a developing System 1 child are expected to present a united front to the world, including the child, displaying less public disagreement than the parents of representatives of any other system. Where discrepancies do occur between the parents of the System 1 child, it is expected that these discrepancies reflect the efforts of the mother and father to meet their respective role definitions; for example, the father is likely to be the more dominant parent in accord with the socially prescribed role. These parents are expected to maintain an air of propriety toward the child and thus respond more aloofly in terms of status and role characteristics than in terms of personal warmth and affection. The absolutism, conceptual closedness, unidimensional approach, reliance on external standards, etc., which characterize System 1 functioning are thought to arise from a history where the parents: permit little diversity among family members in their beliefs about issues of high involvement; use explanation sparingly and physical punishment frequently as responses to rule violation; and reward consistently those behaviors which conform to the parents' standards with the result that adherence to the rule becomes an end in itself rather than a means of achieving a superordinate goal. These parents are expected to instill the dominant American motif and push the child toward success in terms of these criteria; to imbue the child with concern about reflecting unfavorably upon the family; and to treat the child in a markedly discontinuous fashion as he grows older, being highly restrictive and controlling when the child is young but more permissive once the child has shown evidence of incorporating the standards of the parent by behaving in accordance with these standards in a consistent way. Both parents are likely to stress religion and attend church frequently. Perhaps because of a somewhat Spartan conception of manhood and acceptance of the traditional notion of the delicacy of womanhood, certain differences are expected in the treatment of males and females by these parents. It is expected that both parents show more approval and affection toward a daughter than toward a son; while the father in particular makes more demands of a son, is more concerned with a son's success and failure in meeting the established standards, and in general is more strict and punitive toward a son than toward a daughter.

Antecedents of System 2 Functioning

Functioning in this manner is thought to result from a developmental history where the parents, and other training agents, in addition to acting omnipotently, also behave capriciously in the giving of love and the administration of other rewards and punishments. These parents are expected to manifest inconsistencies in their own responses toward important social norms and institutions as well as in the demands they make of their children regarding adherence to rules and regulations and also by frequently falling short of the standards they expect of their children. Parents of a System 2 child are likely to allow him a considerable amount of freedom not out of respect for his ability but as a result of indifference or neglect. These parents may frequently evaluate the child's performance negatively without having previously provided any clear indication of the criteria for evaluation and/or arbitrarily vary their responses to the same behavior, sometimes evaluating it positively, sometimes negatively; in addition they probably provide the child with very little explanation for the demands that are made of him. As a result of the conditions described above, the developing child might well come to associate unstructuredness with anxiety, insecurity, and parental rejection rather than seeing it as an opportunity for exploration and discovery of new alternatives.

It is expected that more disagreement occurs between the parents of a System 2 individual than between the parents of the representatives of any other system, and that there is no effort to conceal the relatively frequent family discord. In addition, it is quite likely that the father is less dominant than the mother, less concerned with the child's activities and less personally involved in the day to day child rearing. Discrepancy between the mother and the father is also expected in the area of religion with the mother displaying a relatively high religiosity and church attendance while the father remains indifferent or gives only lip service to values in this area.

Antecedents of System 3 Functioning

This style of functioning is assumed to be the consequence of overindulgence and/or overprotection by one or both parents, which prevents exploration of the physical world and encourages manipulation of the parents, producing in the developing child inflated notions of power and possibly a feeling of anxiety regarding his inability to cope with problems except by the control of others through dependency relationships. The mother of a System 3 child is believed to be very similar to what has been described by Levy (1943) as overprotective. While reluctant to use physical punishment, she exerts tremendous control over the child through a dependency relationship coupled with overindulgence and the potential threat of love withdrawal. In praising the child, she is more likely to focus on the child than on his accomplishment. The father may or may not behave similarly to the mother; however, if he does not, it is thought that, rather than providing a balance or compensation for the behavior of the mother, he is likely to display a sort of indifference toward the whole matter and remain somewhat distant and affectionally isolated from the child. This pattern of behavior probably enhances the dependency relationship between the mother and the child. The father may even disapprove of the mother's methods of dealing with the child, but is unlikely to interfere in their interactions or to confront the mother about it. In general, disagreements between the mother and the father are likely to be camouflaged by a pervasive lack of communication.

Possibly both parents, but especially the mother, are thought to be very attentive to physical safety and opposed to physical aggression and also to be very concerned with the social acceptance and social achievements of the child as long as these do not endanger the mutual dependency bond between the parent and the child.

Antecedents of System 4 Functioning

This more abstract manner of functioning is thought to arise from childhood freedom to explore both the social and physical aspects of one's environment and to evolve one's ideas, beliefs, goals, and solutions independently through direct experience with the environment and without fear of punishment for deviation from externally imposed standards. It is believed to be important that the freedom allowed be within limits which are appropriate for the child's level of physical and intellectual development, rather than absolute or total freedom which may involve more diversity, uncertainty, and/or danger than he is able to cope with at his current level of functioning. Too much freedom may be overwhelming and inhibit the development of abstractness rather than facilitate it.

The parents of the developing System 4 child are expected to foster independence by allowing, possibly even encouraging, diversity of opinions, by permitting exploration of both the physical and social worlds, and by encouraging the child to test out ideas, assumptions, and possible solutions to a problem and to select the most effective course of action on the basis of his *own* experience. It is felt to be important for the parents to provide the child with a basic sense of security, treating him as a person of intrinsic worth, distinguishing between affect toward the child and evaluation of his behavior, and using explanation frequently to clarify both the demands that are made of the child and the punishments that are administered to him. In general, it is expected that these parents establish a consistent framework with meaningful limitations within which a maximum degree of flexibility is possible so that the child is free to select among several alternatives, modify these alternatives and/or create new ones. Also it is anticipated that the mother and father of a System 4 representative are more equally and mutually involved than parents of representatives of the other systems in both the definition and the implementation of child-rearing practice.

RESEARCH METHODS USED

From a large pool of introductory psychology students at the University of Colorado, 106 were selected to serve as subjects (Ss). Of this number, 15 males and 15 females were from System 1, 19 males and 7 females were from System 2, 15 of each sex were from System 3, and 15 males and 5 females were from System 4.

Subjects (Ss) completed two questionnaires administered on separate occasions in group sessions, one for the purpose of identifying the four belief systems and the other to obtain information about their relationships with their parents.

Classification of Belief Systems

The "This I Believe" Test (TIB) was used to classify individuals into one of the four belief systems. The TIB, devised specifically for this purpose (e.g., Felknor and Harvey, 1963; Harvey, 1963a, 1964, 1965, 1966; Harvey and Ware, 1967; Ware and Harvey, 1967; White and Harvey, 1965), requires S to indicate his beliefs about a number of socially and personally relevant concept referents by completing in two or three sentences the phrase, "This I believe about_____," the blank being replaced successively by one of ten referents, such as "the American way of life," "religion," "marriage," "friendship," etc.

Ss are classified as representing System 1 if their completions denote such attributes as high absolutism, high tautologicalness, high frequency of platitudes and normative statements, high ethnocentrism, high religiosity, bifurcated evaluations, and identification with the dominant American motif.

Ss are categorized as representing System 2 if, in addition to being highly evaluative and absolute, they express strong negative attitudes toward such referents as "marriage," "religion," and others reflective of the dominant American theme without giving much thought to the possible results of negating these referents or consideration of alternatives.

Responses are scored as indicating System 3 functioning if they indicate more relativism and less evaluativeness than Systems 1 and 2, and at the same time express strong positive beliefs about friendship, people, and general humanism and imply that friendship and/or people are a necessary and critical aspect of their existence.

System 4 functioning is inferred from responses that imply a high degree of novelty *and* appropriateness, independence without negativism, high relativism and contingency of thought, openness to new information, and the general usage of multidimensional rather than unidimensional interpretive schemata.

Responses to the TIB were scored independently by three trained judges. Agreement between at least two of the judges was required for classifying a respondent into a particular system. Over several years in many different research projects the interjudge reliability for scoring TIBs has ranged between .85 and .95. With regard to test-retest reliability, one sample with a lapse of one week between the first and second administrations of the TIB showed a reliability of .90 between the two scorings, and for a second sample with a lapse of eight months between the two administrations there was a reliability of .85 between the two scorings.

Assessment of Parent-Child Relationships

The Parent-Child Relationship Questionnaire (PCRQ), developed specifically for this research project, was designed to assess several areas of parent-child relations, such as punishment, approval, control, etc. With the aim of discovering possible changes or trends in the relationship as the child grew older, many of the questions were repeated for three age levels: before age 6, age 6 to 12, and age 13 to 17. These age levels were selected so as to coincide with the early childhood, middle childhood, and adolescent periods of development which are characterized by changes in the role of the child *outside* of the family setting (i.e., preschool, elementary school, and junior-senior high school).

In its final form the questionnaire consisted of 70 items, 62 dealing with parent-child interactions (answered separately for each parent), six focussing on the relationship between the parents, and two concerning church attendance.

It should be noted that this questionnaire requires retrospective reporting by the respondent and that probably what is being tapped is some combination of the respondent's memory of his interactions with his parents, his interpretation of what he remembers, his current feelings about his parents, and his willingness to report what he remembers. It seems likely that all of the latter elements of this combination might be influenced by the respondent's system of conceptual functioning and thus, make it impossible to determine if differences between systems reflect actual differences in developmental experiences or differences in the way respondents construe these experiences. This issue in no way denies the questions which have been raised about retrospective reporting (Haggard *et al.*, 1960; Robbins, 1963; Yarrow, 1963; Yarrow *et al.*, 1964). Rather, what is being suggested is that not only are there inaccuracies in retrospective reporting but that these inaccuracies may occur in a systematic fashion determined by the individual's mode of conceptual functioning.

Thus, System 1 respondents might have a tendency to err in the direction of making the parents fit the American social ideal. Representatives of System 2 might be expected to maximize negative characteristics of their parents. Representatives of System 3 may selectively emphasize different characteristics for the mother than for the father. System 4 respondents might be the most accurate in their reports, being able to accept and integrate both the negative and the positive characteristics of their parents.

COMPARISONS CONSIDERED

The concern in this paper is on differences among the four systems and differences within each system between males and females and between mothers and fathers. This involved six sets of comparisons:

1. Differences among representatives of the four systems, males and females combined, in recall of childhood relations with each of their parents.

2. Differences among the four systems in recall of relationships with each parent, separately for males and females.

3. Differences between males and females *within* each system.

4. Differences *within* each system between mothers and fathers.

5. Differences among the four systems in recalled frequency of attendance by their parents at religious services.

6. Types of punishment and reward recalled by male and female representatives of each system as having been used by each parent.

In order to simplify some of these comparisons, cluster analyses (Tryon and Bailey, 1966) were employed separately for the mother-child and father-child relationships. Limitations of space do not permit a full reporting of the results of the cluster analyses; however the 11 mother clusters are summarized in Table I and the 11 father clusters are summarized in Table II.

A cluster or factor score for each of the clusters (22 in total) was calculated for each S on the basis of his responses to the defining variables of each cluster. These cluster scores have a mean of 50 and a standard deviation of 10. The mean score and the standard deviation on each of the mother clusters for representatives of each of the four belief systems is shown in Table I, the corresponding information for the father clusters is shown in Table II.

All comparisons in this study were made by t tests; an appropriate adjustment was made in the calculation of the t value in those instances where the variances were determined to be unequal. Because of the exploratory nature of this research it was decided to use two-tailed tests and to set the significance level at .10 rather than the more stringent levels which are frequently used. It is hoped that this procedure will facilitate the identification of areas of relevance which can then be examined in a more specific manner in future research.

DIFFERENCES AMONG SYSTEMS IN RECALL OF PARENT-CHILD RELATIONSHIPS, SEXES COMBINED

Table I presents the mean scores on the *mother clusters* for representatives of each of the four belief systems, males and females combined. Significant differences were found between systems on six clusters:

TABLE I

MEAN SCORES ON THE PCRQ MOTHER CLUSTERS FOR EACH BELIEF SYSTEM

Mother Clusters	System 1 Mean	SD	System 2 Mean	SD	System 3 Mean	SD	System 4 Mean	SD
1.[a] Fairness; rapport between mother and child	54.09	8.38	44.77	10.44	50.34	9.86	50.14	9.73
2. Variety of rewards before 6 through 17	48.86	9.38	49.54	9.63	50.78	12.03	51.14	8.72
3. Variety of punishments before 6 through 17	48.51	9.19	49.74	9.59	49.74	10.44	52.95	11.37
4. Arbitrariness before 6 through 17	49.46	11.80	52.07	10.54	50.04	8.79	48.06	8.44
5.[a] Disagree with father re: child; lack of support for father	46.63	6.85	55.00	12.99	50.06	9.83	48.38	7.72
6. Strictness and control before 6 through 17	50.04	9.70	50.49	10.60	50.56	11.04	48.47	8.78
7.[a] Freedom and independence before 6 through 12	48.12	10.90	48.74	10.19	50.75	10.51	53.33	7.12
8.[a] Dependency on mother before 6 through 17	52.31	9.24	50.25	10.37	50.51	10.19	45.43	9.83
9.[a] Social concern	49.78	9.96	48.87	9.31	53.15	11.47	47.07	8.08
10. Frequency of punishment before 6 through 12	50.29	9.42	52.34	12.48	48.74	9.54	48.42	8.12
11.[a] Warmth and approval	51.36	9.76	45.50	10.09	51.59	10.30	51.43	8.93

[a] Clusters on which representatives of the belief systems differed significantly, p = .10 or less.

fairness of the mother and rapport between mother and child; disagreement between mother and father over the child, and lack of support by mother for positions established by father; freedom and independence allowed by the mother through age 12; dependency on the mother; concern of the mother with social criteria for evaluating the child; and warmth and approval shown by the mother.

Representatives of System 1 recalled the most fairness and rapport while System 2 respondents recalled the least.

System 1 respondents indicated the lowest disagreement between their parents while System 2 Ss recalled the most.

System 1 respondents recalled their mothers as allowing the least freedom and independence through age 12 and System 4 Ss rated their mothers allowing the most.

System 4 representatives reported less dependency on their mothers than did individuals from any other system.

System 3 Ss indicated their mothers were the most concerned with social criteria while System 4 Ss reported the least concern.

System 2 Ss rated their mothers as being the lowest in warmth and approval.

Table II presents the mean cluster scores for each belief system based on Ss' rating of their relations with their *fathers*. Significant differences

TABLE II

MEAN SCORES ON THE PCRQ FATHER CLUSTERS FOR EACH BELIEF SYSTEM

Father Clusters	System 1		System 2		System 3		System 4	
	Mean	SD	Mean	SD	Mean	SD	Mean	SD
1.[a] Fairness; father's respect for child and support for mother	53.52	7.91	46.16	11.66	49.49	10.06	50.48	9.41
2. Variety of rewards before 6 through 17	49.12	9.00	49.81	9.64	50.22	12.20	51.29	8.99
3. Variety of punishments before 6 through 12	49.56	9.73	48.11	7.44	50.29	6.59	52.72	16.37
4. Arbitrariness before 6 through 12	50.72	10.74	51.41	9.84	49.68	10.95	47.44	7.68
5.[a] Disagree with mother re: child	47.25	7.18	54.26	12.76	50.67	10.60	47.45	6.83
6.[a] Strictness before 6 through 12	52.19	9.15	49.70	11.36	49.32	11.45	48.03	6.73
7.[a] Control; lack of freedom before 6 through 12	54.40	9.56	47.60	10.11	50.08	10.51	46.21	7.76
8.[a] Dependency on father before 6 through 12	52.46	9.82	48.85	11.07	50.50	9.47	46.90	9.52
9. Social concern	49.74	8.79	49.21	10.75	52.27	11.60	47.80	8.07
10. Frequency of punishment before 6 through 12	51.24	8.69	49.22	10.77	51.35	10.12	47.14	10.91
11. Strictness; arbitrariness; control; lack of freedom 13 to 17	49.74	10.20	49.15	11.59	51.44	10.48	49.26	6.63

[a] Clusters on which representatives of the belief systems differed significantly, p = .10 or less.

between systems were found on five of the father clusters: fairness and respect shown by the father; disagreement between mother and father over the child; strictness of the father through age 12; control and restriction of freedom by the father through age 12; and dependency on the father through age 12.

Representatives of System 2 reported the least fairness and respect and System 1 respondents indicated the most.

System 2 Ss recalled the most disagreement between their parents.

System 1 respondents indicated the greatest strictness by their fathers through age 12 while System 4 individuals indicated the least.

System 4 Ss recalled the least control and restriction of freedom by their fathers through age 12 and System 1 individuals recalled the most.

System 1 Ss reported the greatest dependency on their fathers through age 12 and System 4 Ss reported the least.

DIFFERENCES AMONG SYSTEMS, MALES AND FEMALES CONSIDERED SEPARATELY

The preceding section dealt with differences between systems without regard to the sex of the respondents. In this section the sex of the subject will be taken into account through an examination of between system differences on the 22 clusters for male and female representatives separately.

Males

The mean scores on the *mother clusters* for male representatives of each system are presented in Table III. Significant differences were obtained between systems on four clusters: fairness and rapport, parental disagreement, dependency, and social concern.

Males of System 1 recalled the most fairness and rapport.

System 2 males reported the most disagreement between their parents.

System 4 males recalled the least dependency on their mothers.

System 4 males also reported the least social concern by their mothers.

Table IV contains the mean scores on the *father clusters* for male representatives of the four belief systems. Significant differences between the systems occurred on five of the father clusters: parental disagreement; strictness of the father through age 12; control and restriction of freedom by the father through age 12; dependency on the father through age 12; and frequency of punishment through age 12.

TABLE III

MEAN SCORES ON THE PCRQ MOTHER CLUSTERS
FOR MALES OF EACH BELIEF SYSTEM

	System 1		System 2		System 3		System 4	
Mother Clusters	Mean	SD	Mean	SD	Mean	SD	Mean	SD
1.[a] Fairness; rapport between mother and child	52.66	9.25	44.27	11.05	49.11	11.14	49.27	10.12
2. Variety of rewards before 6 through 17	50.42	11.30	49.39	10.13	47.57	8.98	51.66	8.87
3. Variety of punishments before 6 through 17	48.65	10.62	49.76	10.62	50.13	12.88	51.64	9.67
4. Arbitrariness before 6 through 17	50.94	11.49	53.55	10.31	49.52	8.15	48.22	8.78
5.[a] Disagree with father re: child; lack of support for father	46.44	4.65	53.54	11.00	49.95	9.44	49.11	7.99
6. Strictness and control before 6 through 17	50.01	9.49	50.03	11.13	51.22	11.66	48.48	8.74
7. Freedom and independence before 6 through 12	49.16	11.67	48.97	11.36	48.44	11.45	53.76	7.95
8.[a] Dependency on mother before 6 through 17	50.53	8.61	49.95	10.82	50.55	8.51	43.10	9.51
9.[a] Social concern	49.61	10.18	50.06	9.18	54.58	10.43	47.87	8.58
10. Frequency of punishment before 6 through 12	49.30	9.86	52.08	12.21	49.30	9.44	48.51	8.70
11. Warmth and approval	49.16	8.19	46.12	9.43	49.44	10.59	50.44	9.49

[a] Clusters on which male representatives of the belief systems differed significantly, p − .10 or less.

TABLE IV

MEAN SCORES ON THE PCRQ FATHER CLUSTERS
FOR MALES OF EACH BELIEF SYSTEM

	System 1		System 2		System 3		System 4	
Father Clusters	Mean	SD	Mean	SD	Mean	SD	Mean	SD
1. Fairness: father's respect for child and support for mother	50.00	7.81	47.51	10.98	47.48	10.90	49.17	9.56
2. Variety of rewards before 6 through 17	50.41	10.91	50.46	9.95	47.56	7.42	52.09	8.89
3. Variety of punishments before 6 through 12	52.38	10.82	48.11	7.66	50.44	7.39	50.67	9.14
4. Arbitrariness before 6 through 12	54.55	11.57	50.85	9.89	49.86	10.35	48.47	7.59
5.[a] Disagree with mother re: child	46.92	6.36	52.49	11.24	50.02	10.09	47.84	7.01
6.[a] Strictness before 6 through 12	55.55	8.37	47.48	12.02	51.86	10.44	47.65	7.52
7.[a] Control; lack of freedom before 6 through 12	52.71	9.75	46.66	10.48	49.76	11.15	46.22	8.35
8.[a] Dependency on father before 6 through 12	51.95	8.20	48.65	10.99	49.77	9.38	44.51	9.89
9. Social concern	51.18	9.88	50.42	11.01	53.64	10.18	48.25	8.43
10.[a] Frequency of punishment before 6 through 12	54.47	8.81	50.00	11.83	51.67	11.00	46.66	12.14
11. Strictness; arbitrariness; control; lack of freedom 13 to 17	50.03	10.75	48.98	11.25	50.77	10.34	48.10	6.37

[a] Clusters on which male representatives of the belief systems differed significantly, p = .10 or less.

TABLE V

MEAN SCORES ON THE PCRQ MOTHER CLUSTERS
FOR FEMALES OF EACH BELIEF SYSTEM

	System 1		System 2		System 3		System 4	
Mother Clusters	Mean	SD	Mean	SD	Mean	SD	Mean	SD
1.[a] Fairness; rapport between mother and child	55.51	7.46	46.13	9.25	51.58	8.61	52.77	8.93
2. Variety of rewards before 6 through 17	47.31	7.03	49.93	8.86	54.00	14.03	49.58	9.05
3. Variety of punishments before 6 through 17	48.37	7.88	49.68	6.67	49.38	7.97	56.90	16.15
4. Arbitrariness before 6 through 17	47.98	12.30	48.05	10.88	50.56	9.64	47.58	8.24
5. Disagree with father re: child; lack of support for father	46.82	8.70	58.98	17.75	50.18	10.54	46.33	7.32
6. Strictness and control before 6 through 17	50.06	10.24	51.75	9.71	49.89	10.74	48.45	9.93
7. Freedom and independence before 6 through 12	47.07	10.37	48.11	6.70	53.07	9.30	52.06	4.13
8. Dependency on mother before 6 through 17	54.09	9.80	51.07	9.81	50.48	11.94	52.42	7.79
9. Social concern	49.46	10.09	45.63	9.57	51.72	12.62	44.66	6.55
10. Frequency of punishment before 6 through 12	48.14	9.18	53.04	14.18	48.17	9.93	48.14	7.01
11.[a] Warmth and approval	53.57	10.94	43.80	12.35	53.74	9.90	54.39	7.04

[a] Clusters on which female representatives of the belief systems differed significantly, p = .10 or less.

Male representatives of System 1 recalled significantly less disagreement between their parents than males of System 2.

System 1 males recalled the greatest strictness and the most control and restriction of freedom by the father.

Males of System 1 recalled significantly more dependence on their fathers through age 12 than did System 4 males. They also recalled the highest frequency of punishment through age 12.

Females

The mean scores for female representatives of each system on the PCRQ mother clusters are presented in Table V. Significant differences were found between female representatives on only two of the *mother clusters*: Cluster 1—fairness and rapport, and Cluster 11—warmth and approval.

Like the males, female representatives of System 1 recalled the most fairness and rapport. System 2 females rated their mothers as being the lowest in warmth and approval. No significant differences occurred on this cluster for male representatives.

The mean scores on the *father clusters* for female representatives of the

TABLE VI
MEAN SCORES ON THE PCRQ FATHER CLUSTERS
FOR FEMALES OF EACH BELIEF SYSTEM

	System 1		System 2		System 3		System 4	
Father Clusters	Mean	SD	Mean	SD	Mean	SD	Mean	SD
1.ᵃ Fairness; father's respect for child and support for mother	57.04	6.49	42.47	13.51	51.49	9.07	54.43	8.66
2. Variety of rewards before 6 through 17	47.83	6.73	48.05	9.24	52.89	15.42	49.03	9.91
3. Variety of punishments before 6 through 12	46.73	7.88	48.12	7.41	50.14	5.95	58.47	29.64
4. Arbitrariness before 6 through 12	46.90	8.60	52.91	10.31	49.49	11.87	44.57	8.02
5. Disagree with mother re: child	47.58	8.13	59.08	16.20	51.32	11.40	46.38	6.93
6.ᵃ Strictness before 6 through 12	48.83	8.90	55.71	6.79	46.78	12.19	49.10	4.20
7.ᵃ Control; lack of freedom before 6 through 12	56.08	9.40	50.16	9.26	50.41	10.21	46.17	6.69
8. Dependency on father before 6 through 12	52.96	11.49	49.41	12.17	51.23	9.39	53.58	3.75
9. Social concern	48.29	7.62	45.92	10.01	50.89	13.09	46.65	7.81
10. Frequency of punishment before 6 through 12	48.01	7.52	47.10	7.50	51.02	9.52	48.58	6.77
11. Strictness; arbitrariness; control; lack of freedom 13 to 17	49.45	9.98	49.63	13.40	52.11	10.94	52.27	7.03

ᵃ Clusters on which female representatives of the belief systems differed significantly, p = .10 or less.

four systems are presented in Table VI. Female representatives differed significantly on three of the father clusters: fairness and respect, strictness through age 12, and control and restriction of freedom through age 12.

Females of System 1 recalled their fathers as showing significantly greater fairness and respect than females of System 2 and System 3. Females of System 2 also rated their fathers lower on this factor than females of System 3 and System 4.

System 2 females recalled their fathers as being the most strict through age 12.

System 1 females recalled the most control and restriction of freedom by their fathers through age 12.

Summary of Differences between Systems on the PCRQ Clusters

In some instances the pattern of differences between systems on a mother cluster was quite similar to the pattern on the comparable father cluster. In other instances, the patterns of responses for mothers and fathers were quite different. Some clusters revealed differences between systems for one parent but not for the other, while other clusters showed no significant differences for either parent. Also evident is the similarity between males and females on some clusters and the apparent differences on others.

For the areas of fairness, parental disagreement and dependency the differences between systems on the mother clusters were quite similar to those on the father clusters.

For males and females considered separately and for the sexes combined, System 2 individuals recalled their mothers as lowest in fairness and rapport, while System 1 individuals rated their mothers as most fair and recalled the best rapport with their mothers. On the comparable father cluster a significant difference occurred for females but not for males with System 2 females recalling their fathers as showing less fairness and respect than was recalled by females of the other systems. For the sexes combined and for females only, System 1 respondents recalled their fathers as showing more fairness and respect than representatives of either System 2 or System 3. Although the differences were not significant, System 1 males showed the same tendency to rate their fathers highest, while males from Systems 2 and 3 tended to rate their fathers equally low on fairness and respect.

In the area of mother-father disagreement (both the mother cluster and the father cluster) System 2 individuals recalled the most disagreement while System 1 Ss recalled the least, when data for the two sexes were combined and when males were rated separately. For females only, the results were not significant but showed a tendency for System 2 Ss to recall the most disagreement while representatives of Systems 1 and 4 recalled the least.

For the sexes combined and for males only, System 4 respondents recalled the least dependency on either parent, significantly less than System 1 Ss for dependency on the father and significantly less than Ss of Systems 1 and 3 for dependency on the mother. There were no significant differences between female representatives, however, in contrast to the results for males, System 4 females tended to recall the most dependency on their fathers while the least dependency was indicated by System 2 females. For dependency on the mother, System 1 females tended to recall the most while females of Systems 2 and 3 indicated the least.

In the areas of strictness, control, and freedom, Ss' relationships with their fathers indicated many significant differences between systems. Responses for mothers in these areas tended to follow a somewhat similar pattern but system differences were generally not significant.

On the mother clusters relating to strictness and control and to freedom and independence (clusters 6 and 7), there was a significant difference in only one set of comparisons: for both sexes combined, System 4 Ss recalled more freedom and independence than representatives of System 2 and System 1. For males only, there was the same tendency for System 4 Ss to recall the most freedom and independence, however, the least was recalled by System 3 males; while for females, System 3 individuals tended to recall the most freedom and independence followed closely by System 4 Ss. No significant differences occurred on the mother cluster concerned with strictness and control. For all three groupings (i.e., sexes combined, males only and females only) System 4 respondents tended to recall the least strictness and control. For males the most strictness and control by the mother was recalled by System 3 Ss while for females the most was recalled by System 2 Ss.

On the comparable, although slightly different, clusters for fathers (No. 6, strictness, and No. 7, control and restriction of freedom) significant differences between systems occurred in all comparisons. With data from both sexes combined, System 1 Ss recalled significantly more strictness by their fathers, than individuals of System 4. For males only, System 1 respondents were again highest, recalling more strictness than males of System 4 and System 2. In contrast to the results for males, System 2 females recalled significantly more strictness than females of any other system, while System 3 females recalled the least. The results on the control-restriction of freedom cluster are quite similar for all three groupings. For both sexes combined and for males only, System 1 Ss recalled significantly more control and restriction of freedom by their fathers than individuals of Systems 2 and 4, and for females System 1 Ss recalled significantly more control and restriction than System 4 Ss.

In the area of social concern, significant differences occurred on the mother cluster but not on the father cluster. For both sexes combined and for males only, System 3 representatives recalled significantly more concern by their mothers with social criteria than individuals of System 4, and the same tendency occurred for females. Although none of the comparisons on the father cluster were significant, System 3 Ss tended to recall their fathers as more concerned with social criteria than individuals of the other systems for all three groupings.

The pattern of the four systems in their responses regarding frequency of punishment by their fathers was markedly different from the pattern for punishment by their mothers, although there was only one significant difference between systems on this pair of clusters. Male representatives of System 1 recalled more frequent punishment by their fathers through age 12 than did System 4 males. For the sexes combined, System 4 representatives also tended to recall the least frequent punishment from their fathers. However, looking at females only, the lowest frequency of punishment by the father was recalled by System 2 Ss while the highest frequency was recalled by System 3 females. In contrast to this pattern for fathers, the data for mothers showed System 2 Ss recalling the highest frequency of punishment by the mother, while representatives of System 4 recalled the lowest frequency for the sexes combined and considered separately.

On the cluster regarding warmth and approval shown by the mother, representatives of System 2 were significantly lower than representatives of the other three systems for both sexes combined, males only and females only. System 4 males and females showed a tendency to recall the most warmth and approval. There was no comparable father cluster.

The father cluster concerned with strictness, arbitrariness, control, and restriction from age 13 to 17 did not yield any significant differences between the systems. For males, System 4 Ss tended to rate their fathers lowest on these variables while System 3 Ss tended to make the highest ratings. For females, however, Ss from Systems 3 and 4 were about equally high on this cluster while Ss of Systems 1 and 2 rated their fathers the lowest (although not as low as the System 4 males). There was no comparable mother cluster.

On the remaining clusters, variety of reward, variety of punishment, and arbitrariness, there were no significant differences between systems for either mothers or fathers. The data for male and female representatives combined showed a tendency for System 4 Ss to recall the greatest variety of rewards and punishments from both mother and father. The least variety of rewards from both mother and father was recalled by System 1 Ss who also tended to recall the least variety of punishments from their mother; System 2 Ss, however, tended to recall the least variety of punishments from their father. System 4 representatives tended to recall less arbitrariness from either mother or father than representatives of the other systems for sexes combined and considered separately. Among males System 2 Ss tended to recall the most arbitrariness of the mother while for females System 3 Ss recalled the most. Arbitrariness of the father was rated as highest among males by System 1 Ss and among females by System 2 Ss.

WITHIN SYSTEM DIFFERENCES BETWEEN
MALES AND FEMALES

The results in the preceding section focussed on differences *between* systems. This section will be concerned with differences between males and females *within* each system in how they recalled their childhood relationships with each parent. In order to pinpoint the differences as specifically as possible they will be presented in terms of *individual items* on the PCRQ rather than the clusters dealt with in the preceding section.

Male-Female Differences Regarding Relationship with Mothers

The number of mother items on which males and females showed significant differences were relatively few within every system, from two for System 2 to seven for System 4. Thus the male and female representatives within System 2 tended to recall their childhood relations with their mothers as being quite similar, while there was only slightly more difference between males and females in Systems 1, 3, and 4. The items on which significant differences occurred are included in Table VII.

TABLE VII

MALE-FEMALE DIFFERENCES REGARDING RELATIONSHIP WITH MOTHERS
(ITEMS ON WHICH SIGNIFICANT DIFFERENCES OCCURRED)

Item	Direction of Difference and Significance	Males Mean	SD	Females Mean	SD
System 1 control before 6	females > males p < .05	2.93	1.22	2.13	.74
approval before 6	females > males p < .05	2.86	1.03	2.00	.85
approval 6 to 12	females > males p < .05	2.87	.99	2.00	.96
mother attending religious services	males > females p < .10	1.93	.96	2.47	.74
influence while growing up	females > males p < .05	2.27	.88	1.60	.74
System 2 reminded about family reputation	males > females p < .10	4.26	1.88	5.71	1.89
agreed with mother when parents disagreed	females > males p < .05	4.00	1.32	2.57	1.27
System 3 No. of types of reward 6 to 12	females > males p < .10	1.60	.91	2.53	1.60
encouraged to express opinions	females > males p < .05	4.33	1.54	3.00	1.73
try to please mother	females > males p < .01	3.27	1.16	2.07	1.10
influence while growing up	females > males p < .01	2.67	.82	1.80	.77
influence currently	females > males p < .01	4.73	1.10	3.33	1.23
System 4 freedom and independence 13 to 17	males > females p < .05	1.53	.64	2.20	.45
approval before 6	females > males p < .10	2.47	1.19	1.80	.45
dependence 6 to 12	females > males p < .01	3.80	.94	2.80	.45
dependence 13 to 17	females > males p < .10	4.60	1.06	3.40	1.52
participation by mother in child's activities	females > males p < .10	4.73	1.39	3.40	1.52
mother disapprove of friends	males > females p < .05	5.27	.88	6.40	.89
influence currently	females > males p < .05	4.33	1.45	2.80	.84

Male-Female Differences Regarding Relationship with Fathers

There were more significant differences between males and females in their relationship to their fathers than in relationship to their mothers in Systems 1 and 2, fewer differences in System 3, and the same number of differences in System 4. Only two items showed significant differences between System 3 males and females in their relationship with their fathers, while in System 1, the males and females were significantly different on sixteen items, the largest number within any system for either parent. Table VIII contains the father items on which the systems differed significantly.

The differences between males and females within systems can be summarized in the following way. Within System 2 and within System 3, males and females tended to be fairly similar in their recalled relationships with their parents; System 2 males and females showed the least

TABLE VIII

MALE-FEMALE DIFFERENCES REGARDING RELATIONSHIP WITH FATHERS
(ITEMS ON WHICH SIGNIFICANT DIFFERENCES OCCURRED)

	Item	Direction of Difference and Significance	Males Mean	SD	Females Mean	SD
System 1	no. of types of punishment 6 to 12	males > females p < .10	2.00	1.07	1.33	.72
	fairness of punishment before 6	females > males p < .02	2.64	1.45	1.53	.74
	fairness of punishment 6 to 12	females > males p < .02	2.40	1.12	1.53	.64
	strictness before 6	males > females p < .10	2.73	1.03	3.47	1.06
	strictness 6 to 12	males > females p < .10	2.73	1.22	3.60	1.24
	arbitrariness before 6	males > females p < .05	3.87	1.51	4.87	.99
	arbitrariness 6 to 12	males > females p < .10	3.73	1.44	4.60	1.18
	approval before 6	females > males p < .05	3.29	.99	2.40	1.24
	approval 6 to 12	females > males p < .05	3.40	.91	2.47	1.19
	encouraged to express opinions	females > males p < .10	3.73	1.71	2.73	1.49
	reminded about family reputation	males > females p < .05	4.07	2.02	5.60	1.45
	make you feel your ideas were important	females > males p < .10	3.87	1.46	2.93	1.33
	father listened with an open mind	females > males p < .10	3.93	1.62	2.80	1.47
	father nosey about your affairs	males > females p < .10	5.27	1.28	6.00	1.07
	father attending religious services	males > females p < .10	2.27	1.22	3.00	1.13
	try to please father	females > males p < .10	2.67	1.59	1.73	1.10
System 2	strictness before 6	females > males p < .10	3.94	1.52	2.71	.95
	dependence 13 to 17	males > females p < .10	4.47	.96	5.29	1.11
	father living up to standards expected of child	males > females p < .05	2.53	1.54	4.29	1.80
	similar to father	males > females p < .02	3.00	1.41	4.57	.98
	agreed with father when parents disagreed	males > females p < .05	4.00	1.46	5.43	1.13
System 3	encouraged to express opinions	females > males p < .10	4.67	1.45	3.47	1.88
	try to please father	females > males p < .05	2.87	1.36	1.87	.83
System 4	freedom and independence 13 to 17	males > females p < .01	1.54	.52	3.00	.71
	dependence 6 to 12	females > males p < .01	4.08	1.04	3.00	0.00
	try to please father	females > males p < .10	3.00	1.22	1.80	.84
	influence while growing up	females > males p < .05	2.69	1.60	1.60	.55
	similar to father	females > males p < .01	3.46	1.56	1.80	.45
	agreed with father when parents disagreed	females > males p < .10	4.69	.95	3.60	1.52
	got along with father	females > males p < .10	2.86	1.17	1.80	.84

difference with regard to their mothers, while System 3 males and females showed the least difference with regard to their fathers. The greatest amount of difference between male and female respondents occurred in System 1 regarding relationship with fathers. In contrast to the other systems, the System 4 males and females differed on the same number of items for relationship with mothers as they did for relationship with fathers.

In System 1, the females recalled more approval from their mothers than did males but also more control and more influence, while the greater approval from the fathers for females was supplemented by a memory of him as more fair, less strict, and less arbitrary through age 12. Possibly related to the females' recollection of their fathers as encouraging them to express their opinions, making them feel their ideas were important, and listening to them with an open mind, the females more frequently than the males recalled trying to please their fathers. On the other hand, the males more frequently recalled their fathers as reminding them about the family reputation and as nosey about their affairs; they also recalled both parents attending religious services more frequently than females did.

In System 2, in contrast to System 1, the females (rather than the males) recalled their fathers as more strict, and the System 2 males recalled their mothers (rather than their fathers) as reminding them about the family reputation more frequently than did the females. Within System 2, the males more frequently than the females agreed with their fathers, while the females more frequently than the males agreed with their mothers. The basis for these two differences was the wide discrepancy for females in the frequency of agreement with mother versus father (a high frequency of agreement with their mothers and a very low frequency of agreement with their fathers), while for System 2 males the mean frequency of agreement with mothers and fathers was the same. Also indicative of the lack of a positive bond between System 2 females and their fathers, the females recalled less dependence as teenagers on their fathers, felt less similar to their fathers, and less frequently recalled their fathers living up to the standards which the fathers expected of them. It should be noted that System 2 females are lower than either sex in any system on these three items.

Within System 3 the between-sex differences showed that females were more frequently encouraged by both parents to express their opinions, and tried to please both parents more frequently than males. In addition, the females recalled their mothers using a greater variety of rewards from age 6 to 12, and more influence by their mothers both while they were growing up and currently than did males.

Within System 4, the responses of the females indicated a strong positive bond with their fathers during the time they were growing up, as reflected in the females' recall of dependence, influence, similarity, and agreement—in general getting along well with their fathers and trying to please them. As well as being significantly different from the System 4 males, the System 4 females are higher than either sex in any system on several of these dimensions. The System 4 males and/or the System 2 females were generally the lowest on these dimensions. The System 4 females also showed a stronger bond with their mothers than did System 4 males. The relationship with the mothers, while not quite as pervasive as it was for the fathers, covered the areas of approval, dependence, participation in the child's activities and current influence. The outstanding characteristic of the relationship of System 4 males to both of their parents was the high amount of freedom and independence which they were allowed from age 13 to 17. As well as being significantly different at this age level from the System 4 females, the System 4 males tended to recall more freedom and independence from both parents at all age levels than either sex in any system.

Although not a within system difference, it can be seen from the results presented in this section that there was a striking difference between System 4 females and System 2 females in their recalled relationships with their fathers. System 4 females tended to portray a strongly positive relationship and an apparent identification with their fathers, while System 2 females indicated strongly negative feelings toward their fathers along with the psychological tendency to move away from them.

WITHIN SYSTEM DIFFERENCES BETWEEN
MOTHERS AND FATHERS

Within each system the ratings made of mothers were compared with the ratings made of fathers, for male and female respondents combined. Since, in several instances, the clusters for mothers were quite different from those for fathers, the comparisons in this section were made on single items, which were common to both parents, instead of on clusters.

The number of items on which the ratings for mothers differed significantly from the ratings for fathers were relatively few for all systems, ten for System 1, twelve for System 2, eleven for System 3, and only two for System 4. Comparisons on these items are summarized in Table IX.

System 1 Ss recalled their mothers significantly more often than their fathers as expressing approval from age 6 to 12, as expressing warmth and affection, as expressing concern about their physical safety, as being

TABLE IX

DIFFERENCES BETWEEN MOTHERS AND FATHERS WITHIN EACH SYSTEM

Item	System 1					System 2					System 3					System 4			
	sig diff	Mothers Mean	SD	Fathers Mean	SD	sig diff	Mothers Mean	SD	Fathers Mean	SD	sig diff	Mothers Mean	SD	Fathers Mean	SD	Mothers Mean	SD	Fathers Mean	SD
strict before 6	F > M	3.63	1.13	3.10	1.09		3.79	1.14	3.58	1.47		3.75	1.29	3.59	1.37	3.85	1.14	3.84	1.01
strict 6 to 12	F > M	3.79	1.05	3.17	1.29		3.54	1.36	3.31	1.44		3.63	1.25	3.47	1.41	3.65	1.04	3.44	.78
control and reg 6 to 12		3.33	1.12	3.40	1.10		3.77	1.14	4.31	1.12		3.63	1.13	3.86	1.46	4.05	1.15	4.39	1.20
approval before 6		2.41	1.02	2.83	1.20		2.65	1.27	3.35	1.19		2.29	1.18	2.67	1.30	2.30	1.08	2.42	1.35
approval 6 to 12	M > F	2.45	1.06	2.93	1.14	M > F	3.00	1.23	3.42	1.06		2.30	1.18	2.93	1.31	2.20	1.11	2.39	1.20
approval 13 to 17		2.57	1.25	3.00	1.34	M > F	3.08	1.29	3.50	1.36		2.27	1.23	2.97	1.47	2.30	.92	2.78	1.35
dependence before 6	M > Fa	2.13	1.14	2.67	1.37	M > F	1.96	.64	3.04	1.33		2.30	1.15	2.83	1.26	2.63	.83	2.94	1.26
dependence 6 to 12	M > F	2.72	1.03	3.00	1.02		2.81	1.13	3.50	1.21		2.90	1.03	3.23	1.04	3.55	.94	3.78	1.00
allow C think for self	F > M	3.10	1.24	2.33	1.18		3.58	1.72	3.81	1.86		3.10	1.54	3.37	1.75	2.95	1.19	2.50	1.50
concern about safety	M > Fa	2.17	1.34	3.00	1.53	M > Fa	3.65	1.74	4.62	1.42		2.53	1.33	3.70	1.62	3.10	1.68	3.72	1.96
urge social activities	M > Fa	3.20	1.54	3.97	1.69	M > F	3.92	1.79	5.12	1.40		3.50	1.70	4.40	1.73	4.15	1.76	4.33	1.71
solves problems for C	M > F	5.30	1.09	5.47	1.36		4.73	1.19	5.42	1.03		5.17	1.05	5.43	1.19	5.30	1.30	5.78	1.22
listen with open mind		3.03	1.69	3.37	1.63	M > F	3.69	1.85	3.92	2.00		3.30	1.95	4.17	2.00	3.15	1.57	3.56	1.72
not have time for C	F > M	5.60	1.35	4.73	1.86	F > Ma	5.42	1.58	4.72	1.70		5.70	1.02	4.77	1.50	5.21	1.23	4.53	1.74
nosey about C's affairs	M > Fa	4.93	1.51	5.63	1.22	M > F	4.19	1.90	5.73	1.22	M > F	4.87	1.36	5.47	1.20	5.30	1.26	5.94	.80
C free to talk to parent		3.80	2.02	4.33	1.77	M > F	4.42	1.68	4.65	2.02		3.93	1.95	4.97	1.77	4.10	1.68	4.39	2.00
parent attend religious	M > Fa	2.20	.89	2.63	1.22	M > Fa	2.96	1.25	4.08	1.06		3.17	1.56	3.40	1.13	3.10	1.37	3.72	1.49
allow C to do like peers	M > Fa	4.97	1.13	5.50	.86		4.75	1.19	4.92	1.44	M > F	5.00	1.20	5.17	.97	4.85	1.04	4.94	1.21
express warmth	M > Fa	2.37	1.54	3.13	1.68	M > F	3.38	1.58	4.69	1.35		2.67	1.42	3.47	1.70	2.70	1.42	3.61	1.85
C close to parent	M > F	2.23	1.36	2.50	1.38	M > F	2.81	1.27	3.88	1.45		2.47	1.28	3.23	1.43	2.50	1.24	2.94	1.55
C agree with parent		3.87	1.31	4.03	1.19		3.58	1.44	4.42	1.50		3.85	1.13	4.30	1.32	4.06	1.21	4.39	1.20

M = Mother   F = Father   C = Child

[a] level of significance < .01

nosey about their affairs, as permitting them to do like their peers, and as urging participation in social activities.

Fathers of System 1 respondents, on the other hand, were recalled, to a significantly greater extent than the mothers, as being strict both before age 6 and from 6 to 12, as allowing the respondents to think for themselves, and as not having time to spend with them.

For System 2 Ss, mothers were recalled significantly more often than fathers as trying to control and regulate the respondents' lives from age 6 to 12, as expressing approval before 6, as expressing general warmth and affection, as expressing concern about their physical safety, as urging social activities, as solving problems for them, as being nosey about their affairs, and as attending religious services. In addition, System 2 Ss reported more dependence on their mothers than on their fathers both before 6 and from 6 to 12, feeling closer to their mothers than to their fathers, and agreeing with their mothers more often than with their fathers when their parents disagreed.

Mothers of System 3 Ss were recalled significantly more often than fathers as expressing approval from age 6 to 12 and from age 13 to 17, as expressing general warmth and affection, as expressing concern about their physical safety, as urging social activities, as listening with an open mind, and as being nosey about their affairs. System 3 respondents also recalled being more dependent on their mothers before age 6, as feeling closer to their mothers as they were growing up, and as feeling free to talk to their mothers more often than to their fathers. Fathers were recalled by System 3 respondents more often than mothers as not having time to spend with them.

There were only two items on which mothers and fathers of System 4 Ss were significantly different. Mothers were recalled as being more nosey about the respondents' affairs and as expressing warmth and affection more frequently than the fathers.

The two items, on which mothers and fathers of System 4 Ss differed, also showed a difference in the same direction between mothers and fathers of representatives of each of the other systems. Thus, it would appear that mothers in general are more nosey about their children's affairs and more frequently express warmth and affection than fathers, but that these differences are much greater for parents of System 2 individuals than for parents of representatives of the other systems. As can be seen in Table IX, there is a general tendency for the magnitude of the mother and father differences to be the greatest for System 2.

Systems differed not only in the frequency and magnitude of differences between mothers and fathers, but also in possibly revealing ways with regard to the content of the items on which differences between parents occurred. Thus parent differences in the areas of strictness, allowing the child to think for himself, and allowing the child to do like his peers occurred only within System 1. Parent differences in control and regulation, solving problems for the child, attendance of religious services, and child's agreement with one parent in instances of parental disagreement occurred only within System 2. Differences between mothers and fathers regarding listening to the child with an open mind and the child's feeling of freedom to talk to the parents occurred only in System 3. The items regarding nosiness and expression of warmth and affection (as noted above) were the only items where significant mother-father differences occurred for all systems. In addition, two items showed the same significant mother-father differences for Systems 1, 2, and 3. Representatives of all systems except System 4 recalled their mothers more frequently than their fathers as being concerned with physical safety and as urging participation in social activities.

Also in the area of approval there were significant mother-father differences for Systems 1, 2, and 3. However, the pattern of these differences was somewhat different across the 3 systems. Within System 1 both parents were recalled as maintaining a fairly consistent frequency of approval as the child grew older; at the 6 to 12 age level, mothers were rated as expressing approval more frequently than fathers. For System 2 representatives, fathers were recalled as expressing approval less frequently than mothers before age 6, but after 6, the frequency of approval by the mother dropped and there was not a significant difference between mothers and fathers at the two subsequent age levels. In contrast to System 2, there was not a significant difference between mothers and fathers of System 3 representatives before age 6, but the mean frequency of approval from fathers dropped after age 6 while the mothers maintained essentially the same frequency through all three age levels; thus the frequency of approval from mothers was significantly greater than that from fathers in the last two age levels. As can be noted in Table IX, at all age levels and for both parents there is a tendency for frequency of approval to be lowest for System 2 individuals and highest for System 4 individuals.

The greater paucity of differences between mothers and fathers in System 4 may very well indicate that they, to a greater extent than parents within other systems, are both involved, interested, and active to a more or less equal degree in the child-rearing venture. It may be particularly relevant that the System 4 respondents recalled a high frequency of approval from both parents. The differences that occurred between mothers and fathers in System 1 might suggest that both parents are involved and active in the child-rearing process but that each has their specified role to fulfill (i.e., for some differences the fathers are greater than the mothers, for others the mothers are greater than the fathers). In both Systems 2 and 3, it would appear that the mothers play a more prominent role than the fathers and that the child feels closer to the mother than to the father.

DIFFERENCES BETWEEN SYSTEMS IN RECALL OF ATTENDANCE BY PARENTS AT RELIGIOUS SERVICES

The items from the PCRQ which asked about the frequency of attendance at religious services by mothers and by fathers were not included in any of the clusters. However, as indicated in the introduction of this paper some differences between systems were expected in this area. Therefore, results regarding parents' attendance at religious services are being included as a separate section.

Table X presents the mean scores for representatives of each system for recalled frequency of attendance at religious services by their parents. System 1 individuals recalled their parents attending religious services more frequently than representatives of any other system. Representatives of System 2 recalled their fathers attending religious services the least frequently.

TABLE X

RECALLED FREQUENCY OF ATTENDANCE AT RELIGIOUS SERVICES

(1 = MORE THAN ONCE A WEEK   5 = NEVER)

	System 1		System 2		System 3		System 4	
	Mean	SD	Mean	SD	Mean	SD	Mean	SD
Mothers	2.20	.89	2.96	1.25	3.17	1.56	3.10	1.37
Fathers	2.63	1.22	4.08	1.06	3.40	1.13	3.72	1.49

TYPES OF PUNISHMENT AND REWARD AMONG SYSTEMS AND WITHIN SYSTEMS

The subjects were asked to indicate for each of the three age levels the predominant type of punishment and the predominant type of reward which they recalled as being used by each parent. Six categories of punishment were provided: physical, bawling out-nagging, verbal explanation, restriction of freedom, withdrawal of affection, and denial of pleasures. There were eight types of praise or reward: praise of accomplishment, praise of person, praise for improvement over past performance, praise with urging to do better, physical affection, material reward, granting of privileges, and comparison with others.

These results will be discussed only in terms of trends at the present time. The intent here is to examine and compare overall patterns of punishment and reward rather than to determine the degree of difference.

System 1

The highest percentage of Ss reporting physical punishment by father and by mother occurred in System 1 (the very highest incidence being the 87 percent of the System 1 males who indicated this category as the primary form of punishment by their father before age 6).

In reporting punishment by mother, physical punishment was never the most frequently checked category for either sex at any age in any system except in System 1.

Explanation was never the most frequently checked category by System 1 males, and for females it was the most frequent punishment only for the last age level (for both mothers and fathers).

Praise of accomplishment was the primary form of reward used by mothers and fathers of System 1 females at all age levels.

Fathers of System 1 males also used primarily praise of accomplishment, but praise with urging to do better was checked with almost equal frequency for the first two age levels and was the second most frequent category for both males and females in the third period—a higher percentage of System 1 Ss checked praise with urging to do better than Ss of any other system.

Mothers of System 1 males were most frequently recalled as praising the person during the first two age periods.

System 2

These individuals were the only Ss who indicated a decrease in the use of explanation as they grew older.

Bawling out-nagging was the most common punishment used by mothers of System 2 males and it tended to be the most common punishment for females from both parents.

Males recalled their fathers using physical punishment and then shifting to restriction of freedom in the last period.

Both parents tended to focus on the accomplishment in giving praise but responses were widely distributed.

System 3

Mothers used primarily bawling out-nagging as punishment for System 3 males and explanation for System 3 females.

The responses of System 3 males for punishment by father were widely distributed at all age levels with no category appearing as predominant.

An unexpectedly high percentage of System 3 females indicated physical punishment by their father before age 6, responses were widely distributed in the second period and bawling out-nagging was predominant in the third period.

The only instance where praise of person was a primary category (i.e., no other category having a higher frequency of response) for both sexes at all age levels was for System 3 individuals in reporting reward by their mothers.

As with punishment, the responses of System 3 males for reward by father were widely distributed, praise with urging to do better being the only category which was checked consistently at all three age levels.

System 3 females recalled praise of accomplishment as the primary form of reward from their fathers.

System 4

The females in this group recalled primarily verbal forms of punishment from both parents, with bawling out-nagging most common in the first period, a shift to explanation in the second period, and almost exclusive use of explanation in the third period.

System 4 males also recalled primarily verbal punishment from their mothers but with less emphasis on explanation than indicated by the females.

In reporting punishment by their fathers, System 4 males indicated a shift from physical punishment in the first period to bawling out-nagging in the second period and restriction of freedom for the third period.

To a greater extent than representatives of the other systems, System 4 individuals recalled praise of accomplishment as the primary type of reward used by both parents at all age levels.

CONCLUSIONS

In this final section, an effort will be made to briefly summarize the major results for each system and to relate these findings to the assumptions made at the beginning of the paper regarding the development of each of the four types of functioning.

System 1

Representatives of System 1 (both male and female except where otherwise indicated) differed from representatives of one or more of the other systems, in that they reported:
1. the least disagreement between their parents;
2. both parents as highest on fairness of punishment and related items;
3. their fathers as highest in strictness (males only), and as highest in the amount of control and restriction of freedom through age 12;
4. their mothers as allowing the least freedom through age 12;
5. more dependency on both parents than System 4 Ss (males only); for females there was the same trend for dependency on their mothers and they were second highest for dependency on their fathers (nonsignificant);
6. the highest frequency of punishment by the father through age 12 (males only);
7. more warmth and approval by their mothers than System 2 Ss;
8. the most frequent attendance of religious services by both mother and father.

With regard to differences between males and females within System 1, it was found that:
9. the largest number of differences between males and females of any system and for either parent occurred between males and females of System 1 regarding their relationship with their fathers;
10. males recalled less fairness, more strictness, more arbitrariness, more concern with family reputation, more nosiness, and less acceptance of their ideas and opinions by their fathers than did the females;
11. females recalled more approval by both parents than the males did.

With regard to differences between mothers and fathers within System 1, it was found that:
12. unlike the other systems, almost half of the significant differences between the mothers and fathers of System 1 representatives showed the fathers to be higher than the mothers on certain variables, possibly indicating that both parents were involved but played different roles in the child-rearing process.

In general these findings tend to support the assumptions that individuals who develop a System 1 style of functioning have been raised in a home environment which stressed intrafamily agreement, consistency and fairness within a structured framework, family reputation and religiosity. As expected there seemed to be an emphasis on different role definitions for males and females, for parents as well as for children, the latter being especially evidenced by the differences between males and females in their relationship with their fathers. As anticipated, System 1 individuals experienced a great deal of control, strictness, and restriction of freedom prior to age 12, as well as a sense of being dependent rather than independent. Also as predicted, physical punishment was used frequently and explanation was relatively uncommon, especially for males. While praise of accomplishment was the most common reward there was also an indication that fathers frequently urged System 1 representatives to do better and that mothers of System 1 males focussed on praise of the person during the preadolescent years.

System 2

Representatives of System 2 (both male and female except where otherwise indicated) differed from representatives of one or more of the other systems, in that they reported:
1. the most disagreement between their parents;
2. the least fairness of both mother and father (as well as related items such as meeting standards expected of the child);
3. their fathers as lowest in strictness (males only), while females reported their fathers as highest in strictness;
4. less freedom and independence by their mothers than System 4 Ss (similar to System 1), but also less control and restriction of freedom by their fathers than System 1 Ss (similar to System 4);
5. the least warmth and approval by their mothers (Cluster 11), as well as being lowest on the separate approval items for both mother and father at all age levels;
6. their fathers attending religious services the least frequently and the greatest discrepancy between attendance by their mothers and fathers;
7. their parents as the most arbitrary and their mothers as administering punishment more frequently than other mothers (nonsignificant tendencies).

With regard to differences between males and females within System 2, it was found that:
8. females indicated a lack of a positive bond between themselves and their fathers, while males appeared to have a less negative relationship with their fathers;
9. there was very little difference between males and females in their relationship with their mothers.

With regard to differences between mothers and fathers within System 2, it was found that:

10. there were more differences between mothers and fathers of System 2 Ss, and more of these differences were significant at the .01 level than in any other system;

11. for all of these differences, the mothers were higher on the variables involved than the fathers, perhaps indicating lack of involvement of the father with the child.

These findings tend to be in line with many of the assumptions about the antecedents of System 2 functioning. As expected these individuals experienced considerable disagreement and discrepancy in their home environment in almost all areas from religion to social activities. In accord with predictions the parents were seen as being unfair, as falling short of professed standards, as giving little warmth and approval, and as using explanation sparingly. The fathers, but not the mothers, allowed considerable freedom with some indication that this may have been related to an indifference or lack of involvement on the part of the father. In addition there was a strong tendency for System 2 Ss to recall their parents as being arbitrary and their mothers as administering punishment frequently.

System 3

Representatives of System 3 (both male and female except where otherwise indicated) differed from representatives of one or more of the other systems, in that they reported:

1. more fairness of their mothers than System 2 Ss (similar to System 1) but less fairness of their fathers than System 1 Ss (similar to System 2);

2. more dependency on their mothers than System 4 Ss (similar to System 1);

3. the highest concern by their mothers with social criteria in the evaluation of the child's behavior; the same tendency for their fathers (nonsignificant);

4. more warmth and approval by their mothers than System 2 Ss;

5. more strictness, arbitrariness, control, and restriction of freedom by their fathers from age 13 to 17 (nonsignificant tendency).

With regard to differences between males and females within System 3, it was found that:

6. there was very little difference between males and females in their relationship with their fathers and only slightly more difference in their relationship with their mothers.

With regard to differences between mothers and fathers within System 3, it was found that:

7. the fathers, more often than the mothers, did not have time for the child (significant at the .01 level); the remaining 10 items on which a difference occurred can be viewed as reflecting concern, interest, or closeness to the child, and all showed the mother to be higher than the father.

Relating these findings to the assumed antecedents of System 3 functioning, shows that, as expected, mothers of these individuals tended to promote dependency, to provide a great deal of warmth and approval, to be concerned with social acceptance, to be limited in the use of physical punishment (especially for males), and to focus on the person in administering reward. Also evident were marked differences between mothers and fathers indicating that the fathers were recalled as less fair, as more often not having time for the child, and in general as being more distant and less interested in the child. In addition the pattern of reward and punishment for the mothers appeared more clearly defined than for the fathers in the responses of males but not in the responses of females.

System 4

Representatives of System 4 (both male and female except where otherwise indicated) differed from representatives of one or more of the other systems, in that they reported:
1. more fairness of their mothers than System 2 Ss; more fairness of their fathers than System 2 Ss (females only), (same tendency for males but nonsignificant);
2. less disagreement between their parents than System 2 Ss;
3. less strictness by their fathers than System 1 Ss (males only), and less strictness by their fathers than System 2 Ss (females only);
4. the least strictness and control by their mothers (nonsignificant tendency);
5. the least control and restriction of freedom by their fathers;
6. the most freedom and independence by their mothers;
7. the least dependency on both parents (males only);
8. the least concern by their mothers with social criteria in evaluating the child; same tendency for fathers (nonsignificant);
9. more warmth and approval by their mothers than System 2 Ss (Cluster 11), as well as being highest on the separate approval items for both mother and father at all age levels;
10. their parents as being the least arbitrary (nonsignificant tendency).

With regard to differences between males and females within System 4, it was found that:
11. females experienced a strong positive bond with their fathers, being

higher than either sex in any system on items such as influence by the father, similarity to and agreement with the father;

12. females also indicated a stronger bond with their mothers than did males, especially in the areas of approval and dependence;

13. System 4 males tended to recall more freedom and independence from both parents at all age levels than either sex in any system.

With regard to differences between mothers and fathers within System 4, it was found that:

14. there were only two items on which a significant difference occurred (a comparable difference occurred on these two items in each system) perhaps suggesting that parents of System 4 individuals were more equally involved and active in the child rearing process.

Several assumptions regarding the development of System 4 functioning were supported by the findings in this study. As expected, System 4 individuals experienced parent-child relationships which were low in strictness, control, arbitrariness, and dependency, while being high in fairness, freedom, independence, warmth, and approval. There was a low level of disagreement between the parents and an indication that both were interested and involved with the child but not hovering over him. The use of explanation was higher for System 4 individuals than for representatives of any other system but more prevalent among females than among males. As anticipated, social criteria were used infrequently in evaluating the child's behavior and both parents focussed on the accomplishment more than on the person in administering reward at all ages.

REFERENCES

Adams, D. K., Harvey, O. J., and Heslin, R. E. (1966). Variation in flexibility and creativity as a function of hypnotically induced past histories. In O. J. Harvey (Ed.), *Experience, structure and adaptability*. Springer, New York.

Alter, R. D., and Harvey, O. J. (1968). Belief systems and reaction to high and low status. Unpublished manuscript.

Brown, V., and Harvey, O. J. (1968). Conceptual systems and creativity. Unpublished manuscript.

Coates, C., Harvey, O. J., and White, B. J. (1969). Teacher beliefs, classroom atmosphere and student performance: a replication and extension. Unpublished manuscript.

Felknor, C., and Harvey, O. J. (1963). Cognitive determinants of concept formation and attainment. Technical Report No. 10, Contract Nonr 1147 (07), University of Colorado.

Haggard, E. A., Brekstad, A., and Skard, A. H. (1960). On the reliability of the anamnestic interview. *J. Abnormal and Social Psychol.*, **61**, 311–318.

Harvey, O. J. (1963a). Cognitive determinants of role playing. Technical Report No. 3, Contract Nonr 1147 (07), University of Colorado.

Harvey, O. J. (1963b). Current status of the incongruity hypothesis. In O. J. Harvey (Ed.), Motivation and social interaction. Ronald Press, New York.

Harvey, O. J. (1963c). Authoritarianism and conceptual functioning in varied conditions. J. Personality, 31, 462–470.

Harvey, O. J. (1964). Some cognitive determinants of influencibility. Sociometry, 27, 208–221.

Harvey, O. J. (1965). Cognitive aspects of affective arousal. In S. S. Tomkins and C. E. Izard (Eds.), Affect, cognition and personality. Springer, New York.

Harvey, O. J. (1966). System structure, flexibility, and creativity. In O. J. Harvey (Ed.), Experience, structure and adaptability. Springer, New York.

Harvey, O. J. (1967). Conceptual systems and attitude change. In M. Sherif and C. W. Sherif (Eds.), Attitude, ego-involvement and change. Wiley, New York.

Harvey, O. J., and Kline, J. A. (1965). Some situational and cognitive determinants of role playing: A replication and extension. Technical Report No. 15, Contract Nonr 1147 (07), University of Colorado.

Harvey, O. J., and Ware, R. (1967). Personality differences in dissonance resolution. J. Personality and Social Psychol., 7, 227–230.

Harvey, O. J., Hunt, D. E., and Schroder, H. M. (1961). Conceptual systems and personality organization. Wiley, New York.

Harvey, O. J., White, B. J., Prather, M., Alter, R., and Hoffmeister, J. K. (1966). Teachers' beliefs and preschool atmospheres. J. of Educational Psychol., 57, 373–381.

Harvey, O. J., Prather, M., White, B. J., and Hoffmeister, J. K. (1968a). Teacher beliefs, classroom atmosphere and student performance. Am. Educ. Res. J., 5, 151–166.

Harvey, O. J., Reich, J., and Wyer, R. S. (1968b). Effects of attitude direction, attitude intensity, and structure of beliefs upon differentiation. J. Personality and Social Psychol., 10, 472–478.

Harvey, O. J., Coates, C., White, B. J., and Neva, E. (1969). Conceptual systems of students and performance under stress. Unpublished manuscript.

Hoffmeister, J. K. (1965). Conceptual determinants of strength and certainty of beliefs. Unpublished manuscript, University of Colorado.

Kritzberg, S. F. (1965). Conceptual systems and behavior styles. Technical Report No. 13, Contract Nonr 1147 (07), University of Colorado.

Levy, D. (1943). Maternal overprotection. Columbia Univ. Press, New York.

Reich, J. (1966). Conceptual systems and group performance. Unpublished manuscript, University of Colorado.

Robbins, L. C. (1963). The accuracy of parental recall of aspects of child development and of child rearing practices. J. Abnormal Social Psychol., 66, 261–270.

Symonds, P. M. (1939). The psychology of parent-child relationships. Appleton, New York.

Tiemann, H. A. (1965). Some social and personality determinants of reaction to sensory deprivation. Technical Report No. 14, Contract Nonr 1147 (07), University of Colorado.

Tryon, R. C., and Bailey, D. E. (1966). The BC TRY computer system of cluster and factor analysis. Multivariate Behavioral Res., 1, 95–111.

Ware, R., and Harvey, O. J. (1967). A cognitive determinant of impression formation. J. Personality and Social Psychol., 5, 38–44.

Ware, R., and Harvey, O. J. (1968). Differential effects of different sources and different situations upon representatives of different belief systems. Unpublished manuscript.

White, B. J., and Harvey, O. J. (1965). Effects of personality and own stand on judgment and production of statements about a central issue. *J. Experimental and Social Psychol.*, 1, 334–347.

White, B. J., Alter, R. D., and Rardin, M. (1965). Authoritarianism, dogmatism, and usage of conceptual categories. *J. Personality and Social Psychol.*, 2, 293–295.

Yarrow, M. R. (1963). Problems of methods on parent-child research. *Child Development*, 34, 215–226.

Yarrow, M. R., Campbell, J. D., and Burton, R. V. (1964). Reliability of maternal retrospection. A preliminary Report. *Family Processes*, 3, 207–218.

POSTSCRIPT:
ATTEMPTS AT ANALYSIS AND SYNTHESIS

*Ronald A. Hoppe**

To facilitate the discussion of the interrelationships among the contributions, at least a brief word about each is necessary.

In a unique and impressive way Fuller emphasized the necessity of studying genetic variables so that an adequate understanding of socialization can be gained. His findings, that genetic influences are the greatest on the very behaviors that are the most easily changed by amount of experience, do not permit the continued discharge of genetic factors with the phrase "genetic and environmental factors interact," but force students of socialization to realize their obligation to investigate genetic variables.

The demonstrations by Hess, of the inapplicability of traditional association learning theories to the understanding of the earliest behavior of fast-maturing fowl, cause us to accept the frequently mentioned belief that principles of behavior modification will not apply in a constant way to all socialization periods, especially when considering the slow-maturing human being.

While Fuller pointed out how the same experiences can have different or even opposite effects depending on *individual differences in genetic structure*, Hess pointed out how the same experiences can have different effects depending on the *developmental level of the organism*. From the material presented in the first section, socialization can be said to occur on the foundation of inheritance—inherited factors which are common to the species and genetic factors which are specific to the individual. The acquisition and modification of behaviors are influenced by an organism innately fashioned to acquire and modify some kinds of behavior more easily than others. Studying innate differences between the species as well

* University of Victoria.

as individual genetic differences within the species is necessary to uncover the frameworks which determine *how* socialization occurs.

In requesting that we study the reinforcement history of the organism to understand socialization, Bijou suggested an examination of the development of social stimulus and response functions. Using functional analysis, the ways in which cultural forms of behavior and personality characteristics are established can be discovered.

In offering a substitute for dependency, by way of a more reliably defined collection of behaviors, labelled attachment, Ferguson presented a refined approach to analyzing social interactions in the early life of the individual. By suggesting that both instrumental dependency and the ambiguous motivational construct involved in the notion of dependency be excluded from the concept of attachment, she described ways in which a more determinative collection of behaviors can be studied and how the attachment relation can be used to understand much of the socialization process.

Parke focused on a previously neglected area of experimental study—punishment—by presenting the results of a series of laboratory investigations designed to examine the effectiveness of punishment in controlling behavior. Variables which have been found to affect learning in situations involving either punishing circumstances with nonhuman beings or nonpunishing consequences with human beings were used to thoroughly examine, in a laboratory setting, the role of punishment.

Hartup and Coates exposed an important two part incompleteness in knowledge of imitation: (*a*) a meager amount of information is available on the relation of age to any of the variables associated with imitation, and (*b*) extremely few attempts have been made to empirically generalize the tenets of imitation derived from laboratory settings to natural settings.

It is interesting to note that the contributors to the second section make an urgent appeal for naturalistic studies of the variables and relations that have been demonstrated to be influential in laboratory studies because it is an appeal which concurs with the ideal *modus operandi* of the contributors of the first section. It should also be pointed out, however, that this appeal is for naturalistic studies which are longitudinal, controlled and observational—things which are not typical of past field studies of socialization.

Convincing arguments and demonstrations that *communication* ability is something different from *language* ability were presented by Krauss and Glucksberg. Their experiments illustrated the necessity of studying the acquisition of communication skills—assumed by all to be of primary importance in the socialization process—in a way which is distinct from the study of the acquisition of speech and language.

Harvey and Felknor illustrated how recollections of the behavior of one's parents can be used to provide clues for understanding how individual differences in adult personalities can result from different caretaking styles.

While most of the contributors assumed that we readers use a common definition or description of the socialization process, Bijou and Ferguson explicitly mentioned a broad description: socialization is the development of social behavior. Parke, more specifically, suggested that socialization involves discrimination learning of suitable responses.

Most of the contributors considered the concepts they used to have general applicability to most forms of social behavior. Some of the contributors, Bijou, Hartup and Coates, Harvey and Felknor, used social behaviors in general to expound their notions while others focused on a portion of social behavior. Fuller considered dominance, attachment and activity responses of dogs to illustrate genetic influences; Hess used mainly attachment responses of fowl to illustrate a critical period of socialization; Parke employed resistance to prohibited behavior to interpret punishment, and Krauss and Glucksberg focused on communicative behavior. While Ferguson considered that a set of attachment *responses* could be used to define an attachment *relation*, she also used the concept of attachment to explain a variety of social behaviors. Because of these differences, it is important to realize that any interrelations between the concepts of the different contributors probably involve comparisons of concepts which have been derived from examining different behaviors.

The consideration of individual differences has been a popular point on which to compare approaches to a given area of study in psychology, and different considerations of this point can be seen among the present investigators of socialization. It is perhaps truistic to mention that implicit, if not explicit, in most conceptualizations of socialization is that different socialization procedures produce different individuals. But of the present contributors, a few concentrate most of their efforts on the study of individual differences. Fuller centered on genetically influenced individual differences by examining the interactions of different heredities and environments. Harvey and Felknor concentrated on relating different parent-child interactions to different adult personality characteristics. Ferguson was unique in illustrating how both individual differences in congenital variables (mainly sex) and different environmentally-affected attachment relations can produce individual differences in behavioral characteristics. Bijou emphasized the study of individual differences from the standpoint of different reinforcement histories including different schedules of reinforcement, but he denied that the chronicle of reinforcements affects an organism devoid of genetically produced differences. The remaining contributors discussed individual differences less directly.

When this occurs in a culture which favors considering that "all men are created equal," the implication seems to be that individual differences are a product of mainly different environments rather than different heredities.

A major issue about the proper assumption that should be used when applying principles of learning to the study of socialization has been whether or not to consider these principles as applying in a continuous or discontinuous way; that is, should one set of precepts be expected to apply at one age level and another set at a different age level, or should the same set be expected to apply throughout the entire process? In the past it has been typical of the social learning theories to assume that the principles of learning applied in a continuous manner throughout the socialization process and it has been typical of the developmentally oriented theorist (influenced by at least Piaget) to assume discontinuities in the socialization process. Reviewing the present group of contributors suggests that the mode has changed towards a greater acceptance of discontinuity as a feasible assumption. The change is probably due to an expectation that a close examination of learning throughout the entire developmental period will reveal modifications of behavior which will not fit a set of a few parsimonious rules. Hess was quite emphatic in pointing out how inadequate strict, behavioristically-oriented association learning theories were in explaining the establishment of the imprinting response, but, on the other hand, he did remark how association theory seemed to apply after the critical imprinting period—clearly a suggestion for adopting an assumption of discontinuity in learning during the socialization process. Parke suggested that anxiety and arousal may play an important role in the learning of rules early in the life of the child but might be less important after the rules have been learned, at which time cognitive factors become more significant. He also mentioned that the use of and quality of punishment varied with the age of the child. Hartup and Coates suggested that in general the reinforcements at one age level might be quite different than at another age level, e.g., vicarious reinforcement probably plays a role with younger children but not with older children. In addition they mentioned the importance of discovering the conditions for the origin of imitation in a natural environment. In fact, this was a part of their argument for a developmental study of imitation, rather than assuming a continuity of imitation across age levels. Also, Ferguson pointed to changes in attachment, from diffuse to specific, as the child develops and the occurrence of detachment in a postinfancy period. She also mentioned changes in the objects of attachment with age. Incidentally, the shifts in the objects of attachment suggested by Ferguson parallel, until adolescence, the shifts in the models of imitation suggested by Hartup and Coates. Although Parke, Hartup and Coates, and Ferguson argued for a consideration of different variables at different ages of development, they did not necessarily imply that certain broad principles of learning will not apply to all stages, but rather, qualitative changes in stimuli, responses, reinforcements, and drives will occur. Nevertheless, they did seem to suggest that something more than changes in the values of the parameters of a few social-learning functions is required to account for the modifications of behavior which occur during the socialization process. Bijou's functional analysis, while assuming continuity, certainly does not assume that the specific social functions of stimuli and responses are constant throughout childhood; functional analysis permits the discovery of new reinforcements which might arise at different stages of development. But Bijou did assume that certain principles, such as shaping and schedules of reinforcement, will apply at all ages in a continuous manner.

Several of the contributors indicated an aspect of the socialization process that in the past has not received proper attention: the behavior of the caretaker as a function of the stimulus provided by the young organism's response. Of all the contributors, Ferguson emphasized this interaction the most by describing the development of attachment through reciprocal responses of mother and child. Furthermore, she considered that *matched* reciprocal responses are involved in imitation and are a basis for the development of attachment. This conjoins with Hartup and Coates' view that deliberate *parental* matching may be the instigation of first imitations. On the same point, Bijou mentioned the use of imitation in preschool years *"to prime"* operant behavior, and by this seems to intimate that parental imitation is a response to the child's behavior. When Parke proposed establishing the validity of laboratory results in field settings, he mentioned the necessity of determing what kinds of behavior of the child elicit what kinds of punishment. Parke suggested that the quality and intensity of punishment are functions of the parent's reaction to not only the child's behavior prior to punishment, but also, the parent's reaction to how the child receives the punishment. Hess illustrated reciprocal behavior when he mentioned that the young animal's behavior elicits caretaking behavior from the parent, and Lorenz's notion that the quality of "babyishness" releases valuable behaviors from adults. Finally, the communicative behavior of the adult in reacting to and decoding children's responses was investigated by Krauss and Glucksberg. It is interesting to see that such a wide variety of approaches to studying socialization, as is represented by the present contributors, is concerned with the reciprocal reactions of the young and his parent.

To summarize, a few of the many important points made by the contributors were: (*a*) It is necessary to examine closely the nature of innately determined influences on socialization behavior. (*b*) A developmental approach to the study of socialization through investigations which are observational, longitudinal, and performed in natural settings, is of prime importance. (*c*) The elicitation and modification of the caretaker's responses to the stimulus provided by the young's response deserves a central role in the examination of the socialization process.

AUTHOR INDEX

Numbers in italics refer to the pages on which the complete references are listed.

SUBJECT INDEX

A

Activity index, 9
Adaptive value of behavior, 19, 20–24, 30–34, 70
Adults, socialization of, 162–165
Age differences,
in communication competence, 155–162
in imprinting, 21
Aggression, 17, 33–35
intraspecific, 33
of mice, 16
mode of rearing, 16
punishment, 100–101
Alter-imitation, 39
Anxiety arousal and punishment, 98
Arena test, 8–9
Attachment, 66–77, *see also* Nurturance
development of, 73–75
punishment, 27–28, 99
Avoidance behavior, 24

B

Babyishness, 31
Belief systems,
classification of, 177
defined, 168–173
development, 173–177, 198–203
differences in parental religious attendance, 196
differences in parent-child relations, 180–188
general nature, 168
parental differences, 192–196
punishment and reward, 196–198
sex differences, *see* Sex differences

Breed differences,
chickens, 22–23
dogs, 7, 12, 14–15

C

Classical conditioning, 44
Closedness of cognitive structure, 170–171
Code for observational description (COFOD), 8
Coding, social and nonsocial, 151
Cognitive structure, 46, 170, *see also* Concrete abstractness, and Punishment, cognitive variables
imitation, 118–121, 132-133
Communication competence, 150–152, 155–162
development of, 158–162
young children, 155–158
Complex tasks and imitation, 131–132
Concrete-abstractness,
behavioral manifestations, 169–170
belief systems, 170–173
cognitive structure, 168–169
Conformity and the development of belief systems, 174
Conscience development, *see* Identification
Contact comfort, 69
Critical period, 21–24
and association learning, 27
Cross-sex effect, 74–75
Cultural behavior,
learning of, 50–56

D

Decoding ability of young children, 157–158